FLOWERING DUSK

Other Books by Ella Young

THE TANGLE-COATED HORSE

and other tales; episodes from the Fionn Saga

Illustrated by Vera Bock

THE UNICORN WITH SILVER SHOES

Illustrated by Robert Lawson

THE WONDER SMITH AND HIS SON

a tale from the golden childhood of the world

Illustrated by Boris Artzybasheff

PORTRAIT SKETCH OF ELLA YOUNG
BY THOMAS HANDFORTH

FLOWERING DUSK

DUSK

THINGS REMEMBERED

Accurately and Inaccurately

ELLA YOUNG

LONGMANS, GREEN AND CO.

NEW YORK · TORONTO

1945

TO THE WHITE UNICORN
AND
TO THE TAWNY LIONESS
GREETING

CONTENTS

BOOK I: EIRE

BOOK II: AMERICA

Grateful acknowledgment is made by the author to Mr. Alexander Urquhart of Glamorgan, Wales, and Mr. C. J. Ryan of the Theosophical Society of Covina, California, for permission to quote from the works of Kenneth Morris.

ILLUSTRATIONS

In dream I walked by a lonely bay in the North where the tide crept listlessly on solitary platinum-hued sands. The light was like sunlight filtered through deep water. My Ladye walked with me.

She said: "When you come to riches and honor, will you be kind to my country?"

She spoke of a country not mine. And for sake of that country for which I had no love she was sorrowful: I could see the tears on her face.

"If I am kind to your country: if I come to riches and honor, will you companion me?" I asked.

She put her hand in mine, and gladness was on her face that had the beauty of April.

I knew as I walked there with the tide moving so quietly on the sands that I could choose to hold this dream to me and have these three things: riches, honor, and my Ladye's hand in mine. But I knew that I would refuse the choice, since already I had traveled by a harder road and given my heart to a more chimerical dream.

*Mayhap like bees we garner honey for masters
of whom we are ignorant.*

Book One
EIRE

PORTRAIT OF ELLA YOUNG
BY ROSE McMAHON (DUBLIN)

CHILD'S WORLD

I REMEMBER EARLY CHILDHOOD HAPPENINGS in a series of pictures. One picture is a puzzle-picture: I am looking down from a height at black and white things like teeth, set out in a patterned row—long white teeth, short black ones, in a patterned row! What do they mean? Cows, trees, flowers, mean something that I can understand—a chair, a table, means something—but what do those strange things mean?

Black and white keys of a piano, and a child held up to wonder at them! The person who held me did not strike a note. Sound would have helped me to understand.

I remember an open door with sky and sunshine beyond it, and the sound of singing. I am looking out from the shadow of a room. My mother is in the room. She is singing in a high sweet voice. I am listening to the words while I look at the blueness of the sky:

> *"Kathleen Mavourneen, the gray dawn is breaking,*
> *The horn of the hunter is heard on yon hill.*
> *Dost thou not know how soon we must sever,*
> *Dost thou not know how soon we must part?*
> *It may be for years and it may be forever,*
> *O, why art thou silent, thou voice of my heart?"*

Again I am in a room. I am sitting at a table with a bowl of porridge in front of me. I don't like porridge so I eat slowly, taking small mouthfuls. I have just discovered that if I turn the back of my spoon I can take very small portions

3

at a time, and pieces fall off. I am rather pleased with myself. My grandfather catches sight of my spoon, and comes to my side:

"That is not the way to sup porridge," he says, "you hold the spoon like this." He gently twists the spoon rightside up in my hand. "See how much better it is!"

I look fixedly at him for a few seconds (I can see even yet quite clearly his clean-shaven scholarly face). Does he really believe that I do not know how to sup porridge? He does. How stupid grown-ups are!

In a room again, and sulky. A friend of my mother's has called, and I am brought in to speak to her. I stand in the middle of the room regarding her with disfavour. She is fat, and I don't like her clothes.

"Come here, my pretty dear, and give me a kiss!"

I have no notion of doing anything of the sort. I do not move. She thinks that I am shy, and before I know what she is about she has seized me and is kissing me heartily. I choke and yell with rage. Struggling frantically, I kick and try to bite.

Safe outside that room, I insist, as soon as I get my breath, on having my face washed—again—and again—and again!

TREE OF KNOWLEDGE

I AM LEARNING to spell and to say twice two is four. My father takes an interest in that part of my education. He has a strong bent toward mathematics and hopes that I inherit it. I don't. The multiplication table is a vexation to both of us. My mother has a bent to religion. She concentrates on *The Shorter Catechism*, and lessons from the Bible.

Stories from the Bible set me thinking. Why did God make the Serpent? Or, having made him, why did He let him into

4

the Garden of Eden? God is all-powerful, but He does not seem to have much sense. He might have printed all over the sky: "Jesus is my beloved Son, believe in Him." He never did things like that. He just watched children to find out if they obeyed their parents. He sent people to Hell if they did not believe in Jesus!

Life was not too hard on week-days. There were my sisters, Jennie and Maude; and the garden; and a white rose tree; and the big brown dog, Sam; and the little black and tan terrier, Roger. Sunday was a day to be dreaded: no toys, no picture-books, no hide-and-seek in the garden! My father read aloud from the Bible or from the *Pilgrim's Progress,* and my mother insisted that one answer at least from *The Shorter Catechism* be learned. My mother knew by heart the answer to every question, because she had learned them as a child.

I began to take religion seriously. My mother tells me that one day I came prancing along the garden walk, tearing frantically at my hair, and sobbing out, while I tried to beat away an attentive wasp: "Oh, why did He ever make them? Why did He ever make them?"

I have no recollection of that incident: it was one of over-many that set me revolving in my mind the ways of Providence to man.

Sometimes, with Sam for guardian, I made incursions into a big field at the back of the house. It had tall trees and long grass, and when my nurse was with me she kept me walking about all the time. Sam was different. He liked to run as I did and then sit down and do nothing. One time we sat down by a large flat stone. I noticed small red creatures crawling under it, and lifting the stone, saw an ant-city for the first time. I was entranced. I watched them lift small white bundles and hurry here and there. I noticed the channeled passages, and the brisk air with which the creatures ran about. I would have been content to sit there a long time, if a burning itch had not taken hold of me from head to foot. I felt that I wanted to tear my clothes off, and ran to the house, howling.

I could not forgive those ants. They had attacked me without provocation. I had come to them as a friend. I intended to put back the stone roof of their city. I had restrained Sam from sniffing. Creatures so ungrateful did not deserve to live! I voiced something of this to my mother, but she only said: "It will be a lesson to you! You must keep away from ants."

Had I no friends? Yes, there was Sam! I explained matters to him, and we took occasion to slip away together. I uncovered the ant-city, and directed Sam to do his best. He dug it to pieces, while I stood by feeling as virtuous as the angels who watched the brimstone end of Sodom and Gomorrah.

CIRCUS

THE CIRCUS HAS come to town. Its tents will be in the fields across the river. The noise of it is everywhere. The streets have flowered into elephants, tigers, tawny thick-maned lions, camels, and chariots with brass bands. I stand in a window and see it all go by: clowns with painted faces, riding on asses, riding with their painted faces turned tail-wise; girls about my age in red velvet dresses, dancing on the backs of small ponies; beautiful ladies on white horses; kings on the shoulders of elephants; camels very high and mighty and scornful to look at; dogs with bells on their collars. Running on either side, a crowd of boys and girls and older folk, laughing and shouting as they go. It is like a faery-tale all in broad daylight: and, like a faery-tale, one can't keep it. If God had only thought of a Heaven with things like this in it, everyone would want to go there!

I know now what I want to be for the rest of my life. I will

6

be a circus girl in a red velvet dress dancing on the back of a small black pony. When I grow bigger I will ride a big white horse and have a ruby-coloured cap on my head, with a feather in it: and I will see lions and tigers and elephants and people walking on tightropes every day in the year!

But those lions and tigers, they will be in cages. They growl when the man who is called a lion-tamer goes in to them. Circus girls can't pet them. I begin to think of a picture I have seen. A man in long robes, walking in a country full of mountains. A tiger is walking after him like a tame cat. No one else in that country but the man and the mountains and the strong beautiful tiger. The tiger is walking after the man because the tiger knows that the man is a Great Saint. Whenever the Saint feels like it he can play with the tiger. A tiger has a furry face with white stripes on it. After all, anyone can rub a horse or a donkey on the nose.

I resolve firmly to be a Great Saint.

FLOWERING DUSK

PUT TO BED, by my mother, or by a servant, in the little room that belonged to me, I pressed my face into the pillows and waited for what happened every night—what I knew would happen every night. Great crested serpents would rise, singly and in groups, through the dark softness of the pillow. They would come up, head first, standing erect on their tails: green and multicoloured serpents. I did not love them very much. I called them "The Worms." I was eager for the Lord of them all to rise—a great serpent, dazzling white and covered with feathers. When that serpent rose, I would find myself on a curious machine that glided through the air, keeping fairly close to the ground.

7

I could see the country below me: a strange country that glittered as though the soil of it were star-dust. Flowers that I had never seen elsewhere thrust through the star-dust. They were like delicate flames, and the wind blew them petal from petal as I moved above them. Rivers showed themselves at times, rivers with little waves that curled and broke in a scatterment of jewels. They, too, were star-stuff.

But it was not the strangeness of the country that delighted me most. It was the even gliding motion of the air-traveling machine on which I stood.

I never saw the machine as a whole. I did not wonder about it at all. Without surprise, I found myself standing on what seemed to be an iron bar and leaning with both hands on another bar that ran parallel beyond it—nothing but open space between the bars! Through that open space I contemplated the many-coloured world as it shifted and changed below me, gliding joyously—gliding—gliding—till I fell asleep.

LOSS

I MADE MYSELF obnoxious at home, and was lightly regarded there. I made myself obnoxious at school, and stood high in no one's estimation till I was drafted into the class of a new teacher: a woman with a gracious countenance, and blond hair—lots of blond hair. She believed in me. She praised me in front of the whole class. She listened when I asked questions. I loved her. No need to remind me that I ought to do my home lessons, I thought of nothing else but my home lessons and school. Day followed day, and the sun shone every day.

First period of the Golden Age! I only had one other in my life!

It did not last long. On a day as I idled through a play-hour, kicking a piece of gravel with my toe, she came to me and said: "I am going to teach in the Senior school, you will not see me after today, so this is good-bye!" Another teacher was with her. They stood beside me. I said nothing. I kept my eyes on the piece of gravel. She waited for me to speak. Still I said nothing. "Are you not sorry?" she asked. I could not look at her face. "No!" I blurted out. "I told you so," said the other teacher. "That child is quite heartless." They moved away talking together. I can still see the piece of gravel, and a bit of the school wall—sunshine on both. I knew that if I shed one single tear I would sob for hours and hours. I must endure till bedtime. I did. That night no plumed serpent came up through the pillow—nor any night after that.

I was seven years old. I had lost the world of The Feathered Serpent: and lost my own!

THE UNPARDONABLE SIN

I FELL AGAIN to the contemplation of Providence—a dark contemplation. There was Heaven and there was Hell. Heaven was one continual Sabbath! Dr. Wilson said it was, said it from the tall pulpit in church—the solemn, ugly Presbyterian Church where I sat Sunday after Sunday with my sisters, Jennie and Maude, in the family pew consoled by a monotony of drab walls, the pews opposite, and Dr. Wilson's black-gowned shoulders.

"Heaven is one continual Sabbath!"

I wondered if I could stand Hell. Perhaps one got used to fire. Millions of people were there. I cautiously touched a finger-tip to the hot stove in the kitchen and decided that Heaven was my only choice. But one had to make oneself fit for Heaven. One had to repent of one's sins. I had an idea

9

that I could take care of myself all day long, but night frightened me. I might die in the night and drop into Hell! Before I went to sleep I must repent. I would kneel by my bed trying to squeeze out a tear. One single tear would be sufficient. I never felt sorry for my sins, so I had to think of sad things like the death of my pet bird, or the loss of something I valued—one single tear and then to bed! Sometimes I wakened in the night and did not feel quite sure that I had repented sufficiently. To safeguard myself I recited hymns till I fell asleep. I hated hymns.

It was just like God to corner one. He sent people into the world and made it hard for them, kept them as much as He could from having any fun, and didn't even let them die and be done with it. They had to go to Heaven (if they couldn't stand Hell) and praise Him all the time! I came back always to that thought of praising Him. I didn't mind repenting. It seemed like getting the better of God—but praising Him! I hated God.

Jesus Christ was not so bad—after all, He could not help being God's Son, and He didn't seem to be like His Father. God was the one to be praised. As I repented night after night a resolution was growing in my mind. I just *could not* spend eternity praising God.

"After all," I said to myself, "there is one thing He can't do. He can't make me praise Him: it is one satisfaction He won't get."

I knew it meant going to Hell. I would have to stand it. Millions and millions of people managed to do it. I had an idea that I might like some of those people—I knew I would not like the people who went to Heaven. My mind was made up. I repented for the last time. Next day I slipped quietly into the drawing-room. It was empty. I closed the door, and then said out loud:

"God, I hate you. I wish the Devil had won when he fought against you. The Devil is better than you are!"

I had done it. I had committed the Unpardonable Sin!

I walked out of the room, closing the door behind me. I

was not sorry. No one could frighten me now with a threat of what might happen to little girls who disobeyed their parents. My life was my own: it had some good things in it.

NEW HORIZON

THE FAMILY PEW was in the gallery of the church. It had high walls, and red plush cushions with round buttons that could be pulled off if one worked cautiously for many Sundays. Sometimes I got a button, sometimes my sister Jennie got one. Maude was too young to be enthusiastic. My mother wondered why the cushions had to have buttons sewn on so frequently. My grandmother sat with my father and mother in the pew. She was good-hearted. Now and then she slipped to us children peppermint lozenges with sentences on them. We could show them to each other before mouthing them.

From the sermon and psalm-singing we abstracted our minds, but we sat alert while Dr. Wilson read the chapter from the Bible. After that chapter would come a psalm, and then the sermon, which began: "My brethren, you will find the text which today I shall consider in xxx, Chapter xxx, Verse xxx."

If Dr. Wilson read, as he sometimes did, the chapter which contained his text, I knew when he came to that verse, and conveyed the news by an unobtrusive pinch to my sister Jennie who relayed it to Maude. We were all attention when the sermon began. Had I picked out the text? Yes! We abstracted our minds. Dr. Wilson did not always read the chapter which contained his text. In that case I shook my head, and we abstracted our minds without waiting for the sermon.

Boredom was lightened by the fact that we stood up now

11

and then to sing one of the Psalms of David. We could watch the Precentor striking his tuning-fork, and the Choir waiting for the Jew's-harp sound of it to die away before they let out their voices. The Precentor was always solemn, but we could take note of a chorister giggling at times.

When we stood up I could see into the body of the church since our pew was in the gallery. After all there was nothing to interest one in the body of the church: just people and a sprinkling of children in their Sunday clothes. One day I caught sight of a child that must be, I thought, about my own age—a child with brown-gold hair curled on either side of a pale face. She had her eyes on the psalm-book, and kept them there; but I had eyes for nothing else in the church save that child. She was like the first sunlight on a day of Winter. The ice in my heart broke up. All my ideas about God and the Universe surged and tumbled to destruction. The fact that she existed changed the world. The psalm ended. Everyone sat down. I was no longer a prisoner in a pew. It was not the Sabbath Day. My heart was singing.

So for the first time I saw Brysanthe. She was seven years old. I was nine.

THEATRE

LONGFELLOW WAS MY mother's favourite poet. She read aloud from a big book, gorgeous in tooled leather and gilt edges. We sat on little stools, listening: my sister Jennie, my sister Maude, and myself. The *Saga of King Olaf* delighted us. Soon we found ourselves, we never knew how or why, acting the part about Queen Sigrid the Haughty.

We acted in secret. No one knew for quite a while. When my mother found out, she bestowed on Queen Sigrid several bright-coloured scarves. King Olaf promptly annexed one

12

as a battle-cloak; the maid of honour to Queen Sigrid got another: it consoled my sister Maude for the meagreness of the maid-of-honour part. I was King Olaf. We invented new scenes, and decided that simple prose would do as well as poetry. When we came to that decision, we found that we could make up plays ourselves. We needed another actor, so my cousin Kathleen joined the group. Still we acted without an audience, but now we thought out plots and had exits and entrances. We had a theatre too, for my mother had given us a room that was vacant save for a few boxes and a big trunk containing disused damask curtains, shawls, and other things which furnished forth the theatre wardrobe.

We could be seen studying Shakespeare, but found it difficult to use his material. We felt that we should learn off Shakespeare's words. We did not need to learn off the words in plays of our own constructing. We just settled among ourselves what the actors were to say, left the words of each part to the inspiration of the moment, and got the cues by heart.

High Tragedy was our forte. Every person in the play came to an untimely end, but was allowed the consolation of a dying speech—a supreme declamation which brought tears at times to the eyes of the entire cast.

My sister Jennie, who took the deaths especially to heart, entered a plea for the survival of at least one chief personage. But the standard could not be lowered.

Scenery we never had, except when we made excursion to an old castle—a square, thick-walled keep so strong that time could not ruin it beyond the devastation war and blasting powder had wrought upon it in some long-forgotten struggle and misprise. It yet hoarded dungeons, stairs set in the thickness of walls, turret windows—ruined bowers and banqueting-hall. For such a setting, plays invented themselves. There was nothing neglected except the shining reaches of the strong river that swirled by the castle walls. There should have been a boat—a rescue, and escape by water in our plays

13

—but we had no boat, and felt that we could not upset the realism of the moment by imagining one.

Stone, they say, keeps its memories with more tenacity than earth or sand can muster. The stones of that castle knew heart-break and the blood-bath: how strangely among those memories, among the little flowers and grasses of the ruined walls, must have flowered and foamed our high-faluting make-believe, "our sorrow only sorrow's shade!"

HIGH EMPRISE

A NEW SCHOOL and a chance to gather a clan for myself! At first it was a clan of malcontents in revolt against the head-mistress who was a disciplinarian and not too well beloved. We carried on a guerrilla warfare with considerable success. Punishment had little effect. Those on whom it fell had the clan sympathy. Skirmishes and alarums, defeats or victories, refreshed our spirits.

Then Brysanthe came. She was a model pupil. It had been our custom to make model pupils ridiculous. But Brysanthe was different. She brought something into the school that had never been there. The Head melted into generousness. The other teachers forgot to think up sarcastic remarks. Puzzlement overtook the clan. We experienced a change of heart, and had that welcome extended to us that prodigals extort even from saints and angels.

Guerrilla warfare—all warfare, was abandoned. But the clan must not dissolve, rather under this new sun it must strengthen and extend itself. Why not found a Round Table Fellowship and be Arthur's knights?

Arthur's knights came into being. The Head, who was secretly romantic, was delighted. We pored over Malory and brightened our minds with Tennyson—we sought out armorial

14

devices and obsolete words. Every day was a new adventure. The school (which boasted a clock-tower, a courtyard, and many disused rooms) was the kind of private school that produced a play at Mid-Summer and one at Christmas, in which the pupils shone, or did not shine, according to their abilities. The time in between was mostly spent in preparing for the plays. It was the virtue of the school that it did not harass its pupils with exams. It had a mind above medals and scholarships.

Pages, squires, knights, and paladins—no one wanted to be a damsel, not even with the bribe of being Guinevere. The damsels, like the horses, were imaginary. But the Round Table Fellowship was real and living. It grew and prospered: it routed the customary play and gave a tournament instead at Mid-Summer and Yuletide.

The last tournament was held at Mid-Summer, with ropes of laurel and roses twined from tourney stall to stall, green branches strewn lavishly, blazoned banners, the sound of trumpets and singing voices.

A champion maintained the lists against all challengers, there was tilting at the ring, and casting the javelin. The air hurtled with joy-shouts. Bay leaves sharpened the sweetness of rose and clove-carnation, the heady fragrant thrust of Summer lilies.

A crown for the Queen of Love and Beauty; laurel for the victors; a flourish of trumpets.

The End

Long years afterwards, when I was gray-headed, I met in California a member of that Fellowship—one who had held a page's rank. At once I was eagerly questioned as to whether I remembered those multicoloured, those bannered and joyous days. I have never forgotten them. Once only in my life did fantasy create a world that was rounded and perfect, and too short-lived.

NEW COUNTRYSIDE

*L*ONG, BROAD MEADOWS REACHING AWAY TO the horizon. A wide sky, unbroken by turrets of any city. Pale hills, blue with distance. Cattle walking homeward, loitering even in the one street of the small town, founded years ago by French refugees, and lettering to this day French names on its grocery and dry-goods stores. The little town is sleepy—it stirs itself only on a fair-day when pigs and sheep, goats and horses make a commotion in it. The countryside has a sleepy, well-fed look. The people have too.

But not far off is the Bog of Allen, that spreads itself over half of Ireland; it is many-coloured and beautiful, changing with every hour of the day like the sea. I can visit the fringe of it. Very far away there are pine trees against the sky. I know a place where I can surprise a small group of pine trees. They are wind-worn and twisted. In their shadow there is a spot that must be the Fountain of Youth, for when I stand there I feel a great joy surging through me. It is something that belongs in especial to this spot. I go there when I can, always alone. Always I find the same overwhelming virtue there. I tell no one about it.

DARK WATERS

WHY DID PEOPLE never skate on the three-cornered lake so fantastically fringed with pine trees? Being newcomers, we

16

asked ourselves that question, and had the answer in unexpected fashion. Night after night had been freezing hard, and word came that people were skating on that lake. My sisters and I hurried down. We had been afraid to venture on it by ourselves lest it should have hidden springs and treacherous ice-holes. But everyone was skating on it this afternoon. We skated with the rest. Suddenly, as it grew dusk, everyone deserted the lake, everyone except my sisters and myself. We could not tear ourselves away from the ice. I skated boldly into the middle. It was nicer after all to have the lake to oneself! But was it nicer? I felt that someone was skating noiselessly behind me. I looked over my shoulder, no one there, but still some person was skating behind me. I could not shake that person off—that invisible presence. Outmatched and outwitted, I made for the shore. As I took off my skates I noticed that Jennie and Maude at another part of the lake were taking off theirs. I hurried up to hear the reason. "We can't stay," they said. "Didn't you hear the great splash that something made in the lake?" "I heard no splash," said I. "The lake is frozen solid." "That's just it," said my sisters, "yet there was a splash. We heard a great animal running behind the bank. We heard him leap on the bank, but we saw nothing, then there was the splash. We are going home!" We went home, all three.

Why had that countryside such deeply-haunted waters? The river Barrow ran at the foot of the meadow beyond our garden wall. It formed a great black pool there, a horrible pool. At night sometimes I dared myself to go through the meadow, which belonged to our house, and down to that pool, but I never dared to go: I was afraid. No one else dared to go. No one passed by that pool at night, yet there was no story about it that I could gather except the old Irish legend which said that an evil beast had been flung into the river Barrow long centuries ago.

There was a little wood that frightened folk even in the daylight. It was very beautiful. In Springtime it was blue

17

with hyacinths, yet people went through it in companies; no one lingered there.

SILK ATTIRE

THE HOUSE WE lived in had been built by a French count, a Huguenot. It had large lofty rooms, a walled garden, and several ghosts. My sister Elizabeth had seen a tall figure go whitely by in the dusk. My mother had been held awake by noises in the night, and to my room at times came a gentle ghost that waited to be spoken to, but never answered.

I would waken in the night with a sharp suddenness and the knowledge that someone was standing in the room. A slender figure at the foot of my bed—someone who wished me to be aware and to awaken; someone, I thought, who was fain to speak, and could not. It did not happen every night, it did not happen at the same hour: but always the figure stood there with a gentle insistence—waiting.

At last I took my courage in both hands and sat upright in bed in the dark.

"In the name of the Trinity, Father, Son, and Holy Ghost, speak!" I said, "I am not afraid to listen."

She did not speak. She waited there as she had always waited; then, sighing a little, she moved softly from the room: as she went her silken skirts made a sound about her.

She came on nights afterwards, silent and faintly expectant. Perhaps my adjuration should have been more stubborn. I did not renew it. The sound of my voice seemed too loud and too shattering—almost a menace—as if one fired a pistol-shot in order to begin a conversation.

There should have been some story of this lady, but I could never come on it. Sometimes she stood between the dressing-table and the bed. She could have stolen a glance

18

at herself in the mirror, but I think that she was too heavy-hearted.

In what places did she wander through the long other hours of the night, through the dragging, uneventful hours of the day? Did she walk in the walled garden that had such a plenitude of roses, such a wilderness of green in meadows beyond? They were not meadows one would choose to walk in, for the Barrow wound among them like a black snake, but they were good to look upon from a high window when sunset reddened the waters; or at dawn when a mist half-obscured and silvered them.

At sunset, and at dawn the Earth stirs and sighs like one in sleep, remembering a secret. Do those who have said farewell to life and put off the burden of the flesh, sigh at times and remember?

ARTISAN

THE KITCHEN MADE complaint: saucepans were disappearing, in ones and twos—in a series of saucepans. My mother, who took no interest in the kitchen, forbore to intervene until a shortage was threatened. Then she said that something must be done—no one knew exactly what.

At this juncture my brother appeared with an invitation to the entire household. Everyone must come and see a boat that he had constructed with the help of his chums, Bert and Harry.

The boat was in the loft over the hay-shed.

We trooped out to the yard, and by an untrustworthy ladder huddled into the dusty loft. The boat displayed itself. It did not look very seaworthy—what can one expect from an orange-box? The bottom was flat, the seams were wide, and took the eye, but they were calked (fine nautical expres-

19

sion), yes, they were calked, as my brother pointed out, with the best Archangel tar.

The best Archangel tar!

It was noticeable in saucepan after saucepan. It was on our clothes, on our hands, on everything we touched—it was everywhere!

Sticky with it, smelling of it, we descended to view the launching. The boat was borne by its builders in triumph through the walled garden and orchard and down the slanting meadow to the pool where the waters of the Barrow swirled and darkened. The household followed in a straggling procession.

When we were all lined up, the boat was launched with much ceremony. It sank head first, gaping in every seam.

"It was the best Archangel tar," said my brother dolefully, "and I used plenty of it."

We did not dispute the fact.

VACANT MIND

THE SOUND OF a cracked bell calling the villagers to church. The church sits far off amid green meadows. It has a starved-looking spire. Inside one walks on cool slabs of limestone, and the walls are whitewashed. The Earl of Portarlington has a large thrust-forward pew in that church, and presently his house-guests will fill it. The women, getting a last use of finery outmoded in London, look exotic in comparison with the country-folk. The clergyman drones a sermon.

I am glad that the church sits far off. I wish the cracked bell had not so loud a voice. I do not need to go to church. My father has a sermon preached for his household and himself in his own house by a Presbyterian minister once a month. This is one of the unsanctified Sundays, and I am observing the Sabbath by a lack of occupation. The cracked bell has stopped. A lark is singing now, high in air, a shrill shaken sweetness. In these wet meadows there are many larks. They seem as little a-kin to the prosperous lushness as flame is to a smouldering log.

How heavy the scent of white narcissi in the garden below me! A few pale roses have opened there. If today were not Sunday, I would work in the garden. I am weary of those meadows stretching away, away—away to nothing but little towns alike in a drab ugliness, all furnished with churches, and cracked bells. Somewhere there must be folk who think as I do: people who would greet me as a comrade.

The hours go by slowly.

CLOUD SHADOW

*W*HAT DID I CARRY AWAY FROM THAT COUN-
try of wide horizons? A sense of spacious skies, of great em-
battled clouds, of fiery sunsets and rose-red dawns; of moons
that glowed like copper—full-orbed harvest moons, rising
slowly; a memory of flooded meadows—of a more than usual
flood when boats traversed the one crooked street in the
little town—the sparkle of ice on long reaches of water;
swift motion on skates; the sight of the Bog of Allen flowered
knee-deep in heather and honey-loud with bees in August;
or patched with silver lichen and emerald moss when the
year declined; the Bog of Allen spiced with many scents,
stretching away to where three hills showed blue and faint
in the distance. So might a continent untrafficked-in show
itself beyond untraveled waters: so might cloud shadow,
purpling a wilderness, entice and elude.

OMAR

WE HAVE MOVED with all our belongings to Dublin: not
to the city proper, but to a highly respectable suburb of it,
Rathmines.

The household is not enamoured of the change. No one
could be. The house is small and mean-looking: it has many

rooms but not a single spacious one. Crowding on either side of it are similar houses—their presence heightens the general effect of comfortless gentility.

We console ourselves with the thought that Dublin has theatres and concert halls—perhaps it has interesting people! Inconsolable is the noble Persian cat, Omar. He had lived in a great walled garden with trees to climb and inferior creatures to wonder at him. How could he be reconciled to a pocket-handkerchief of lawn bordering on the roadway, and a meagre garden in the house-rear with a few objects that can only by courtesy be called trees!

We felt a resolution growing in him, and for some days kept him prisoner, plied with cajoleries, flattery, and good things to eat.

He seized the first opportunity to escape, and for three days the most frantic efforts and offers of reward have not recovered him.

Omar is my cat—purchased with money somewhat painfully saved up—the first cat that I have ever owned! It is impossible to say how splendid-seeming he is, how gracious and subtle in all his ways. Now he is outcast, wounded perhaps, and starving!

I sit with my head in my hands, cursing my luck. Everyone knows that I have the worst possible luck! The whole family knows it. But I must do something to break this black bit of it. Omar must be rescued. Suddenly an idea occurs to me. My sister May is lucky. I will give the cat to her. When she owns him things will be different. Omar will have a chance.

It worked. Omar has come back—a pitiful little voice at the kitchen door asking for admittance. He had tried—as I had tried so many times—to conquer Fate, and Fate had bested him! We all exert ourselves to comfort him, and gradually he begins to understand that we are in exile. We have lost the big beautiful garden. That life has come to an end.

A SYSTEM OF EDUCATION

OMAR HAS BEEN carrying out a system of education for some time, carrying it out with perseverance and efficacy. Today it has reached the high-water mark of success.

When I explained to him that the ill-mannered blue-furred kitten (son of Blue-Jacket, the Champion Cat of Scotland) was only here on a visit, he resolved just to ignore him. But Patsey was not to be ignored: also it was evident that he was going to stay for some time. Omar made up his mind. He would train that kitten, train him without ever a growl or a hiss, without even the lightest and most deserved paw-slap. He would train him by example and will-power.

He began at breakfast time. When Patsey left his own well-filled plate and thrust an uninvited head into Omar's platter, Omar drew back with dignity and sat at a little distance, fixing his eyes in a penetrative disapproving stare on Patsey. Patsey did not seem to feel the stare. He ate up all Omar's food and went back joyously to gorge as much as he could of his own.

Later Omar established himself, curled up, in his favourite chair—a chair that even the Master of the House would pass meekly by. Patsey climbed up there and tried to possess himself of the cushion. Omar at once relinquished it. He sat at a little distance directing that powerful stare on Patsey. Patsey slept happily.

Omar continued these tactics during the day.

Next morning at breakfast Patsey thrust a greedy unabashed head into Omar's platter. Omar drew back, sat at a little distance, and turned the full power of his golden eyes on Patsey. That young ruffian showed signs of uneasiness. He glanced from time to time at the golden potentate who sat motionless, splendid in ruff and feathered tail. Finally he crept back to his own food.

During the day Omar withdrew from cushions and lairs with unwearied courtesy.

24

Next morning, Patsey started for Omar's platter, stopped halfway, whimpered a little, and went back to his own. Omar sat motionless.

On the following morning, it was plain that to Patsey's mind there had penetrated the understanding that Omar was a Superior Being. He did not dare to approach his own plate until Omar condescended to begin breakfast.

The Superior Being proceeded to elaborate points of etiquette. He taught Patsey (by the same method) that when a plate of good things was put down between the two cats, Patsey must draw back and sit motionless until Omar signified that he would eat no more.

Today, unwittingly, I put the System to a supreme test. I placed a chicken liver, roasted and savoury, on a plate before Patsey, as a gift to him. Omar was nowhere in sight. Patsey drew back and sat at a little distance regarding the food sorrowfully. Then with an agonized yell, he rushed from the room!

At first, I thought he was smitten with some dread and sudden disease. But when he returned with Omar, I understood things. I divided the liver between them.

Confronted with a system of education that I have neither the patience nor the self-restraint to practice, I also regard Omar as a Superior Being.

Yesterday, when he accidentally upset a case of pencils that I had, in pure laziness, permitted to lie on the floor, I uttered a hasty and unkind criticism of the mishap. Omar regarded me with pained surprise and then he walked out of the room.

I crawled after him and apologized.

A VISIT TO LIMERICK CITY

I ALWAYS LIKE Boss Gibson's house: it is so strange and quaint with its square stone-flagged hall and its stone-flagged corridors. The long narrow rooms opening out of each other are amazingly lofty (there is no second story), yet they keep a cheerful much-lived-in aspect.

Many people of every age and quality have enlivened these rooms, for Boss Gibson loves to gather folk from all quarters of the globe. Just now Annie Besant is a house-guest. With a handful of her most energetic supporters she has come to evangelize Limerick—a sleepy town sunk in Catholicism and Episcopalian orthodoxy.

Annie Besant herself has but newly joined the Theosophical Society. She is slender and gracious-spoken, she has a soft, pleasant voice, arresting eyes, very beautiful hands, and a certain shyness of manner that is unexpected and delightful.

Boss Gibson has forgotten the work-a-day world for the nonce. (He is Master of the Hounds and has a stableful of hunters.) He has abstracted his mind from horses and forgotten his ability to curse out a lazy groom. He is practising concentration and spends an hour each morning sending thoughts of peace and love to the Four Corners of the Universe. His young and charming wife Janie regards this development with skepticism. She remembers that only a few days before the advent of Annie Besant and the New Life, Boss Gibson said to one of the grooms:

"You d—— d—— good-for-nothing rascal, you'll go to Purgatory for this!"

"O no, Sir, that's one place I'll never see."

"You'll never see! Aren't you a Catholic?"

"O yes, Sir, but anyone who spends a year with you has put in his Purgatory—he'll be free of it in the next world."

The house is thronged with eager aspirants who have come to ask Annie Besant for "Rules of Life," and answers

26

to questions—such stupid questions! I think they come mostly to be able to say hereafter that they have spoken to Annie Besant.

She lectures every evening in a dusty little room that is scantily furnished with an audience three-parts skeptical and adverse. Tonight a drunken man occupied one of the front benches and made unseemly and uproarious remarks. Annie Besant sent some of her henchmen to reason with him—to no purpose. Then the tall lean figure of the Boss appeared on the platform.

"You have had good advice, fellow! Take it, and leave the hall."

"I'll see you all damned first," roared the obstructionist.

"What you need," said the Boss, "is not advice, but help. I'll give it to you."

He strode from the platform, gripped the lout by the shoulder and hustled him into the street. Some of the lout's comrades in the back of the hall, who revered the Boss as a horse-tamer, cheered, and the meeting proceeded.

I discuss this episode with Helen Laird. We are both reassured. It would be a pity if Boss Gibson renounced the world. He lets me drive his blood-mare, Athena, and Helen borrows his hunters. We like to hear tales of his fisticuff exploits:

"Did I ever tell you," asks Helen, "about the time he 'wiped the floor' with two cattle men?"

"I don't know that adventure. Let's hear it!"

"Well, the Boss, practising good fellowship, got into a third-class railway carriage—you know the kind—wooden benches and the aspect of a cattle truck! Two big unshaven cattle-drovers were there before him. As the Boss settled down, they took out short clay pipes and began to smoke.

" 'This is not a smoking carriage,' said the Boss in a mild voice.

" 'What's that to us, we are going to smoke here, like it you, or lump it.'

27

" 'There is time to change carriages,' said the Boss. 'If you don't, I'll wipe the floor with the two of you!'

" 'You would! We'd like to see you!'

"The Boss wiped the floor with the two six-footers, and then shunted them on to the platform just as the train was starting. They fell in a heap, and to the delight of the by-standers the train went on without them!"

Happenings of this kind have won for the Boss his nickname. His real name is Robert Gibson. He is not a political boss. He is just a person who seems to be always in the front of things: hence "The Boss" or "Chief."

Limerick has only one railway station—sleepy river-bastioned Limerick Town. Leaving it by train one sees the slender spire of Saint John's Cathedral thrusting heavenwards; one sees the reaches of the Shannon, blue and silver, or leaden-dark: as skies are fair or sullen. One sees the tall time-worn houses—a huddlement of red brick! They have a dull roseate excellence.

Good-bye, Limerick City.

ÆON

"Do you know," said Helen Laird to me one evening as we were doing nothing in particular, "do you know we never hunted up that Theosophical Society Boss Gibson told us about."

"That's true," said I. "Why don't we hunt it up tonight?"

"It's raining," said Helen, "and likely to keep on raining."

"It's likely to keep on raining for ninety nights out of a hundred. Let's go tonight!"

Fortified with mackintoshes and umbrellas, we started on the hunt. The house was somewhere in Ely Place. There are four tall Georgian houses in Ely Place. Which one? The rain was too disturbing to allow us to ponder the question deeply. We decided to start at the left-hand corner with number one.

"Is this the Theosophical Society?" we asked of the trim maid who opened the door.

She regarded us and our dripping umbrellas and our query with disfavour.

"No, it certainly is not!" she said, and shut the door.

We knocked at number two. "Is this the Theosophical Society?"

"Yes, certainly!" said a young, dark-eyed lad of about eighteen. "Won't you come in?"

Dispossessed of umbrellas and mackintoshes, we entered a room to the right of the hall. It opened with folding doors to another room, and both rooms were filled with people who sat on chairs. Somebody was addressing this audience. Helen and I found a seat and sat attentive. The speaker was talking of dream-consciousness, voyages in the astral, cycles of re-incarnation, of many gorgeous things that shone and revolved like worlds in that little cosmos, that dimly lighted cosmos. From the chandelier in the first room there hung a strange pattern of triangles that seemed to form a globe, and from that again hung a serpent. When the speaker had finished, the meeting was thrown open. Anyone could speak or ask questions. Immediately a man in one of the front chairs bounced to his feet.

"You put your souls in jeopardy with this talk," he yelled. "Listen to me, there is only one true way of salvation, and you can find it for yourselves in the Bible, the Word of God."

One or two people heckled him a little, and encouraged by opposition, he burst into a full-bodied Gospel harangue. He ceased only for want of breath, but the people only sat and smiled. Afterwards I learned he did this every night. It was his way of solacing his soul for the secret delight he took in these Pagan orations, and the society of these heretical folk. While he discoursed, I stared at walls and ceilings. The walls had pictures painted on them—perhaps pictures is not the word, symbolic emblems or drawings which made

29

one think of Blake's drawings. In one place a small human figure stood between two great Beings, one blue and the other scarlet, who seemed eager to engage the attention of the man. In another place great serpents, crowned and plumed, reared their heads. The light was dim, and the pictures moved in it like tapestries blown by the wind, now in light, now in shadow.

I had been at Theosophical meetings that were livelier than this one, meetings where you didn't have to listen to Gospelers, and I was just resolving that this first visit to the Theosophical Rooms would be my last when someone rose at the back of the hall and began to speak. It was a wonderful voice, unlike any other I had ever heard. I craned round to see who possessed it. In the dim light at the end of the hall I could see a tall, slender, bearded man. He leaned slightly forward as he spoke. He spoke eagerly, but his talk had nothing to do with anything that had been said earlier in the evening. I don't really know what he said. I could only think that here was the most bewildering person I had ever encountered. He did not seem to be human, but rather the vehicle through which some Being, rainbow-hued and unearthly, manifested itself. When he ceased speaking, I sat for a while in wonderment, till Helen said, "We had better be getting home."

Already many people had filed out of the room. As we turned to go, a girl with very bright red hair and an eager face came up and said, "Wouldn't you like to look at the pictures on the walls?"

"They remind me of Blake's drawings," I said. "Who painted them?"

"Why, Æ, to be sure!"

"Æ?" I queried.

"Yes, Æ, the diphthong of Aeon, the name he writes under. His real name is George Russell. Haven't you heard of him? Don't you know him? It was Æ who spoke before the meeting broke up."

30

He was still at the end of the hall. I looked down at him. He had a group of people round him.

"Tell me more about Æ," I said to the girl.

"Wouldn't you like to meet him? I'll bring him up."

She brought him up, and he moved with us from painted wall to wall.

His eyes were of a strange blue, very luminous. In the dusky room he made a semblance of light about himself. Gods and Heroes, Days and Nights of Brahma, Mountains, Fire-Fountains, Lakes, and Forests loomed and faded and scintillated through his talk.

Was it rain outside, muttering and pattering, or the sound of shaken sistrums, the swish of the boat that oared Osiris on the Sunken Waters at Abydos?

SILENT HOUSE

It is an afternoon in Springtime, all sunshine, green leaves, and bird-music. I find myself in Saint Stephen's Green Park with nothing to occupy me, and say to myself: "It is only a step to the Theosophical quarters in Ely Place."

Turning the handle of the door, I walk in. There seems to be no one about, I have the whole house to myself—a joyous emptiness, space and quiet. Strolling idly, I reach the back office.

Great silence in the back office, but two people are there: Violet North, and the strong-visaged, red-haired poet, Paul Gregan. They are seated on chairs at either side of the fireplace. Their chairs are tilted back, and their feet are set squarely on the mantelpiece. Each one is solemnly smoking a long churchwarden clay pipe. I am about to speak, but a gesture from Violet stops me. It means silence. I sit down

31

meekly and dumbly. Perhaps they are conducting an occult experiment.

They smoke solemnly for ten minutes more. Then Violet says:

"We can speak now. I'm Carlyle and he's Tennyson."

"It gives me a new idea of those personages," say I, "but why this silence? I thought that Carlyle was a great talker, and Tennyson well able to put words together."

"That's just it," says Violet, "the only time they ever loved each other was one time when they sat and smoked together without speaking a word for one hour. Now we've done it!"

"Yes," chimes in the poet, "nothing like being thorough! I didn't think Violet could keep it up for an hour."

"I didn't think *he* could," says Violet, "but we did, you see!"

We sat there, the three of us, and talked of many things, and as we talked my eyes came to a halt on the door of the inner office. It was covered with inscriptions in what looked like Arabic lettering. Inscriptions of the same kind diverted themselves on the walls.

"Aren't they nice?" queries Violet. "Kenneth Morris and I did them this morning."

"Yes," say I doubtfully, "but what are they?"

"Texts from the Koran. Kenneth and I are reading the Koran, and we have been converted. This is an idea of spreading the gospel!"

"An excellent way truly: the less intelligible a gospel is, the stronger its grip! Perhaps you'll convert the whole Society!"

"Alas, no. Æ says we've got to clean them all off."

Kenneth Morris slipped into the room at this moment—tall, slender, dark-eyed, with an eager clear-cut face; Kenneth Morris, the young Welsh poet, who was afterwards to write, *The Book of the Three Dragons*, and foredate Spengler in the discovery of Cycles of Culture and Civilization. Kenneth, shy and very young, sat silent while Tennyson and Carlyle, recuperating from that unwonted hour, talked with

32

vigour and munificence. How could anyone foreknow that Kenneth, beautiful then as a young knight carved on a tombstone, would keep his poet-heart and his high noble dreams, and his beauty, the length of a lifetime when the rest of us, faltering, showed the dust and sweat of the road.

Presently Æ came in. He had in his hands a drawing of an airship, a drawing in coloured chalk. He had seen the airship at Kilmashogue. We fell to talking of airships and of the sacred mountain of Kilmashogue.

"The Folk of Dana have these ships," said Æ. "I think they go about in them often, and we spy on them now and then."

Violet had seen airships. They were like this one that Æ had drawn.

"You can see them at Newgrange, too," said Violet. "Over the mound of Angus a group of us saw three in broad daylight."

"They must have seen them in ancient Ireland too," said I, "for, in the annals, it is recorded: 'This year, a wonder—three ships in the air over Tara.'"

How far back all these wonders reached in Ireland! One heard faery music on the sacred mountain: did not Finn, thousands of years ago, on a night of the nights, encounter a god from the sacred mountain of Slieve Gullion who brought music with him and devastated Tara.

At Kilmashogue, an old and gracious Master, like a king out of the Golden Age, showed himself at times and instructed disciples. Kilmashogue could open: in a fire-body one could enter it to find a vast chamber and learn wisdom from the Master. Æ had been in there many times. Violet had been there. A French poet that I knew had entered and had found an altar. And the Master had said, "This is the altar on which souls are fashioned."

Outside, the sunshine took on the colours of evening.

"I think the folk of the gods come out at twilight," said Æ. "Do you remember what Yeats said: 'There is one hour when everything is beautiful.'"

33

A hush fell on all of us till Violet began to recite in her beautiful chanting voice the poem that Yeats had made about Inisfree.

Talk had come to an end. The sky was changing from rose to amethyst. Shadows purpled the streets.

Kilmashogue would be darkening, retreating into its radiant heart.

I walked home, thinking of that mountain.

THE HERMETIC SOCIETY

THERE HAS BEEN a split in the Theosophical Society: Æon, followed by all the young writers and poets, has renounced Mrs. Tingley. The house in Ely Place has shut its doors against us.

We call ourselves "The Hermetic Society," and meet in a room, found after much searching, in a house empty but for ourselves. One climbs two flights of stairs to reach it. First one has to find the stairs: newcomers search for a long while before discovering the blind alley and the dusty entrance to the half-deserted house whence those stairs lead up to the deserted room. Tallow candles light it. It is full of shadows and dust. The members are supposed to clean it up now and again, but they don't think of it very often. A fire burns in the grate when anyone remembers to bring sods of turf.

Opening dimly from that first room is a second, dignified with the title of library—it has much emptiness and a few books and pamphlets.

In contrast the walls of the chief room are covered with papers more or less securely pinned there. Close inspection discovers them to be sonnets and lyrics in the hand-writing of the authors. There are questions and replies in verse—

34

mock-serious criticisms and compliments. Neatly written on a large piece of paper is a query which purports to come from Helen Laird—though in reality Æ wrote it in a spirit of mischief. It begins:

> Dear God, I wonder if you've heard
> Of me—my name is Helen Laird,

and goes on to complain that in the Hermetic everyone has a different idea of God and it is hard for a beginner to choose. I wish I could remember this masterpiece, but unfortunately I can only recall a verse referring to myself:

> My sister, Ella, takes of you (God)
> A territorial sort of view:
> I think an Island is her notion
> Somewhere in the Atlantic Ocean.

Seumas O'Sullivan, slender and graceful, brings in lyrics which he is too shy to read. James Connolley has a fine sonnet about a ship. Padraic Colum is concerned with ballad poetry.

Æ lectures on occultism every Thursday evening, and when the lecture is over he discusses poetry and criticizes the work of his young poets. He thinks it will be possible to collect enough material for a small book of verse: with a foreword from him it would find a publisher.

At times we persuade Æ to recite his own poetry. He does so in a rich chanting voice. Sound, he insists, is one of the great things in poetry. Keats and Shelley he praises, Swinburne he does not mention.

STANDISH O'GRADY

IT WAS LATE when I got to the Hermetic Rooms last night. The meeting was over and members were standing in little

groups discussing everything—or nothing—as the case might be. Æ was a little apart talking with a clean-shaven distinguished-looking man, whom he brought up to me with:
"You know who this is—Standish O'Grady!"

Standish O'Grady whose books we knew by heart—all of us—whose *Critical and Philosophical History of Ireland* was a second bible, whose *Red Hugh*, whose *Cuchulain* were household words!

Whatever I might have felt of awe at meeting one whom I had long regarded as a master-patriot and scholar was dispelled by the ease and charm of the man himself.

Standish was planning a crusade and was all a-fire with the idea. The landed gentry needed only to know some truths about Ireland and about themselves. If they were made aware of what a proud and ancient culture they could claim as Irishmen, they would claim that inheritance—if they realized that they must throw in their fortunes with their countrymen, or lose both lands and authority, they would save themselves: they would head the "New Ireland Movement" rather than lag behind and be destroyed by it!

He is so sure of this, but as he talks my mind slips back to something that Æ has told me: Standish O'Grady had qualified as a barrister, and with his talent and the help he could expect from titled friends he had a brilliant career before him.

He chose to interrupt success: he pored upon old manuscripts and Gaelic Sagas; he wrote the *Critical and Philosophical History of Ireland;* he followed it up with the *Bardic History of Ireland.* One of his high-placed friends read a few pages of the latter, and said to him:
"If you intend to do anything in life, you will cut free from this kind of stuff: *Cuchulain! Fardia!* the very names are an abomination!"

Standish, with a pedigree that goes back a thousand years; with lands that have been in possession of his ancestors for as long as anyone can remember, feels that he can gauge and speak for the landed gentry.

36

With all my heart I wish that he could, but I know that they are not patterned after his fashion. Into my mind flashes another of Æ's stories (for Æ reveres Standish and loves to talk of him): Standish owns a strip of ancestral lands that produces nothing but an upcrop of stones, sparse grass, and slender-stemmed wild flowers. This land has three castles—all in ruins. A man with a money-making instinct offered a big price for one of the castles—it would make a fine hotel!

Standish drove him indignantly from his presence.

I think to myself (all crusaders are drunk with the heady wine of another world) this man will not be without followers, though on the fingers of one hand he will be able to number those from the landed gentry.

PORTRAIT

I HAVE BEEN seeing a good deal of Margaret O'Grady these days. Someone has said that Standish O'Grady's wife is like a splendid ship in full sail, and the comparison is apt. She is big, blonde, and handsome, with a way of getting what she wants.

Just now she has her hands full: for in addition to her own plans and projects she has to see that Standish sets out every morning for the studio where John Butler Yeats is painting his portrait. Standish doesn't want to sit for his portrait, but a deputation of citizens has begged him to forego his own wishes in the matter because the National Gallery needs to have a portrait of the man who has done more than anyone else to awaken interest in the Irish Sagas—more than anyone else to revive the National Spirit.

It is a matter of form to say that Standish is "sitting." He walks about most of the time, stands with his back to the painter, because he wants to look out of the window, gesticulates and waxes wroth when he thinks on what might be, and is not, in Ireland, or lapses into gloomy silence when he adds up in his mind the hours that he might have spent elsewhere.

Yesterday he came home unexpectedly.

"What has happened?" asked his wife anxiously.

"Oh, nothing much," said Standish. "He is only painting me with blue hair. I don't mind looking as grim as Lucifer after the rebellion in Heaven— If Yeats puts 'This Lost Land' on the portrait, it will explain the grimness! But I *won't* have blue hair!"

He will have to be coaxed back, but Mrs. O'Grady seldom fails in what she undertakes. Once only did Standish get the better of her. It was when she escorted him to the breakfast given in his honour by John Quinn of New York. The breakfast awaited them in the Shelbourne Hotel, a short distance from their own house. As they walked along (Mrs. O'Grady triumphant at the thought of an early start) Standish stopped short and looked at his wrists.

"I've come out without cuffs, Meg—I must go back for them."

"You can't, Standish: we are due at the breakfast."

Standish walked in silence for some minutes, then he said: "Grandy's shop is close by. I'll step in there and buy cuffs."

"Don't waste time in the choice, Standish—take anything and hurry back! I'll wait outside the shop."

She waited. Standish did not appear. She waited some more. Then she went inside, and discovered that Grandy's shop had two doors: the one where she stood guard, and one round the corner of the block. Standish was not to be found. He was probably safe at home.

The breakfast progressed without him.

FIRST GLIMPSE OF THE WEST

ENTER MRS. O'GRADY flourishing two scraps of paper.
"We're going to Connemara, you and I!"
"What has happened?" I enquire.
"Well, the Western Railway Company wants Standish to give the country a write-up. They offer two tickets. Of course, Standish wouldn't write it up, so we're going, and you can write it up."
"I'll write it up," said I.
We started. Our tickets took us everywhere that the railway went, and franked us along the famous drives where the railway didn't go.
How splendid to be going West, to Gaelic Ireland, to the unspoiled, beautiful West! The trees grew smaller, the grass sparser. The little fields had stone walls around them. One passed sedgy lakes all bright with water-lilies. It is true the little train, with its self-important panting engine, loitered. It had a pleasant sense of taking its time. It stopped for the engine-driver to light his pipe in a cottage and have a talk with a friend. On one occasion it slowed up to let an old mother goose and her goslings get off the rail. Mrs. O'Grady was much amused, and while I sat down to write the kind of article that would please the Railway Company, she indited a letter to Standish in which she described and embellished these happenings. Standish was delighted. He much preferred it to my article. To please the Railway Company, he published mine; to please himself, he published hers.
Unfortunately, the Railway Company studied the copy of *The All Ireland Review* that he sent them, and came across Mrs. O'Grady's letter. As a result, while we were sunning ourselves in Achill, a lament arrived from Standish. The ingratitude of humanity! That Railway Company had sent a young man to demand an interview and tell Standish what

the Company thought about it! The young man surprised an interview.

"I am glad he did," said Mrs. O'Grady. "I'm glad that Standish had to listen to what the Company thought. Perhaps it will make him careful."

"It will make the Railway Company careful," I said. "We'll never get another ticket!"

We never did.

But how the wind and the sea welcomed us, and the mountains deploying in companies. What joy we had of the wide bog lands stretching to wider skies; what colour there was of greenness in the sparse grass; what splendour of orange in tangled sea-wrack caught among the ancient granite-gray boulders.

My first glimpse of the West. My first experience of an enchantment that has held me all my life. Those little lakes with the sedges, those unplowable bogs, those untameable mountains, those wind-blown trees, those reaches of sand where the waves lap and make a song for the sea-birds—lonely, untrodden reaches by the sea, how well I remember them!

How well I remember the stone-walled cottages so securely thatched; the generous fireplace with its ingle-neuk; the raftered ceiling; the stories by the smouldering turf-sods; the dawns, the sunsets, the unbelievable beauty!

ANOTHER GLIMPSE OF THE WEST

IT IS ALMOST dusk, and I am walking along a road that is strange to me. Someone should have met me at the little railway station with a jaunting-car. Nobody did. I am bound for a farmhouse. Some kind folk have pointed out the road. I must walk. There is a strange delight in following an unknown road at dusk. It lengthens out, it takes strange shapes; some adventure lies at the end of it, one seems to think. I had no idea how far off the house was or how long it would take me to get there. The magic of the West held me, as it always did. It didn't seem to matter whether I found a house.

Why had no one come to meet me at the railway station? I had taken such trouble to find out from a railway guide exactly when that train would arrive at Cong. (And this, of course, was silly, since everyone in the West knew exactly when a train arrived, an event like a thunderstorm or a meteor.) Why hadn't they come? This question was beginning to eat into my mind, beginning to spoil the mystery of the unknown road, and the twilight with song of thrush and blackbird in it. The emptiness of the road, the darkening sky, gave me a sense of going on and on, over the edge of the world. But a clatter of horse hooves and wheels asserted itself and round a corner an Irish jaunting-car came into sight. The man who drove was standing on the dashboard to drive more effectively. He drew up with a flourish.

"Are you the lady from Dublin?"

"Yes, I am," I said in an injured tone. "Why did no one meet the train? Did you get my letter?"

"We got no letter. We thought you were not coming. But a while ago my mother said, 'Take the car and go out to meet her. She is on the road.' "

"What could have happened to the letter?" I asked, safely ensconced in the car. "Oh, it's the postmistress," said he. "She keeps the hotel in the town and opens all the letters from tourists. If no one meets them at the train she is there to talk about the hotel." That made me suddenly remember that someone had spoken to me of the hotel and suggested that I spend the night there. But I was determined to be far from the sound of a railway train.

A warm welcome awaited me in the small farmhouse. The woman of the house, dignified and pleasant-faced, came out to help me from the car. The daughter, a shy young girl with red-gold hair, was there too. In the background stood

41

the father of the family. My driver was the red-haired, only son. Firelight and tallow candles made a brightness in the house.

My bedroom smelt heavily of peat smoke. (I learned afterwards that in some occult fashion that room gathered to itself any smoke that might be going loose about the house.) But dominating the peat smoke, dominating the room, was a sense of the country outside, passionately alive, rejoicing in itself—strong, strong and beautiful in the darkness. I could hardly wait for dawn light to see it.

A country of stone, with colours no grassland can take: purples that lightened to amethyst, pale reaches of silver, blue that rivaled lapis lazuli, faint fugitive touches of rose. The lakes it had did not give greenness. Their waters were still and black. What did that country remember? Something too old for man. He had no part in the fantasy of its rocks, in the dark steely glitter of its waters. Hawks could live there. Hawks and the Gods of Dana. Like jewels, like the colours of dawn and sunset, like unearthly flowers, the Gods of Dana moved in the desert of stone, showed themselves in the haunted knolls. White horses, a flaunt of many-coloured mantles, strange head-dresses they had. Like a hound before them and following them went the wind. Music swirled and sounded about them. It was good for a man to veil his eyes as they passed. They were out of the old, old life of the earth—before the glaciers had ribbed these rocks and scooped these hollows—they would be there when ice again gave quietness to the world.

The country-folk had stories of giants and dwarfs, of kings whose burial mounds made the only hills in the landscape. A great battle between gods and demons had raged once from horizon to horizon.

"Do you see yon tall standing stone?" said the son of the house as the jaunting-car rattled past it. "A great king lies under it. His name was Lugh Lamh-fada."

How well I knew that name! Lugh the Long-handed, the Sun God, Lugh Ildana, the Master of every Craft, the Cham-

42

pion of the Gods—Lugh, under that stone, dead! But his great white Hound still coursed the heavens, and dying folk yet prayed for dawn.

By the turf fire in the stone-flagged kitchen we sat, night after night, talking: the household and myself. Candle-light made slight inroad on the darkness, but the turves were warmly red. We talked of prophesies; of saints that had the power to bless or curse; of golden cups and buried treasure; of boats that sped over lonely inhospitable waters where the living dared not venture; of folk who made fortunes in America, the New Island, as they called it—feeling it closer by them than Dublin town, nearer than Tara, once so spend-thrift of wine and song—Tara, where their ancestors had foregathered with kings.

At last I had to go. The horse was in the shafts of the jaunting-car, my meagre traveling kit hoisted across the threshold, and the household gathered in the open air to bid me farewell: the man of the house, the golden-haired daughter, the son who had handled the reins on so many journeys across bog and stone-land, and the woman of the house. In Gaelic Ireland the woman is always the head of the house. This woman, gracious, kindly-featured, nimble-witted, had been most kind to me. I thought of her as I thought of the country itself, with joy and respect. She came forward now to speak for the group. She said:

"You will go far away from here, and with time you will forget this place and us, but we will never forget that a great saint once stayed in our house."

She kissed my hand. I could not find any words.

"A Great Saint!"

Would I in the long years of a lifetime forget that! I never dared to publish it. I never dared make trial of it on my family. But one reason why I write these memoirs is that I may record it here.

CAVE OF THE RED STEEDS

ONE EVENING AS we sat by the wide hearth in that raftered house at Cong, the talk was of a cave not more than a few miles from the farmhouse. A strange cave, said the folk of the house. I had to take it on hearsay, for no one knew by actual hazard what the cave was like. It has the name of being demon-haunted, and wise folk keep their distance. Everyone believes that the cave extends for miles underground, but it is marked only by a small opening in a field that has little else to boast of. It is a treasure-cave, say the country-folk, and piled within it are cups with jeweled rims, shields of gold and silver, bronze swords and hammered necklets.

Lured by that glittering hoard, foolhardy individuals have, in times past, braved the entrance: but have either returned hurriedly—sans the treasure—or have never returned. There is a tale that once a piper ventured in, playing lustily on his war-pipes. The music could be heard growing fainter and fainter till it ceased. The piper never came out.

But at times things came out of that cave. Horses came out—red, small-eared steeds! Two hounds came out, and gamboled on the scant grass of the meadow—a black hound and a white hound. Water came out in a torrent flooding the low-lying ground. Broken fragments of soil with grass-roots and heather came out. It was plain to the country-folk that a river must be somewhere underground, a river that no one could put a name on, a river that was not charted on a map.

One person, tradition said, came back with a story of having encountered the river. It had by the brink of it a woman who was rinsing blood-stained warrior-gear in the waters.

At once I thought to myself: I could name that River, and name the Woman too. It is the River that separates the world

44

of the living from the world of the dead: and the Woman is the Washer at the Ford, her name is Macha.

Cu-Cullion on his death-journey met with her. She is well-known in the ancient sagas.

How is it that the country-folk who have forgotten the old tales invent them anew with no greater stimulus than a hole in the earth that a badger might scoop? What are those hounds but the Hounds of Annwn—the breed that bays behind the Wild Huntsman? Those sods of flowered turf from a far country—should the flowers not be asphodel, or red-chaliced lilies from the Honey Plain?

I announced my intention of exploring the Cave. The household was filled with consternation.

"No one will go in with you," said the Woman of the House —"It is a terrible thing to think of you going in by yourself."

I assured her that I was used to caves. I had crawled into caves. In caves I had sat solitary. I had gone by boat into caves where the sea groaned and snorted like a wounded beast. Caves were in fact a thing that experience made me fit to handle!

The talk stretched far into the night before I could win consent to the enterprise. At last it was agreed that I should take with me three wax candles which had been lit on Saint Brigit's Feast, and specially blest for an emergency; I should take also a ball of twine to unwind as I went. Friends would stay at the Cave mouth to keep God and the Saints acquainted with my whereabouts.

Next morning the Woman of the House climbed up beside me on the jaunting-car, which was driven as usual by the Son of the House. We had the candles and the twine.

The Cave was just a small opening in a neglected-looking field, with a house near by—a small thatched farmhouse. Our advent drew everyone from the house (the only one in sight) and the news that I meant to enter the Cave stirred protest and advice. Not a soul had entered the Cave within memory of the oldest inhabitant, but there was a tradition that people —strangers from a long way off—had taken a treasure of gold

45

and silver cups from the Cave: had taken weighed-out gold, and golden candlesticks. No one had word of what befell that spoil or the marauders who snatched it, but the by-standers opined that ill-luck followed and overtook them.

I asked the folk of the nearby house if they had ever seen anything come out of the Cave. "Yes, certainly: water came out in the Wintertime, enough to almost flood the field; it was known that hounds came out of it and horses too."

I took my candles, I took my ball of twine, and squirmed into the Cave. The entrance was so low that one could not stand up or even stoop. The passage became roomier as I advanced, and presently I came to a lofty chamber, the floor of which was raised about a foot and a half above the level of the passage I had traversed. I climbed to the floor, which seemed marvelously devoid of heights and hollows after the rough road I had scrambled and stumbled along. The chamber was symmetrical as if it had been hewn from the living rock. The roof arched away to a point beyond my flickering candle-light. I could see the opening of the passage I had come by, a cave of darkness below floor-level.

But was it the passage?

Not far off I spied another cave of darkness—also below floor-level—and while my gaze traveled round the central platform, another, and another, and another.

As I realized the significance of those caves of darkness my fingers clutched instinctively at the ball of twine. I placed it carefully on the floor, in full view of my three candles which I had set upright at equal distances. There was a great silence everywhere. The world of days and weeks and years did not exist any longer. My thoughts went back to another silence—silence and darkness in the Brugh of Angus, the artificial chambered mound at Newgrange by the Boyne.

I sat alone once in the Central Chamber of the Brugh (having bribed the custodian to absent herself and her candles). The roof arched above me in blackness and there was a great silence about me, penetrated by the chill joyous-ness of the Brugh.

46

Suddenly I became aware that the Chamber was filling with pale light that surged like water through the narrow tortuous entrance passage. Like water, it seemed to have weight and substance. Washed by this pale liquid slow-moving light the pillar-stone of the Brugh suddenly flamed silver, shot up like a column of moon-fire. The Sun, journeying westward, had touched it with an out-stretched finger.

The Chamber in the Cave of the Red Steeds was more wonderful, the silence more penetrating, the joyousness more intense. I felt that if I sat there long enough I might attain to a state of spiritual perception in which Time, Space and Fate shriveled to nothingness.

The joyousness for the time being engrossed me, but just as I said to myself: "I shall stay here a long while," I became conscious of the minds of the folk outside. They were growing anxious. After all, I was having the whole pleasure in this expedition. They were sitting dully outside. I took one last look at the ribs of rock arching into blackness, one last look at the dark openings that stood like doorways—leading God knows where! By what doorway, what passage had I entered? I could not tell. They all had a similar aspect. But the clue of cord was there to guide me. I carefully collected my candles, extinguished two of them, and followed the clue. It brought me to daylight and a group of people who asked me if I had seen the river or found traces of treasure. They were disappointed when I said that I had not.

I keep thinking of that Cave. Assuredly a Fountain of Youth jets upward in it from the heart of the Earth even as a Fountain of Youth and Joyousness jets upward in the Brugh of Angus. To this day it can be felt in the Brugh by practically everyone who goes there. They find themselves talking and laughing: it seems, on dull overclouded days, as if the Sun came forth.

The Cave of the Red Steeds is natural—the Cave of the Brugh of Angus has been carefully fashioned. The Ultonian kings paid honour to it, and at the Samhain Festival processions wound among the standing stones that still, in broken forma-

47

tion, circle the mound. Fire leaped on the summit. Five great roads converged on it.

Did kings, and druids, and joyous processions ever pay homage to the Cave of the Red Steeds?

KILKIERAN

MAUD JOYNT, MARY SCARLETT, and myself have arrived in Kilkieran. We wanted a wild, God-forsaken place, and this seems to be it. We occupy the only house that can harbour visitors, and they have to be hardy, much-enduring visitors. The house is of stone, it is two stories high, and has all the comforts of civilization: linoleum in the chief room, a sofa and several dingy stuffed chairs. The house belongs to the postmistress. Her children wear shoes, and are called "the little ladies." Nobody else wears shoes among the children of Kilkieran. The other houses are one-story high, crouching among the walls of their little fields. Everywhere there stretches a desolation of mountains and of waters. Not a tree, not a bush. It is a country of lonely waters, black bogland, and stone—purple, silver, and amethyst stone—a country that is not green, a country that no one can exploit, beautiful and wild, untameable as a hawk. I regard the linoleum and the tawdry chairs with disfavour, and look out of the window. There is a low stone wall near the house, and beyond that the sea. On the wall a man is sitting. He is bearded, he looks like a Greek of the age of Pericles. He has the air of not being occupied with anything, not even with his own thoughts. So might an Athenian have sunned himself. There is not another person in sight.

I rehearse in my mind a few sentences of Gaelic. I am going to try them on that man. I try them. They are successful. My Gaelic does not smack too much of school books and Dublin. Presently we are talking. His name is Padraic Greene. We talk of sailing-boats and the sea. He has a sailing-boat, one that is never used for fishing, the fastest boat on the water. We become friends at once. Padraic is not afraid of the sea. He plays with it. It is a joy to him, he says. He doesn't want to fish, he just wants to feel the boat leaping on the water. He is a man after my own heart. Certainly we will take that boat out and go sailing.

We take it out first thing next day. I persuade Maud Joynt and Mary Scarlett to come with me. Padraic manages the boat and there is a boy to help him, called Mat. When we start, Padraic dips the long oars in the water. He lifts an oar-blade of water and lets it drop back into the sea. He does this three times for sea-luck. He says it is to honour the Trinity, but I think of the three waves of Mannanaun and of folk who invoked the sea-god centuries ago beneath these mountains, on these turbulent waters.

Many days we go out sailing, sometimes with my two friends, sometimes without them. They tire of sailing; I do not. We talk about old sagas. Padraic knows the fine points of a story. He knows many of the old Gaelic stories. I tell him stories of Greece, episodes from the *Iliad*. Padraic praises the best and the second and the third best as they should be praised. Stories in Greece and in Ireland are much the same.

Wide skies, the wind, the foam-curled waves, a boat that lifts to the waves and the wind, days that repeat themselves, sunshine and dusk.

THE SCHOLAR

PADRAIC GREENE is taking Maud Joynt, Mary Scarlett, and myself from Kilkieran across to Inishmore, the largest of the Aran Islands, in his sailing-boat. The wind is fresh, the waves promise a dance for the boat. It is a dance, and rather too much. My two friends say it is too much to be endured. Inishmore is like a faery island beckoning, enticing as the song of a siren, but my friends are obdurate. We turn back. The wind freshens, the sea is more mountainous. Padraic suddenly runs the boat into a long, green inlet of the sea. Mountains keep out the wind. The water is still and of a marvelous greenness. Two or three other boats have found shelter in the inlet. The men are leaning over the sides, the tall, slender, dark men of Connaught. They are gazing idly at the water as their ancestors might have gazed a thousand years ago. They do not lift their eyes to stare at us. They are too proud to stare at strangers. Padraic, without appearing to stare, takes stock of them, and presently announces:

"There is a great scholar on one of those boats."

A scholar! We prick our ears. Maud Joynt is a Gaelic scholar. Mary Scarlett speaks Gaelic fluently. I speak it a little.

"Padraic," I say, "has the scholar any of the old stories?"

"He has," says Padraic, "stories that came down through generations."

"Do you think," said we all three, "that he would come aboard and drink tea with us?"

"He would do that," said Padraic.

Padraic was ambassador. He returned with the scholar, and a number of his friends. We had tea and then we begged the scholar for a story. He got to his feet, and we arranged ourselves on either side of him in a half-circle. The story would be prose, so we could sit. Had it been poetry, everyone would have been obliged to stand. It was a long and a splendid story. I could not follow it very well. I hoped that my friends did, but everyone in the half-circle listened with reverence and made the appropriate remarks. That is to say, at every pause we cried out:

"What a jewel of a story!"

"Wasn't that hero the champion of the world?"

50

"If I were to cross the ocean to see a fight, 'tis that fight I would choose to see."

"Oh, it's great that story is entirely!"

We sat in a circle, listening reverently, and making the traditional remarks, all of us except Mat, the boy whom Padraic had with him in the boat. Mat went forward into the bow, leaned over, and spat meditatively into the sea. When the scholar had gone and there was no one in the boat but ourselves, Padraic said to Mat:

"Isn't it a shame for you to disgrace yourself, you that had a decent rearing, and couldn't behave yourself like the son of your honest father."

"Yes," I chimed in, "Mat, why did you go away from the others? Why didn't you listen to the story?"

"Because I didn't understand a word of it!" said Mat.

"Understand a word of it!" said Padraic. "Did I understand a word of it? Did anyone understand a word of it?"

"What!" cried I, "Padraic, aren't you a native-born Irish speaker?"

"I am, thank God," said Padraic, "and my father's before me."

"Well, why didn't you understand a word of it?"

"Because," said Padraic, "it's old, old Irish out of the old times, and this man had the words of it from his father, and he from his father again, and back and back, till an eagle couldn't remember it—or the oldest tree! He has the very words. He didn't change them."

Then suddenly I understood what a marvelous happening it had been. This man came of a family of story-tellers, his ancestors may have told this story to pleasure the kings of Connaught in the days of Ireland's Golden Age. Of course no one understood it. English-speaking folk would not understand the *Saga of Beowulf* if someone recited it as the first singer had recited it for the Saxons. If, somewhere in England, one discovered in a remote cottage a man who could recite the *Saga of Beowulf*, a man whose ancestors from father to son had handed it down to him, what a to-do there

51

would be. The story this man recited came from an older age. Probably it would die with him. It was a story of the Fianna, and Cunnaun, the Connaught warrior, was the hero of it: a tale of how he took the shape of a great bird and went to the rescue of Finn, who had been carried away by a king from overseas.

We were all sober-minded as our boat headed for Kilkieran. I was thinking how much a sojourn in England as potato-picker had spoiled Mat's manners, how much the potato-picking world was spoiling all our manners, how soon it would invade every place, triumphant, chock-full of confidence and common sense.

GREEN WATER

PADRAIC, MAT, AND I, and the slim, eager sailing-boat are wave-riding. We have oilskin helmets on our heads, and oilskins reaching to our feet. Padraic is maneuvering the boat so that a wave will hit her on the bow, and rise over the side in a tongue of spray that will leap clear over the open body of the boat (she is only decked on the bow) and out beyond the stern with scarce a drop of water spilled. At least it would not be spilled if no one sat in the stern, well to the left of the tiller. But I am sitting there. Part of that glorious rush of water will strike my shoulder and dash on my face and be gone!

How the boat leaps and lifts. No motor holds her down. She is alive, she sports in the water like a dolphin, she veers and turns like a sea-gull, she takes the wave like a sea-hawk striking prey.

Now Padraic is maneuvering so that the wave will come over the stern, brush my shoulder, dropping a glitter of spray in my lap, leap clear of the open body and dive over

52

the bow. It requires skill. If Padraic, or the boat miscalculates, the wave will come aboard and swirl about our feet. One wave would not swamp us, but it would be a mishap.

We are out of sight of Kilkieran village. We have the sea and the sky and the barren mountains to ourselves. That is a good thing. The villagers think we are all three mad, and tempters of the Almighty! But we know that we have sea-luck. This is a boat that will not drown, nor will any one of us three at any time, unless we decree it ourselves.

Presently we will return to the harbour with dignity and seemliness, displaying that craftsmanship which sets Padraic above every sea-expert in Kilkieran. We will be talking of magical lakes, and of horses, gray to whiteness, that lift dripping shoulders and neigh shrilly in the hours before dawn, of faery music that echoes among the reeds, of strange lights that move on the waters.

MAUD GONNE

I HAVE NEVER SEEN Maud Gonne, but I want to see her. I wonder how I can bring it about. I hear that she is going to lecture in some small room to a gathering of ultra-patriots. It is likely there will be free fights in the audience. She has the art of stirring her hearers to that pitch of enthusiasm. My folks will certainly never allow me to go by myself. I try to think of some respectable person who will take me. Finally I bribe my young brother.

There is not a free fight after all, and quite a lot of boring people speak before Maud Gonne comes on the platform. She reads her speech, a tall wax candle on either side of the desk. I am disappointed in the speech, but not in the beauty of Maud Gonne. She has a beauty that surprises one—like the sun when it leaps above the horizon. She is tall and like

53

a queen out of a saga. Her hair is burnished gold and her eyes are gold, really gold.

I do not see her again for many months. Then I see her standing with W. B. Yeats, the poet, in front of Whistler's *Miss Alexander* in the Dublin gallery where some pictures by Whistler are astonishing a select few. These two people delight the bystanders more than the pictures. Everyone stops looking at canvas and maneuvers himself or herself into a position to watch these two. They are almost of equal height. Yeats has a dark, romantic cloak about him; Maud Gonne has a dress that changes colour as she moves. They pay no attention to the stir they are creating; they stand there discussing the picture.

I catch sight of them again in the reading room of the National Library. They have a pile of books between them and are consulting the books and each other. No one else is consulting a book. Everyone is conscious of those two, as the denizens of a woodland lake might be conscious of a flamingo, or of a Japanese heron if it suddenly descended among them.

Later, in the narrow curve of Grafton Street, I notice that people are stopping and turning their heads. It is Maud Gonne and the Poet. She has a radiance as of sunlight. Yeats, that leopard of the moon, holds back in a leash a huge lion-coloured Great Dane—Maud Gonne's dog, Dagda.

Destiny swept them closer to me. These two moved through my life for some years, with a background at times of Paris, at times of Irish play-houses, at times of Irish mountain and pine-wood, always with a sense of far-off splendid happenings, of queens of long ago, and of that prince who had the strangeness of hawk-feathers in his hair.

THREE DAYS AGO Phyllis MacMurdo came to me in a state of great excitement.

"We must go on pilgrimage to Slieve Gullion. Do you know it is the mountain of Manannaun?"

"I know it is the mountain of Cullion the Smith. Probably Cullion was a god, since Setanta, the Northern hero, called himself Cullion's Hound—Cu-Cullion."

"I had a vision about the mountain," said Phyllis. "I saw first of all a line of countryside with the sea beyond it. Then between land and sea there sat a great Being, a God, enormous. His head leaned on his knees. But of a sudden he rose up. It was the God Manannaun. And the next moment the mountain appeared. Slieve Gullion is the mountain of Manannaun."

I did not know that it was the mountain of Manannaun, but I have a great respect for pronouncements made by Phyllis. She has considerable psychic power, and is always very honest with herself. Though she has lived for the most part in England and been nurtured in the British tradition, ignorant alike of Irish mythology and of Irish history, she comes of Highland stock and Ireland has wakened the Seer in her.

Yesterday we went on pilgrimage to Slieve Gullion. We had to go part of the way by train, part of the way on a jaunting-car, and part of the way on foot. Where the makeshift road ended, the jaunting-car, perforce, came to a standstill, and we approached the mountain over slanting meadows of sparse grass set thick with wild pansies, blue and milky amber. Slieve Gullion is not a peaked mountain. It crouches—humped and enormous—a territory, a bastion fronting the sea on one hand, and looming on the other above the approaches to the country of the North. So sacred was it once that men, animals, and even household goods brought within its shadow were in sanctuary. Its widely extending summit was known as the White Radiant House of Lir. This mountain had thronged processions once and sound of singing men and blown trumpets. On the day of our pilgrimage it was silent save for the sound of bees, velvet furry black-and-gold wild bees that rioted in the blossomed heath and heather—a bourneless paradise, since as far as the eye could travel the mountainside was garmented in a multi-coloured magnificence of purple blossom, of carmine, and pale rose.

Phyllis, eager to see all that time allowed, started at once to climb. I threw myself upon the heather, so honey fragrant, and closed my eyes. What memories the mountain must hold in its heart: memories shared by the lake that it bears shoulder-high and hidden—the lake of the goddess! Unforgotten still must be the night when Cu-Cullion possessed himself of the Faery Steed, the Grey of Macha, seizing it strong-handed as it thrust from the lake-bed dripping and silver-pale in the moon-path. Unforgotten still must be the sunlight that clung about Fionn, son of Uail, when the White Hind that he had followed so tirelessly led him solitary and joyous-hearted to the lake margin, led him to the wan adventure that waited beneath its waters. Unforgotten must be Allyn son of Midna faring forth to avenge the spear-theft, faery lissome, shod with music, plumed with every splendour of sun and star-shine.

The myriad-throated song and silence of the mountain was about me. Sharp tang and savour of the sea mingled in my nostrils with the honey fragrance of heather; a wild bee blundered past from time to time; shadow and sunshine raced on the mountain-slope. It was so until Phyllis returned.

She had not found the lake, but joining company with a man and a woman of the district, she had news of it. They told her that the lake is shaped like the moon when the moon is new, the marge is desolate-bare and coloured like a sword of hammered iron. The water is wine-red. The lake is bottomless, and round about it are set powerful strange

56

stones with carvings upon them. No one knows the meaning of the stones, or who set them there.

"We are fortunate to be here," said Phyllis. "Let us gather heather, white and red, and go tonight to the play that the Daughters of Ireland are putting on to honour the Festival of the Lughnassa. There should be heather from Slieve Gullion on the stage and in the hands of people in the audience."

We gathered armfuls of heather, and set our feet again upon the scant grass of the slanting meadows. The jaunting-car was a small blot in the enameled countryside. I turned for a last look at the mountain. It sentinelled the horizon. The sky was violet-dusk behind it. I would fain have invoked it for strength to serve Ireland, but I dared not. The Mountain was too august. I made haste to overtake Phyllis, and at that moment Slieve Gullion reached out to me in a graciousness unbelievable—a ray of benediction from a god.

All the way to Dublin our minds hurried the train that puffed so contentedly along. We had to give up supper—or the play! We gave up supper.

That night the little room in a back street of Dublin city—where the Daughters of Ireland were celebrating the Lugh-nassa, the Marriage Feast of Lugh the Sun God to the Royal Sovereignty of Ireland—that little shabby room with its improvised stage had a luck-gift of heather, red and white, from Slieve Gullion.

The play was *Red Hugh's Captivity* by Alice Milligan, always a delight—Red Hugh escaping through the window that does duty on the stage for Dublin Castle—Red Hugh climbing into the night with the stars alone for spectators is the symbol of Ireland escaping.

When the shouts and cheers and snatches of song had subsided the curtain went up on the Prologue to *The Last Feast of the Fianna,* a second play by Alice Milligan, dealing with the Fionn Saga.

It had been arranged that Maud Gonne should read the

legend which Alice Milligan was using in the play. The raised curtain showed her, seated in an ancient carved chair, with an illuminated parchment book on her knee. She had a splendid robe of brocaded white poplin with wide sleeves, and two little pages in medieval dress of black velvet held tall wax candles on either side of her. The stage was strewn with green rushes and branchlets of blossomed heather.

Maud Gonne has a sun-radiance about her. The quality of her beauty dulled the candle-flames. I spoke to her that night for the first time, presenting red and white heather from Slieve Gullion.

"OF SO MUCH FAME IN HEAV'N EXPECT THY MEED"

THERE ARE so many things to do, to learn, to see, in Dublin City that I wonder how I find time to hammer away at verse and prose. I have tried for years to carve something beautiful out of words. I am trying harder than ever, now! When I lived with those lush sleepy meadows, those uneventful days in the Midlands, I had plenty of leisure but no one to hearten me. I cannot be sure that I have found anyone to hearten me over-much in this place, but I have found comrades: and Æ gives to me, as he gives to all his poets in tutelage, much advice. He thinks, even, of sponsoring a small book of verse selected from our best attempts.

"Seumas O'Sullivan," announces Æ, "has a thin streak of genius." This is heartening for Seumas who has, perhaps, more than a streak. Æ has not made such a comment in my case. Indeed when I bring him some carefully wrought stanzas, he says: "Why don't you get music into them? Sound is what matters. You should know your Keats and Shelley better!" I balked when, on hearing some of my blank verse,

58

he suggested Milton. "To me Milton's blank verse is heavy and monotonous. At times he has a splendid line, or the flash of an image at white heat—but for the rest!" The rest was silence.

I am working hard at prose. Arthur Griffith takes my articles, and Standish O'Grady publishes everything that I send to him. But these two people are more concerned with what one says than with how one says it. I am concerned very much at present with how one says it. I have progressed a good deal, I think, from those childish days when I covered exercise books with high-faluting phrases. Perhaps I have only moved from one set of high-faluting phrases to another— yet without the jeweled phrase, prose does not repeat itself in the mind, or ask to be read a second time. I am proud, at least, of one piece of prose that I have written, and because of my fondness for it, and because the incident it embodies has left an ineradicable stamp on my imagination, I set it in the wake of this chapter. I have named it: "The Rose Queen."

THE ROSE-QUEEN

I SAW HER when I was coming out of church. Church was hateful, but I had to go there. I sat through the hours of it resentfully, pretending to myself that I did not see the blank walls or the dingy pulpit. The people looked ugly. I had a half-formed, childish suspicion that I looked ugly myself. It did not matter. Nothing mattered but the clock. If one counted the red velvet buttons on the pew-cushions, and the heads of the people who sat opposite, and the squares of glass in the window, and then looked cautiously back to the clock, the hand would have moved five minutes.

The hands of the clock had crawled through the last minute. The Benediction had been pronounced. I was escaping. How I hated the slow, shuffling crowd. People pressed upon me from behind; they pushed into the corridor in front of me; they swarmed on every side. It seemed hours before I came to the stairs leading from the gallery.

The descent began—shuffling, hateful, intolerably slow. I was sick with rage. Beneath me I could see the mass that emptied itself into the vestibule through the central doors— a sluggish, monotonous, loathsomely-familiar ugliness: increasing every moment. I turned my face to the drab-painted walls and began to count the imitation bricks. I had counted them often before. One (I counted sullenly to myself)— Two—Three—Four—Five—then someone laughed very softly and joyously, and looking down I saw her. She was standing on the threshold of the outer door and she had laughed.

I did not think that anyone could be so beautiful. She was like queens I had read about—queens of Avalon and Joyous Garde, beautiful as roses—I thought they had all been dead long ago. Her hair was pure gold finely spun. Guinevere had hair of that colour; such hair, too, had the tallest of the queens who wept for Arthur wounded in the boat, the boat from Avalon, drifting, drifting on a sea without waves—a sea milky-white, coloured at the heart like an emerald.

She passed through the doorway and down the narrow entrance-alley into the street. It seemed that no one wondered at her as she passed—I was the only one that knew: I and the queens in Avalon.

The house in which she lived had trees before it and long sloping lawns. A heavy iron gate shut it away from the rest of the world, and through the bars I could see a winding path with laurels on either side of it and great branching crimson roses.

It was an enchanted garden! The grass was very green and smooth, as if it had been clipped that demoiselles might trail their cloaks of vair upon it. But no one ever came to gather the roses. A mysterious quiet was on the trees, a strange brightness on the leaves of the laurels. Perhaps they had been brought from a far country, and dreamed of stars

60

no one else had seen: perhaps the witch, Vivien, had woven a spell about them, and quiet would hold them for ever as it held Merlin in the oak-wood of Brocielande. It was a marvelous hidden pleasaunce. I could believe almost that no one knew about it save myself; that no one ever walked there save the Rose-Queen.

She came upon me once as I thought of these things and stared at her roses. She came behind me: for she, like myself, was outside the gate.

"I see that you love roses," she said.

It was undreamt-of and overwhelming. I began to move shamefacedly away.

"Do not go," she said. "I will give you a rose—only wait!"

I waited. She must have walked along the path where I had so often seen her in my thoughts: but I do not know what she looked like among the laurels and roses, or what she said when she came back and gave me the rose. It was only when she had gone that I knew my feet were in the dust of the roadway and I had a rose in my hand—a rose from the enchanted garden! To me also, as to the Knights of the Siege Perilous, had come the Miraculous Happening.

Petal by petal the rose withered: yet the virtue of it remained with me, and now I can always see the garden. It has grown larger: its lawns are like those lawns that lie translucent between seas of gold in twilight skies, its roses are fiery-hearted like the dawn. I am not a child outside the gate any longer. I can go in now. The garden is so vast that I have never come to the end of it. It is full of strange shadows and pale beautiful light. The Rose-Queen is there, faintly smiling, ivory-white, subtle as flame. She is as wise as the tallest of the queens in Avalon: and in her hands, kissed by such diverse lovers, she holds the million-petaled Rose of Dreams.

ALYS

I HAVE BROUGHT away roots of white iris from the garden of a woman who is beautiful as the iris flower. Her garden has trees of apple-blossom, and white roses. I shall never be there again, for the Lady of the Garden is going from Ireland—very far overseas.

I have written of many people in these memoirs, but of this woman whom I remembered from a past existence—whom assuredly I shall remember in whatever life comes after this one—I have said nothing.

The things that are most deeply cherished in the heart cannot be snared in words. Scarcely can thought encompass them. Like flame they cannot be prisoned; like granite embedded in the sea-floor they cannot be dredged to the surface. They are one with the dark mysterious life of the Earth: potent, invisible, unescapable.

Who could make known, to one ignorant of it, the wind's path among reeds; cloud-shadow on a mountain; the feather-flower of falling water; or the miraculous way in which flame, extinct in a pall of billowing smoke—with no foothold—re-kindles itself beyond the murk?

I have brought roots of white iris from her garden.

WHEN THE GORSE WAS IN BLOSSOM

I THINK IT was the riot of greenness in bough and laneway that stirred in me the wish to spend a few days in that hill-perched cottage which commends itself so jocundly to Margaret O'Grady, chiefly I think because of the mountains that turn their gaze in its direction. My sister, May, promised to come with me, and we both thought it a good idea to invite

Maud Gonne. I found her in her Nassau Street apartment with the great lion-coloured dog, Dagda, beside her. A fire sparkled in the grate. Spring sunshine pushed its way through the windows. William Butler Yeats sat at the far end of the room with the air of one who has retired from a controversy. He held an open book in his hands: Poems by John Keats. He was not too pleased to see me, and the pleasure lessened when Maud Gonne consented to accept my invitation. His mood changed, however, when I suggested that he might like to come. "I know who ought also to come," said Maud Gonne, "Arthur Griffith loves mountains, and works too hard—we must persuade him!"

In a company of five we progressed to the cottage on the hillside. It had been there long enough to establish comradeship with the moss and stones and the fine wind-nipped grass about it. Across the narrow alley the Golden Spear, Slieve Cullen Mór, lifted itself: naked of trees, patined in silver and amethyst by upcrops of living rock, austere and unlichened.

"We must climb that mountain," said Maud Gonne, "the sea is beyond it—the sea where the sun rises!"

"There is a wood more close at hand," said the Poet. "The trees have all young leaves and there will be flowers underfoot."

"Ah, but think of the flowers the mountain will have—the small hidden flowers!"

Enthusiastically we started for the mountaintop. The air was keen, the slanting sun had urgency in its deepening gold. The mountain itself was urgent. It was as though the strength of that upward thrust compelled us to the summit, so lightly and joyously did we achieve the ascent. Hawk-empire it was, with a countryside spread below us, multicoloured against the far-reaching pallor and radiance of the sea. Sound and silence had empery in that uplifted place, solitude and a sense of myriad-throbbing life. We could snatch but moments of it for the sun was hurrying to the low Western horizon, and dark-fall stood half-irresolute in the firmament to the East. We turned, reluctant, to the valley already full of shadow.

"Next day we will go to the little wood," said the Poet, with conviction.

"I must return to Dublin tonight," said Arthur Griffith whose mind does not whole-heartedly disport itself in forests, and who is not overfond of Yeats.

"Give yourself a longer stay!" we urged. "You love mountains."

But he was resolute, and soon we lost him striding townward in the thickening dusk.

Next morning Yeats led the way to the little wood. We sat there very happily, talking of nothing in particular till Phyllis MacMurdo arrived. At once she caught sight of the peak of Djouce showing in a gap of neighbouring hills. It suggested a weighty question: "Has a mountain a symbol and a colour?"

"Certainly a mountain has both," said the Poet, and the talk ran on symbols for some time. I quoted Æ to the effect that Kilmashogue has for symbol interlaced triangles in green and mauve. Phyllis told of a Mountain that she invoked once, on a night when she lay sleepless, and of how the strong power of the Mountain invaded the room and took such whirlwind possession of mind and body that she feared exceedingly and could scarce endure the anguish.

"Sacred Mountains are too strong for mortals," said Maud Gonne. "It is like inviting a lion to play with you!"

"We might try for the colour of Djouce," said the Poet, "that would not be harmful."

We shut our eyes, fixed our minds on the peak of Djouce, and tried to see a colour. Soon everyone announced success. Colour had manifested itself. But we had each seen a different colour: Yeats saw green; Phyllis, red-gold; Maud Gonne, red; myself, amethyst; my sister, blue. A long discussion followed on planes of perception; complementary colours; and the moods of mountains.

Suddenly Maud Gonne recollected that she was to speak

at a political meeting that night. It was not a meeting that could be ignored, and we decided that we would all of us return with her. We would walk down the hillside and along the winding country road until we could hail a vehicle and possess ourselves of our valises. It was a loitering, straggling, happy-hearted procession in the waning light. Already the thrush had taken up his evensong, and gorse and blackthorn outbreathed a honeyed and sharp-tanged fragrance. Yeats abandoned himself wholly to the magic of the moment. He would swoop down on a stray twig and toss it in the air; he would gather a stone from the roadway, make it skip from one hand to the other, then fling it skyward.

All too soon there was a sound of hoof-beats. All too soon Dublin house-roofs patterned the sky.

"In an old ballad," said Yeats, "this town is called: 'Dublin of the Curses'!"

THE BRIGHT RING OF DAY

I USED TO ENVY those folk who lived in the days of Wolfe Tone or of Emmet: days when Ireland was vibrant, when an ideal, a hope, a common cause knit people together. I did not foresee that I would find myself, as I do now, in the days of a more dynamic awakening, a struggle closer banded. It is true that we have no hope of an armed thrust at the might of England, but we can tear to pieces the calumnies with which she strives to hide her exploitation. We can revive our ancient culture and our language. The sagas and hero-tales even now are spreading amongst us as oil spreads upon water, iridescent and unescapable. We have such captains of imagination, such image-makers as Standish O'Grady and Padraic Pearse; such fire-bringers as Thomas Clarke; such scholars as Whitley Stokes and Kuno Meyer: indeed

65

the broad-shouldered, blue-eyed, bronze-bearded German is more than a scholar. He is a champion. He defends our literature with a fierceness that makes some of us think that he must have lived in Celtic Ireland centuries ago. Not alone is he engaged in translating from the ancient manuscripts and defending the sagas, he is giving lavishly of time and energy to the establishment of an Irish School of Learning, in order that Ireland may provide more and more of her own scholars.

The sagas, the tales of gods and heroes, the poems well-hammered and riveted with assonance and rhyme—these that belong to us, our joy in discovering them, our determination to know them and to make them known, Padraic Pearse's determination that Ireland shall be worthy of them—these are building up our nationhood: these and the Gaelic language. Comradeship, nationhood, is nourished upon a cause which all may espouse, an effort in which all can take part, each working for the good of the whole. Such a cause, such an effort, we have in the revival of Gaelic. To win success we must all share in the labour, and in the enthusiasm that spurs the labour: sharing so we reach back to the splendour of Ireland's heyday and forward to the Ireland of our heart's desire. Doctor Douglas Hyde did a thing, perhaps, greater than he knew when he founded the Gaelic League.

Out of imagination that is fire of the brain; out of a tenderness that is magic of the heart; out of a hard endurance that is pride of the body we are building—all of us, great and small—the Ireland that our poets have dreamed of, and our seers foretold. Ireland herself—the substance, for our dream is but a shadow of her—Ireland herself, the Sacred Land, the Dark Rose, for ever lovely and beloved blesses the work, enlightening our minds and our hearts, and strengthening our hands.

THE SWORD

THE TREES BY the river had young leaves, all rain-washed. The river, named for a goddess, spread itself like molten silver in the rainy light. We had glimpses of it many times while Robert Gibson (Boss Gibson) urged his fleetest mare, Athena, along those narrow roads and winding lanes. The river, at every encounter, was lovely: and lovely, beyond it, was the long low softly curving line of the Clare hills. It was not to see the hills or the river that we journeyed. Boss Gibson was searching for a yew tree, any yew tree that had the mark of centuries on it: or, better still, a split bough! That morning Boss Gibson, Janie his wife, Kuno Meyer and I (who are house-guests) had talked of ancient Ireland, of dunes, and forts, and lisses. Kuno learned with delight that the Limerick countryside has for its chief adornment raths and forts and lisses—or rather the remains of them—places where faery laughter can be heard, places where white horses flash by, leaving the grass untrampled. In Kuno's mind these strongholds of long-dead kings, these more than ruined palaces, took again form and magnificence. He spoke of the palisades and moats of them; of the war-gear they held once; of the beaten copper fashioned to the likeness of birds and of beasts and set upon the walls of the feast-chamber to give back the candle-flame and wink redly with carbuncle eyes. The door lintels were of red yew, carved skillfully. Kuno wondered how red was the yew. The Boss was helpful at once. The heart of a yew tree is red—as red as a cleft pomegranate. Moreover he had an idea that he knew where to find a yew tree, one that age or hardship had cleft. All afternoon we drove about in search of it. We did not find it where the Boss thought it was. We chanced, however, upon a tree elsewhere. A strong-thewed great-limbed yew that tree was, and miracle of miracles, the giant trunk showed newly split and red indeed as the heart of a pomegranate!

After dinner the Boss insisted that we set out for the house

67

of a well-known Limerick priest, famed as a patriot and an antiquarian, who had a collection of bronze ornaments and bronze weapons, together with pieces of carved yew that had blackened for centuries in bog-water.

Gathered in the stone-flagged hall of the priest's house, we looked at pins and brooches, shield-bosses, and carved yew.

"These are mostly from Lough Gur," the priest was saying.

I thought of Lough Gur, as we four had seen it so short a time ago, desolate and strange among low treeless hills and flat hunger-bitten stretches of bogland: Lough Gur that once was sacred to Aunya, the Mother-Goddess of the Celts!

The priest was talking of battles:

"There must have been many a stiff fight on that lake-shore, among the marshy pools. Peasants, digging turf, still uncover bronze ornaments, fragments of shields, and now and then a bronze sword, perfect save for the hilt—a hilt that may have been a sea-beast's tooth."

One such sword lay in the glass case in front of us: a bronze sword of the finest leaf shape, large and long. A sword that a king, in dying, may have flung to the morass, saving it thus from alien hands. Kuno saw nothing but that sword!

"Would you like to handle it?" asked the priest, unlocking the case.

Kuno took the sword in his hands. As he stood there he looked more like a warrior than a great scholar. Broad-shouldered, bronze-bearded, tanned by sun and wind, he was that Kuno who had run away from school as a boy, all for sake of the feel of a boat and the salt smell of the sea. His eyes caressed the sword. He seemed to grow taller, holding it.

"You love that sword," said the priest, whose eyes caressed it also. "I will give it to you!"

Kuno Meyer had no words for a moment: nor had anyone. Silence acclaimed most fitly this gift. We felt that the priest spoke for Ireland. It was Ireland herself proffering a sword to the man who had championed the cause of her literature, her scholarship, and her honour, in so many encounters: and

68

won victory; who had toiled unremittingly to establish for her "The School of Irish Learning"; a sword to this man from overseas who loved her more than some born within her borders; to this man a gift out of that past of which he had revived the glory.

This splendid happening was the moon of that night—a moon that did not wane for days. It was still resplendent when I took leave of my friends and of Limerick on a chill dark-skied morning. A few stragglers loitered by the railway station. Boss Gibson stood, holding the head of his fidgety mare, while the vanguard of a Spring snowstorm glittered by: snowflakes on his coat and on his gloved hands.

Snow on the long line of the Clare hills.

"UNDER THE OPENING EYELIDS OF THE MORN"

STANDISH O'GRADY, PALADIN of Ireland, is conducting a crusade. He speaks and writes "winged words" to those who are sympathetic and those who are not. Scholars and artists respond, but the landed gentry are indifferent for the most part, though warned that now they must either come forward on Ireland's side; or perish, dupes of their own foolishness and of England's statesmanship. The chief convert is Captain the Honorable Otway Cuffe, brother and heir to the Earl of Desart and owner of an estate in Kilkenny, who is establishing a Guild of Woodworkers and a Guild of Woollen-Workers in Kilkenny town. The idea is to strengthen the country economically by founding and supporting home industries, whilst reviving in pageant and drama a knowledge of that past which England, banning Irish history in the schools, seeks to obliterate. Standish has re-told the Cu-Cullion Saga in language worthy of that great epic: and a Kil-

69

kenny printing-press is now at work on those sound-empano-
plied words.

The National Spirit has more than stirred, it has lifted its
head and shouted. Everywhere little clubs are springing up
for the study of the Irish language and of Irish history. Those
who have a knowledge of the sagas and the history, lecture
night after night to eager listeners. Classes are held at all
hours for the teaching of Gaelic. The language is a difficult
one, but the struggle to master it creates a bond that links
the earl's son and the street-urchin. It is one thing that we
can all do for our country. Æ is writing the story of Deirdre
in dramatic form. Maud Gonne has secured a promise that
he will give the play to the Society of which she is President:
"Inghinidhe-na-hEireann" (The Daughters of Ireland).

The Daughters of Ireland come new to the art of play-
acting: indeed they come new to the Gaelic, to the sagas,
and to everything! It does not hamper their enthusiasm—on
the contrary it affords them occasion for a fiery and untrammeled assault on things as they are. The Society is composed
of girls who work hard all day in shops and offices owned
for the most part by pro-British masters who may at any
moment discharge them for "treasonable activities." To be
dismissed in such wise means the semi-starvation of long-
continued unemployment. These girls dare it, and subscribe,
from not too abundant wages, generous amounts for the hire
of halls to be used as class-rooms and for theatre rehearsals.
I have undertaken, under their auspices, to teach Irish history by a re-telling of the sagas and hero-tales.

In a room perched at the head of a rickety staircase and
overlooking a narrow street, I have about eighty denizens of
untamed Dublin: newsboys, children who have played in
street alleys all their lives, young patriot girls and boys who
can scarcely write their own names. Outside there is a continuous din of street cries and rumbling carts. It is almost
impossible to shout against it if the windows are open, and
more impossible to speak in the smother of dust if the windows are shut. Everyone is standing, closely packed—no room

70

for chairs! They stand there, in ages ranging from nine years to eighteen, ready to listen, if there is anything worth listening to, ready to boo or come to fisticuffs the moment that they are not interested. But they are interested. I do not need to say to anyone, "These are *your* heroes!" They have relinquished the luxury of a devil-may-care idleness, and whatever adventures may wait round a street corner, to live in heart and mind with Ireland of long ago: to adventure with Fionn, defend the Ford with Cu-Cullion, and crack jokes with Conan the Bald. Eager-eyed, drawing in breaths of rapturous admiration, their thin hardship-sculptured faces flushed with wrath and pride, they stand there adding new names to the hero-names that they have cherished ever since they could put names together: Cu-Cullion, to Parnell; Brown Diarmid, to Robert Emmet; Fionn, the hero-avenger, to Wolfe Tone.

As they tumble down the narrow stairway, homeward bound, I hear shouts of:

"I'm Cu-Cullion!" "You're not—I took it first!" "Fionn was a bigger man!"

"It's Diarmid that's my choice!" "I'll fight you on it!"

In other rooms the Daughters of Ireland have classes for Irish dancing, Gaelic songs, and the Gaelic language. Since we are reviving everything at once, we pay attention to the ancient Festivals. There are four which divide the year into periods of three months: the Festival of Brigit, the Pure Perpetual Ashless Flame, in February; the Festival of Beltane, the coming of the young Gods who succour the Earth, in May; the Marriage-Festival of Lugh, the Sun, who weds the Sovereignty of Erin in August; the Festival of Samhain, that opens the Inner World, in November. W. B. Yeats was eager to revive these Festivals, and at one time planned with Maud Gonne pageants and dances, but the scheme fell through. The Daughters of Ireland, in honour of these Festivals, put on short plays: acting in them eagerly and dauntlessly as soon as they have memorized the words—and sometimes before! Alice Milligan's play, *The Escape of Red Hugh,* is a

71

prime favourite. The young prince, kidnapped by the English and treacherously imprisoned, is looked upon as a symbol of Ireland: and the cheers that greet his prison-break are not all for the hopes that blossomed once and died with him.

Just now the Daughters of Ireland are preparing strenuously for Æ's *Deirdre*.

Æ'S DEIRDRE

PLAYS ARE THE order of the day. Everyone is trying to write a play in verse, prose, or Kiltartan. Even I am trying— without success! All this is because Standish O'Grady says that the drama can be a great agent of national regeneration. Towering images from the Heroic Age, tales of half-forgotten splendid happenings, must surely mould and enrich the lean imagination of the present: strength from a strong-sinewed past must lend a strength to us! Irish drama should hold the mirror not to Nature but to the Heroic Age.

Æ's play was written with this pronouncement in mind. He has chosen the famous and tragic story of Deirdre for whose foretold and foredoomed beauty Concobar, the High-King, broke oath; fire blackened the palaces at Emain Machan; and the close-knit comradeship of the Paladins of the Red Branch dissolved.

I think that Æ made choice of this saga for sake of the heart-piercing loveliness of Deirdre's lament when she takes farewell of the craggy heights and the tree-rich glens of Alba, where she and Naisi had lived in such a splendour of love, and turns herself to what she knows is a death-journey. For this lament, upflung superbly in the second act of the play, Æ has searched for and fitted together his noblest and most regal-sounding words: and since he thinks that every one in the Heroic Age should be heroic (for the sake of posterity)

72

he has even tried faint-heartedly, to whitewash Concobar.

The Daughters of Ireland, with the sanction and support of their President, Maud Gonne, are putting on the play. It is to be an effort on a grand scale. Æ is designing the dresses. He has a colour-scheme in amethyst, emerald, and sapphire: and his mind is an armory of swords, double-edged javelins, daggers, and bull-hide shields with hammered bosses. The actors, drawn chiefly from the ranks of the Daughters of Ireland, are being drilled ruthlessly by Willie and Frank Fay who have high standards in acting and elocution, and are not wanting in ideas as to how High Kings and damosels renowned in saga should stand, move, and utter words.

At a hall in Camden Street rehearsals are in progress. Maurya Walker, slim and good to look at, is to play Deirdre. Dudley Digges, young, enthusiastic, new to the stage, and well-esteemed by the Fays, is to be Naisi!

Night by night work goes on in Camden Street. The hall is unlit, but the stage is faintly illuminated. Hard austere benches, unravished of dust, stand starkly in the auditorium. Somewhere midway on one of them Maud Gonne, Æ, and I sit attentive. Æ puts in a word now and then of approval or remonstrance, Maud Gonne whispers a comment to me, late-coming members of the cast slip unostentatiously to their places.

"Go over those lines again!" comes the voice of Frank Fay.

"You are standing too far to the right. Stand here!" from Willie Fay.

A door opens and slams, there is a shuffling of feet, and the Poet, William Butler Yeats, enters. He finds his way to a seat on the bench behind Maud Gonne and sits silent, but not for long. He has crossed from England the night before, and these players and the dim many-shadowed almost empty hall intrigue him.

"This," he says, "is what I have so often thought of—a theatre drawn from the people. Ah, but that is not how they should speak the words!"

He springs to his feet and stumbles through the dust and

73

murk to the stage-platform to instruct Frank Fay. That personage is not grateful, and the Poet returns.

"I must write a play for these people; for this theatre. But why do they stand that way? They lose the effect!"

He is about to essay another foray when Maud Gonne restrains him.

"Willie," she says, "I wish you would put your mind on your play."

"It is a play that I will give to you when it is written."

But the rehearsal is ending. The folk clamber down from the platform. Talk is general, and Yeats has captured the Fays. Perpetually enthralled and encoiled by the idea of the moment, the Poet has developed an oratory of exposition that saves him from arguments of defence. The Fays bear up under it until Æ gently detaches him, and we all surge toward a street corner and tram-cars.

RUMOUR

There is quite a surge of excitement in some Dublin circles tonight—a turmoil and a pother. It is rumoured that George Coffey has taken the gold ornaments from their cases in the Museum—the collars and armlets and torques from the ancient times—and loaned them to a set of Dublin players! And these same Dublin players, pampered to this unheard-of and criminal extent, have refused an invitation to play before the Lord Lieutenant and his court! I should be able to gild the refined gold of this rumour—or ungild it—since I am one of the players. Ungild it I shall.

It all came about because my sister Elizabeth, the actress, was greatly taken with Deirdre's farewell to Alba in the second act of Æ's Deirdre. To please herself she committed the words to memory, and to please herself recited them.

74

One or two people who heard her noised the thing abroad. Elizabeth has a beautiful voice. Æ was fascinated. He planned a colour-scheme for Elizabeth, who is tall and slender with masses of red-gold hair and eyes that have green and amber lights in them. He made sketches of long-sleeved gowns and superbly folded shoulder-mantles as if Elizabeth were really going to appear in the rôle of Deirdre. Suddenly, from some brain or other, sprang an idea full-panoplied like Athena from the brain of Zeus. Why should she not play? Why should we not gather a few enthusiasts and bring the Second Act to life? Æ was more than ever delighted; he said that he, himself, would play Naisi. A young poet—James Cousins—and the young writer and revolutionist, Ryan, offered for the brothers, Ainnle and Ardan. In a weak moment I consented to be Lavarcham. George Coffey, who looks like a princely warrior, took the part of Fergus. We had Mrs. Coffey's drawing-room for rehearsals, and George Coffey's experience as an antiquarian to guide us in the manufacture of armlets, torques, and bronze swords which we made out of cardboard—very lavish and effective!

Everyone in the cast was ignorant of the art of play-acting with the exception of Elizabeth who had played lead in London when tragedies by Webster, and comedies by Beaumont and Fletcher were put on the boards of the Court Theatre, regardless of everything but art for art's sake. She was cast for the rôle of the Duchess of Malfi when the much-too-good-to-last Court Theatre came to a much-regretted bankrupt ending.

Elizabeth busied herself at once with the work of production. She was concerned with how the actors should stand and how they should speak. Æ cared only for word perfection. He decided to assume the prompter's burden. He could whisper a word to anyone on the stage. He knew every line. This was all very well if he had not taken the office too seriously. So occupied was he in assuring that no one omitted jot or tittle of any passage, improved or altered any line, that he quite forgot whether he was, as Naisi, to go up-

75

stage at a particular moment or come midmost down. He trusted to impulse, and never repeated himself. He was the despair of Elizabeth. Eventually we learned to keep an eye on him and maneuver out of his orbit, taking our own haphazard positions as best we might.

The second act of *Deirdre* was given just once, in Mrs. Coffey's long lofty drawing-room, to an audience of invited guests. It brought down the house. The Daughters of Ireland will shortly present the whole play in a series of public performances.

THE GOLDEN STORM
1903

THE YEAR OF the great storm. Something has happened in the elemental world. I think that the Guards have changed. An invincible wind tore through Ireland. Following it the skies are dark. Mrs. O'Grady reports from Achill that the faery-folk are no longer there. Journeying, later, to Achill myself I find this to be true. They are only in one place, Lough-Na-Keerogue. It is strange what a difference it makes. The heather is still rose-coloured, the sphagnum moss marvelously green, the reeds are silver, but the magic has gone! Will the new elemental life flood this place, or will it burst forth in some district far off—out of Ireland—perhaps in some country that has not known magic in a long while?

I call to mind what Mrs. O'Grady said in 1902 as she stood near Lough-Na-Keerogue and felt herself in harmony with the Inner World.

"There is coming to the Earth a Lord of the Sidhe who has never before taken body. His comrades will proffer gifts as he passes among them. These will be patterned upon a hand outstretched—upon the palm of humanity."

76

In the year 1902, Mrs. Standish O'Grady, Captain the Honorable Otway Cuffe, and I were in Achill. I had rooms in a cottage on the side of Slieve-More. They were staying in Dugort: one at a pension, the other at a hotel. I saw them often. On an afternoon when they came to my hillside, Captain Cuffe said to Mrs. O'Grady: "Look into the future, if you can, for Ireland!" She became very still, turned her mind inward, and almost at once began to describe a battle.

"It rages," she said, "it is furious! Powerful chiefs are fighting. Victory goes one way and another. Fighting will be in Ireland. The heroes that fought long ago will take part in this battle. Cu-Cullion will take part in it, but he will have another name. It is a welter, a confusion!"

At this, the vision was interrupted for a short time, and when Mrs. O'Grady resumed, she said:

"I hear the sound of brazen trumpets blown mightily. This battle is greater and fiercer than before. There are those fighting in it who will draw down the clouds to make helmets. It is a war that spreads like fire— Ah! now a resistless Force is descending. I cannot name it, this Great One! I cannot bear it—this Light that consumes! Nothing can stand against it."

She drew herself from the power of the vision, and for a while was dazed and confused, though, as a general rule, she passes from the inner to the outer consciousness easily and rapidly. She kept saying:

"We must remember this. We three are enjoined to remember this!"

This storm, disastrous yet with a core of fiery joy, this exodus in the Faery or Angelic World must be part of the foretold happening. I have tried, by meditation, to learn something of the new Nature Lords, but only in a dim far-off vision have I been aware of them: ruthless and hard of mien in comparison with the gracious Spirits gone inward. These, who marshal in the New Age in so far as the Angelic World can marshal it, have for colours red and white. Red is the inner colour. The stones are the ruby and the crystal.

What are we to remember, I ask myself—we three? What do we know? The Nature Spirits that have made patterns, lovely and joyous for such as loved them—inexorable in so far as Destiny had weight with them—these are departing. Their colours are green and amethyst; their stones the amethyst, and the emerald: inner, and outer.

There descends an Invincible One. If it be Christ, indeed, He is accompanied by the Twelve Legions of Angels! Before Him the White Fire of Purification devours; with Him is the Ruby Flame of Love that re-fashions all things to its own image. *"Whose fan is in his hand, and he will thoroughly purge his floor."*

SAMHAIN EVE

IT IS MIDNIGHT on Samhain Eve. There is a keen cold air abroad and the sky is brilliant with stars. I have kindled a small fire of aromatic woods, and thrown upon it a branch of heather from Slieve Gullion, the mountain of Mananaun: the mountain of the Smith, the Shaper of the World. Tonight, say the ancient tales; tonight, say the seers who have understanding, the gods throw open the doors of their dwelling-places, their hidden dwelling-places in the Sacred Mountains, and whoso has courage, wisdom, and purity of heart may question the Divine Ones: may cross the threshold of light and be for a moment a god among the gods.

Samhain is, I think, the greatest of the old Celtic Festivals, this Feast of nuts—the Nuts of Knowledge—and of apples—the Golden Apples of the Tree of Life—since in it, symbolically, the Shaper of the World, the Smith of the Stars, of Hades, and of the Nether Hell grants to those who can drink of his cup immortal life, and power to know the true from the seeming.

It is very silent tonight yet there must be everywhere a great surge and pulse of melody could I but hear it. I think of comrades who are keeping this Festival. The fire spurts in little tongues of flame. I send a wish to my comrades. The flame sinks in ashes.

A CHANT FOR SAMHAIN

Mananaun draws the Sword. It is the Ashless Flame. It is Beauty. It is the Enlightener of the World.

Peace be on the sea: the Boat of Mananaun has crossed it.
Peace be on the land: the White Horse of Niav has set foot upon it.

Let song be given to the Flame that is the spear point of Midyir. Let it sing the heart-love of heroes since the beginning of Time.

Lo the gates of the Underworld are broken in pieces.
The Abyss is bridged.

Midyir the Terrible shakes out the locks of his hair, and suns leap in the darkness. He was in the Nether Hell imprisoned. Chaos was about him: in his ears the groaning of torment.

He made himself strong. He lifted the world on his shoulders. He scaled the Abyss. The Hosts of Heaven rejoice over him.

Brigit lifts the Stone. Her hands about it are its monstrance: on it are the names of the gods. No builder fashioned it. No mason hewed it: yet by it the cities of the gods and the thrones of the stars are established.

The Star of Knowledge is risen.
The centuries abase themselves before it.
Peace be in the Heavens.

79

The Feast of Mananaun is made ready. The wine is poured into the Cup. The wine of Lir purples the Cup. Whoso quenches thirst thereat attains to quenchless life. Upon its brim the stars and constellations are jewels. The Divinity that holds it is veiled.

Peace be on the Abyss.
The Boar that slew Diarmid is slain himself.
The Nuts of Knowledge are garnered.

Lir broods upon the Abyss.
He broods in silence.

PADRAIC PEARSE'S SCHOOL, CULLENSWOOD HOUSE

PADRAIC COLUM IS TAKING Maud Gonne and myself to see Pearse's school. We are walking. Suddenly a small child, a grimy little street-urchin, misses its step and sprawls on the pavement, almost at our feet. Padraic picks it up, presses a penny into each hand, and sets it off with the howl it meant to give forgotten. The school has established itself in an old-fashioned Manor House, Cullenswood House, which stands in considerable grounds, and has an air of remembering better days.

Padraic Pearse comes to the door himself. We enter a square hall, and find ourselves confronting a large oil painting of the hero, Cu-Cullion. He is a slender youth, scarce out of boyhood, but he carries the spear and the sword of a full-grown warrior. Lettered in Gaelic about the frame is the hero-vaunt:

Though I live but a year and a day, I will live so that my name goes sounding down the ages.

80

"You know the story," said Pearse.

Yes, we knew the story, knew it in Standish O'Grady's splendid version: Cu-Cullion, the hero foretold, had captured the steeds of the war-goddess, Macha, and demanded the arms of a champion. His uncle, Conacher the King of Ulad, had given his own sword, and his death-dealing spear. But the druids said: "This day is ominous. Whoso takes arms on this day will be short-lived: but his name will live after him." "Choose a luckier day!" cried the King of Ulad. Cu-Cullion said: "I have chosen: though I should live but a year and a day, my name shall go sounding down the ages."

Pearse took us from room to room. The rooms were empty of boys. The sunshine outside had enticed masters and pupils to the walled garden where the boys had little plots to cultivate as they pleased. The rooms were rich in pictures. There was one of a woman sheltering many children under a blue mantle—Ireland herself with a splendour of light behind her, and in that splendour the Lords of the Faery World, the Gods of Dana, rank on rank, till the brightness hid them. There was one of Christ, a little child in a field of flowers, with his arms outstretched in cross-fashion. Small bunnies played about his feet. In one room the names of Irish patriots, in Gaelic lettering, made a frieze. The name of Robert Emmet was not there! I said something about this to Pearse. "You will come upon Emmet presently," he replied, as he led the way to a room where the chief wall held a bas-relief of Emmet, and nothing else. "Cu-Cullion has the entrance hall to himself," I commented, "and Emmet has this room—the fortune-favoured champion, and the ill-starred one."

"One is not less than the other," said Pearse. "I would like the boys to feel that success is not the chief goal: but rather worthy effort in support of what we esteem to be just. I would wish the boys to have the hardihood of Cu-Cullion, and the Christ-heart of sympathy with all living things."

Knowledge of the old legends and of saintly lives might foster such a fellowship; dramatic representations could give body and colour and a chance to image oneself in nobler

81

guise and be for some moments the saint or hero chosen as exemplar.

The boys spend much time in preparing plays, for which they make their own costumes and stage accessories. Just now they are fashioning chariots and spear-heads for an outdoor play, the defence of Ulad by the boy-battalion of youths who held the ford against the great hosting of Queen Maeve—and perished. They stemmed the battle-surge for a short and glorious moment after Cu-Cullion, all but mortally wounded, staggered back from the river-lip. At Christmas the boys will put on a play in one of the Dublin theatre-halls. It will show the thatched cottages of a hamlet in Gaelic Ireland; the stone walls; the small fields; the flower-patterned wayside where the children are playing with a stranger-comrade who leads them in joyous game after game, and only at the end reveals himself as Iosagan, the Christ-child.

"How I wish," said Padraic, as we found ourselves again on the street, "how I wish that my boyhood had been nurtured in such a school!"

ENCHANTED STRAND

I am staying with Maud Lloyd, the artist, in her house at Inch, County Kerry. It is a strong two-story house built of stone and stands on a hill—the only house on the hill, with no other house in sight. Far below stretches a whole country-side: the great strand of Inch, the Atlantic a-wash on its borders; the sand dunes; the deep inlet of the sea beyond and behind the sand dunes; the range of Macgallicuddy's Reeks sharp-pointed against the sky. Maud Lloyd is at home here, for she loves to paint whole ranges of mountains, river-inlets, and meadows.

It is early Spring—the loveliest time of year in this part of

Ireland. The village of Inch (Gaelic-speaking) is some distance away—we seem to own all the territory our eyes can touch. The strand, coloured like pale ivory, stretches for miles—only sea-birds there and ourselves! The full moon edges the long, incoming waves with silver flame—the new moon is silver and rose.

But the strand is the most wonderful thing. It is very slightly inclined to the sea, and when the waves make an onset they run up very far, leaving their comrades as it were bunched in wonderment a long way out.

If one lets oneself listen for a little while on this strand, great bells are heard, deep-sounding and strange. People hearing them for the first time are certain that near at hand must be a cathedral, though if they listened a little more intently they would be convinced that no cathedral ever had such bells.

Always one can hear the bells but one cannot always hear the chariots. They come thundering along the strand, immense chariots driven furiously: so massive are they (by the sound) and so headlong is the pace that of a surety the horses leaping and straining in the traces must be kin to those harnessed by Apollo.

No one that I talked with had seen the chariots or the gods who lean forward urging their steeds. Many of the Gaelic-speaking folk have seen the great horses that come out of the sea and do not find the dry land strange under their feet; many have seen the Faery Riders with fantastic head-dresses and hair that swirls about them like flame, but no one has seen the chariots. They hear the thunder of the wheels and the thud of hoof-beats and are content to enquire no further.

What shall I say of this strand that I have seen patined with gold in the late sunset, and silvered to unearthly strangeness under the moon? It will not go into words, the thing that I would say of it: like an image in a deep pool that a touch disperses, it must remain unsnared by any net the mind can weave.

83

Yet I am fain to share with others the subtle enchantment of the place, the strangeness of it. Perhaps through strength of such a wish it may chance that someone lingering hereafter on the strand at Inch, someone even who will never venture there, may touch hearts with me—myself long dead.

IONA

MAUD LLOYD AND I had a strange adventure on Iona. We owe it in part to Mr. and Mrs. Ritchie, the two artists who live for many months of every year on Iona and take such an interest in the folklore and antiquities of the island. Our stay of several days on Iona was drawing to an end and we called to say good-bye: it was Saturday and our steamer left on Monday.

"Of course you have visited Porth-na-Laragan," said Mr. Ritchie.

"We never heard of Porth-na-Laragan."

"O you must see it," said both the Ritchies. "No one should leave Iona without seeing Porth-na-Laragan."

"Tell us something about it."

"Well," said Mr. Ritchie, "it's a long inlet of the sea with a raised beach stretching landward, and on the beach the prehistoric grave of some chieftain or other, a giant-grave. It's a queer place. If there is ever anyone drowned on the island the body will be washed into Porth-na-Laragan. Bodies of sailors drowned at sea come floating there. I can't stand it myself. I wouldn't stay there alone for five minutes."

"I don't feel that way about it," said Mrs. Ritchie. "It is a strange place, but it exhilarates me: I hear music there, splendid orchestral music."

Maud Lloyd and I decided that we must see Porth-na-
84

Laragan. We had Sunday for the adventure. We set out early, tramping over the fine grass. Iona is a small island but it has many little dells, and inlets of the sea. After we had walked a considerable distance without encountering a living being, we found ourselves on the edge of a cliff about two hundred feet high, looking down on a narrow dark inlet of the sea. A ridge of toothed rocks almost closed it seaward. Opposite to us was another cliff descending steeply like the one we stood on. Below us was a sloping beach of great, round wave-worn stones.

"This is Porth-na-Laragan," said Maud Lloyd with decision.

I demurred. We ought to see a giant's grave. Neither of us could see a giant's grave.

"All the same," said Maud, "this *is* Porth-na-Laragan. I know that it is!"

Just then we heard the sound of a pickaxe from the headland opposite. Someone was striking rock in a casual sort of way. We felt annoyed. This was the Sabbath and the good Iona crofters should all be in the meeting-house. Who could have imagined that one of them would be pickaxing on a barren headland? A piece of ill-luck and likely to spoil things!

Something else made us forget the pickaxing. It was a great burst of baying, as if many deep-throated hounds bayed together.

"The Sabbath-breaker has dogs with him," said Maud. "That makes it worse. I'm going down into the bay before those dogs come around."

She moved in the land direction toward the one place where one can enter the bay. I stood where I was because something seemed strange about the baying of those dogs. They had started with the suddenness of a thunderclap, and they stopped with the same suddenness. Now the pickaxing was going on again. As I turned to follow Maud Lloyd the baying broke out again with the same sharp suddenness and ceased abruptly and completely as before. I hurried to overtake my friend, and even as I turned something darkly in-substantial, as the shadow might be of an enormous bird, swooped past me and descended into the bay.

I overtook Maud Lloyd. She was standing in a perplexed attitude.

"Listen!" she said. "The pickaxing is coming now from below us!"

From where we stood, we could not see the beach directly below us, as the cliff overhung slightly, but it was plain that someone was walking down there and striking the face of the cliff with a pickaxe as he walked.

"This spoils it altogether!" said Maud Lloyd.

Then suddenly she caught my arm.

"What is walking down there? It is not a man. Do you hear how the stones crunch under its feet?"

"Yes," I agreed, "it is not a man."

Whatever walked there made the great boulder-stones of the beach roll and crunch as gravel would crunch under a heavy-footed human. While we held our breath, a strange shout came from almost directly underneath us. It might have been a shout from a cave. It was deep and muffled. Almost instantly a huge stone shot out from beneath us, crossed a little river, and lay on the grass beyond it.

Whatever was beneath us had chucked that stone as a child playing "Ducks and Drakes" chucks flat stones to make them dance on the water. But this stone was one that a man could hardly lift!

There was another shout. It was faint, muffled, and seemed to be far off. Then silence. Complete silence.

"Someone is down there," said Maud Lloyd, "someone badly hurt. We must go down."

I was eager to go down, but I did not expect to find anyone badly hurt. We hurried along the cliff-path seeking a place to descend, or even a spot from which we could view the inlet and its approaches. When we got to a place where the water and beach displayed itself we saw nothing but sky and sea and boulder-stones—and emptiness! It was impossible for

Maud Lloyd to explain this to herself. She had never before had a psychic experience.

"There must be a cave," she insisted. "The person must be somewhere."

"Do you remember how that being walked?" I asked.

She was silent.

We spent the rest of the day examining the place. We went down to where the stone lay. It was a real solid stone, and, strange to say, it had not been taken from the beach where every stone was wave-washed to roundness and smoothness. It was a sharp-edged, weathered stone, one side of which had lain embedded in earth. The earth mark was on it and even the clay moisture. Maud Lloyd could barely lift it. We went back over the ground that we had come and found a ledge from which several stones had been taken, large stones that had lain embedded in the earth there.

We went across to the headland where the dogs had bayed. We found no trace of pickaxing. There were no dogs. We found what might be the giant's grave, but we heard and saw nothing that was strange. The place had an eerie feeling and seemed charged with a pulsing flamelike energy. I found it exhilarating but did not hear music.

We took a stone from what we thought might be the giant-grave and promised ourselves an interview with the Ritchies. We had time to see them before the steamer took us homeward.

"Certainly you saw Porth-na-Laragan," said the Ritchies.

They were both interested in our account of the baying hounds because they knew every dog in Iona and there was not a single deep-voiced large dog in the whole island. The crofters have small shrill-voiced sheep dogs that scant feeding for generations has reduced to jackal-colour and jackal-size. As for a man pickaxing on the Sabbath—that is not a thing that would happen.

We treasured our stone. In Dublin we knew many people who could psychometrize.

DJINNS

BACK IN DUBLIN I asked Mrs. O'Grady to psychometrize the stone which had come from the giant's grave at Porthna-Laragan in Iona. Mrs. O'Grady has very unusual psychic powers: at times she surprises glimpses of the Faery World.

She took the stone in her hand and pressed it to her forehead. Then she said:

"I see a great many huts. They are round-shaped and thatched with grass. People are coming in and out. They are a slender dark-skinned folk and seem to wear only a single garment—I think it is linen. It is dyed blue." (Mentally I said, "Go into one of the huts.") "No, I will not go into one of the huts," said Mrs. O'Grady with firmness and determination, laying down the stone.

The country she described might have been the low-lying country inland from Porth-na-Laragan, but she did not see anything resembling the cliffs or the raised beach.

I gave the stone to Maud Gonne. She took it in her hand, and instantly saw Porth-na-Laragan. She described it exactly, except that she said:

"There is a cave here: the entrance to this cave is very narrow, like a crack in the cliff."

Afterwards she made a drawing which showed everything exactly as we had seen it. She marked the place where the cave was, opposite to the place where we had first stood; it was the place from which the sound of pickaxing had come. Later, on another visit to Iona, I learned that there was a cave in the cliff, a narrow cleft as she described it.

What had thrown the stone? I tried to remember any tale of a stone-throwing spirit. Had I ever heard such a tale? Yes, in County Clare an old man had pointed out one of the highest parts of the cliffs of Mohar which go down eight hundred feet to the sea, and said: "There used to be a great spirit who would sit there all lonesome by himself and pass the hours of the day casting stones into the water to pleasure himself."

Where else did I hear of stone-throwing spirits? I remembered missionary tales of heathen devils that had a resort for themselves in a grove of trees and cast stones at converts on their way to church. I wasn't quite sure that these gamesome spirits were huge: they were not solitary. Arabian djinns seemed to be more like the County Clare or the Iona spirit. Djinns were vast creatures, simple-minded too, for when they came into contact with humans they got into trouble! Was there not a story of a djinn imprisoned in a bottle?

I learned more about djinns from a young Oxford man.

"Djinns," he said, "I never heard of them until a Hindu friend of mine mentioned them casually in conversation. 'What are djinns?' I asked in my ignorance. 'Don't you know about djinns? We have lots of djinns in India. My father's garden is infested with them.' 'Tell me about them.' 'Well,' said the Hindu, 'those djinns in our garden annoy us. We used to eat out there for coolness, but the djinns threw ashes on the food.'

" 'Did you ever see them?' 'No. They are spirits in the air. One day my uncle came. He said, *"Let us eat in the garden."* We said to him, "The djinns do not allow it." He said, *"Djinns would not frighten me. Let us eat in the garden."* The food was spread in the garden. The djinns threw down ashes into the dishes. My uncle cried out to them, *"You call yourselves djinns. You are no good. You can only throw ashes. Why don't you throw down meat-balls and rice?"* The djinns threw down meat-balls and rice.'

" 'Real meat-balls—real rice?'

" 'Yes, real enough.'

" 'Did you taste them?'

" 'Do you think we would eat food thrown down by devils?' "

Poor djinns! Just trying to attract a little attention to themselves. Perhaps they had oblation poured to them in that very garden in times gone by: wine offered and wheat and honey. Or perhaps they were djinns that a magician had tamed and trained to bring dishes. Was there not a story of a magician who gave a feast and boasted that every dish had been lifted from a king's table—from tables at the end of the earth?

WORDS OF POWER

Æ IS GOING from town to town, from county to county of Ireland establishing Land-Banks and Co-operative Dairies for the good of the people. Indeed he is more George Russell the organizer than Æ the mystic. His new self is as much interested in cows and chickens as his old self was in gods and elves. Some elf in his brain, remembering, draws caricatures of the new self—full of a whimsical humour. He showed me one of himself and a farmer walking the roads: himself tall and ascetic, with enormous feet that had measured miles and miles of bogland; the farmer short and squat, with ears that had expanded perceptibly under a barrage of Agricultural Propaganda.

Æ painted spirits of the wood and the mountain: George Russell paints groups of joyous children. He has not quite lost his interest in gods and demons, however, for he still loves to relate the adventure of Yeats and the Djinn. Yeats, who had instructed the old Theosophical Society in Ely Place in the arts of evocation and exorcism, to his own satisfaction if to nobody else's, was a joy to Æ. His adventures are no less a joy to George Russell who loves to remember him stooping to trace a cabalistic sign, or striding sword in hand, purposeful and valiant, with strange-sounding syllables and Potent Names in his mouth. I cannot hope to tell the adventure of the Djinn with the grace and charm that George Russell lends it, but the tale is too good to slip into oblivion.

Yeats was, to borrow a simile from Gaelic Ireland, a candle of knowledge and a road-showing torch to the members of a small and very select group of occultists who had discovered each other and their own powers by grace of the gods: and had, by Destiny, been welded into an Occult Society to be spoken of with that cautious reticence which cuts away the letters from the name of a Tibetan Master.

There came a day when a member of this Society returned from the East with an occult picture. In one corner of the picture there was a seal: under the seal a Djinn was imprisoned. Superstitious Londoners might have trembled had they known what their city housed. The Society felt the responsibility. A Djinn is a mighty and devastating spirit that can wallow in whirlwinds and shake earthquakes from its multiple wings. Its temper could not be supposed to improve in a bottled-up condition. Djinns do not mellow like wine. It is true that when they allow themselves to be inveigled into commerce with humans they get the worst of it. This Djinn did: and one had heard of others. They seem to be an honest trustful race of giants that should at all hazards keep clear of humanity.

What was to be done about the picture and the caged Djinn? After much thought and more debate the Society resolved to appoint Yeats as Guardian. Yeats was a necromancer, a troubler of the wells of knowledge, a gifted Mage, wise in spells and incantations—assuredly Yeats was the person. His mind was not unacquainted with Djinns. Ireland that reared him was a country where Djinns and simplehearted peasants lived together harmoniously by dint of minding their own business.

To the abode of the Poet the picture was heedfully escorted. It was solemnly installed in that room of his with the midnight-blue curtains and the tall wax candles. Left alone with the picture, Yeats contemplated it. His attention was fixed on the seal. His mind ran on incantations. The person who imprisoned that Djinn must have used incantations. If one freed the Djinn, one would remove the seal with a suitable incantation. Yeats thought of several that were eminently suitable.

He thought of incantations all next day. He wondered how long the Djinn had been there. It was cruel to keep the Djinn shut up in a small space. They were bulky creatures when they stretched themselves out. This poor Djinn must be cramped. After all, it was a responsibility to keep a Djinn cramped up. There was such a thing as cruelty to Djinns.

That night, as he contemplated the seal, a fixed and stern resolution came into his eyes. He made sure that he remembered the Names of Power in their proper order; that the light, or want of light, scintillated or flickered as it should; that the incense spiralled in the right direction.

Then with all ceremonies proper to the occasion he struck the seal from the picture.

Nothing happened. The Poet went disconsolate to bed. Had the Djinn evaporated—seeped through the seal centuries agone? Had a Djinn, at any time, behind that seal, ached and agonized for freedom? One believed too readily in tales from the East. Knowledge was moving westward. London had perhaps at this moment magicians more powerful than those of Bagdad.

Before daylight, members of the Society began to arrive, clamouring for an interview with Yeats. The Djinn had given each one of them a taste of his quality. Something must be done—and done at once! A second night was beyond human endurance.

The Poet did not need to rack his brain for an expedient. He knew what should be done. The members of the Society must sit silent and sympathetic in the room with the midnight curtains. The picture must be there: so must fruit and flowers, incense and cabalistic symbols and pale light. The Poet would chant the Words of Power. He did.

The Djinn, who was not wanting in gratitude, attended the seance. He was in a mood to listen to reason when Yeats pointed out that the proper object of reprisals was the adept who imprisoned him. That personage had gone to his account long since: but the East, the widespaced East, still took the heat of the sun and the cold light of stars. London was not the place where a Djinn could find rest for the sole of his foot: its murky air was not the air to disport in. A wise, a well-instructed Djinn would depart forthwith, accompanied by the speed-off and good-luck wishes of every member of the Society.

The Djinn departed.

THE GREEN DOOR

"GEORGE MOORE IS OUTRAGING the sensibilities of Ely Place," said George Russell. "All Dublin will be shocked in a little while: he'll make a splash like a whale!" "Why?" asked I. "What is he doing?" "He's painting the railings and his front door green—bright emerald green. Think of it in a respectable, pro-British locality!"

I was doing nothing in particular that afternoon, so I strolled into Ely Place. Workmen were painting the railings green; workmen were painting the door. Even as I strolled slowly and contemplated this outrage, the door was torn open and a man with a mass of untidy pale blonde hair came out on the steps and stood there gesticulating to the workmen. My first glimpse of George Moore, and the beginning of the Saga of the Green Door.

Ely Place was roused; its railings had never been painted green. Green was a disloyal colour, only flaunted by misguided rebels and by the commonfolk. The inhabitants of the three other houses consulted with each other. They held impromptu indignation meetings. They went to interview the landlord. The landlord, roused to a sense of the enormity of

93

the event, and fearing lest his property deteriorate and his rents fall away, wrote sturdily to George Moore. This was what George Moore had been waiting for. He composed an epistle, a masterpiece, which he sent at once to his landlord and to the newspapers. In it he explained that his house was a symphony: its carpets, its Manets, its mirrors, its curtains, all were phrases in that symphony, but the keynote was the green door! He was anxious not to hurt the feelings of his neighbours or damage his landlord's property. He could change the green door, but then he would have to change all the furniture of the house—change the entire symphony! As he had paid for the first one, it was only reasonable to suppose that the landlord or the neighbours, or both combined, would pay for the second!

The landlord retired from the controversy, but the neighbours hired organ-grinders to play in front of the green railings. They encouraged their dogs to bark at them in passing. George Moore made himself as objectionable as he could, and Dublin elaborated the saga. It was a Dublin that had leisure to talk at street corners, to be witty about trifles, a Dublin of sonneteers and raconteurs.

Moore delighted it: his quarrels with his cook; his conversion to the language movement; his conversion to Protestantism; his Messiahship; his daffodils; his green door; his gray mullet. His thousand and one poses set so much wit a-scintillating that Moore himself seemed dull: he had to think out remarks beforehand and lead up to them in conversation, while almost any corner-boy could be witty offhand.

We undervalued George Moore till *Ave; Salve; Vale;* appeared.

THE PLAYBOY

It is wednesday night and Synge's *Playboy of the Western World* is running at the Abbey. Dublin is concerned about it. The patriots have discovered an insult to their country. The discovery was due to the foresight of Yeats. Everyone would have taken the *Playboy* as an extravaganza, a fantasy, if Yeats had not prevailed upon Synge to write a little notice explaining that the play represented real life in the Gaelic parts of Ireland, studied at first-hand by the author.

Just think of it! In Germany they would learn, and perhaps in France too, since Synge had captured the ear of Europe, that when a man murdered his father in Gaelic Ireland he became a hero, and processions of women brought him butter and eggs and any offering they could gather. They would learn that the Gaelic mouth is full of curses and words that would make Shakespeare blush. It behooved everyone who cared for the reputation of his country to show strong disapproval, and show it in the Abbey.

There was no timidity about the disapproval, especially when the second act came on. That act was insupportable. Hisses and boos overwhelmed it on the first night, Monday. A triumph for the patriots, well-earned. But Yeats, unchivalrously and against the rules of warfare among the Gael, called in the police. Next day an unsympathetic magistrate said, "Two pounds fine, or a month in jail." The patriots went to jail. They repeated their tactics on Tuesday. On Wednesday everyone wondered what would happen.

Police were to be everywhere on Wednesday. They expected to maintain order. They *were* everywhere. They leaned heavily against the passageways where every seat was filled, the burly good-natured metropolitan police, each man six foot high. When the second act came on, the patriots didn't boo. They didn't make a disturbance of any kind. But suddenly the air was full of snuff and pepper. The actors coughed and sneezed; the audience coughed and sneezed;

the big policemen wiped their eyes, and didn't see anyone that they could arrest. When the actors recovered their voices, they went on where the coughing left off. The objectionable parts were passed. Everyone was satisfied. The actors had said the words; there had been a demonstration; no one was arrested. At the end of the play, there were calls for Synge. Synge did not appear, but Yeats did. He was enjoying himself. He strolled slowly to the middle of the stage and surveyed the seething audience. It did not even throw words at him, it made a stillness to let him speak. "He has courage," thought the folk; his tall figure and dark arrogant face caught their imagination— "After all, *he* did not write the play!"

"Let us discuss this later on," said Yeats, naming hour, day, and place. "I invite you."

"We'll come!" said the audience.

It was half a threat, half a promise.

GHOST-HUNTING

"Well," said lucy middleton, as she came into my room one afternoon, "I don't think much of Willie Yeats and Fournier d'Albe as ghost-hunters."

"What have you been doing?"

"Oh, we spent the night in the haunted house in Baggot Street."

I pricked up my ears. Haunted house in Baggot Street! I had often heard of it, and I knew what the outside of it looked like.

"Yes," said Lucy, "we went in there, and strange to say, the house had some furniture in it—old-fashioned, neglected-looking furniture."

96

"I thought people hurried out of that house and took their furniture with them."

"Well, there was furniture there, and that surprised me."

"What did you do?"

"Oh, we walked about from room to room and got the feeling of the place."

"Did you see anything?"

"Nothing at first. I knew we should sit in the dark, but those two men wouldn't do it. So I slipped off by myself and went into one of the rooms. It was dark, but after a while someone, whom I could not see, brought in a lamp and set it on a table. The lamp had a red shade and made a red light in the room. I sat there with my hands in my lap, and after a while I knew there was someone besides myself in the room. There was someone leaning against the mantelpiece. I looked round and saw him, a pale-faced, dark-haired young man in eighteenth-century dress. He tried to speak to me, but I could not hear him. His face was pale and sad. Then I knew that he was gone. After a while, a young girl came into the room. She had on a white dress and she came very close to the lamp. I could see her face. Her face was wet, and water was dripping from her long black hair. She might well have risen from the river. She looked earnestly into my face and tried to speak, but I could not hear her.

"There was nothing after that in the room, and I felt there would be nothing. I went out into the hall where Willie Yeats and Fournier d'Albe were. We decided then to leave. Before we left, in one of the rooms, Willie Yeats asked any spirits that were there to give a sign. There was a crash and a pane of glass splintered in the window. Then we came away."

It was more than a year afterwards that I was driving with a friend. We passed the Baggot Street house.

"I see it's empty again," said my friend.

"I hear it's badly haunted," said I.

"Oh," said my friend, "don't you know the story of that house?"

"I wish I did!"

"That house belonged more than a hundred years ago to a noted rake. He carried off a young girl, a farmer's daughter, and kept her there a prisoner for some time. When she got a chance, she rushed out and drowned herself in the Liffey. That is the story of the haunted house."

GILPIN

GILPIN MUST HAVE a chapter in this book if only because of the delight that certain children take in hearing about him. I don't know how I acquired him, but he soon emphasized, and overemphasized, his presence and personality. I call him Gilpin, borrowing the name that Walter Scott gave to the goblin who plays such a part in *The Lay of the Last Minstrel*, whose pranks, indeed, gave Walter Scott the idea of writing that poem. Gilpin began by causing things to disappear, and re-appear in unlikely places. Things like silver spoons, books, door keys would desert their habitats and re-appear on a cushion, a bedspread, or a rug. He made night lively by a series of knocks on the walls, the windows, and the furniture. He turned somersaults on the floor at midnight with a re-sounding and weighty noise. I tried to see him several times, without success—indeed I have never laid eyes on him—but as I sat talking with Lucy Middleton in a room frequented by the rascally Gilpin she suddenly said:

"O look! There is a mountain elf coming out of your big cupboard!"

"What is he like?" I queried eagerly.

"Just like what they usually are! He has a head large for his body. His ears are big and pointed: they stand out from his head. His mouth takes up a lot of his face. His eyes are round."

"How big is he?"

"About the size of a child ten or twelve years old."

"How do you know that he is a mountain elf?"

"I have seen the like of him, lots of them in Connemara. They go in companies on the hills and grassy lonesome places. The country people call them 'The Good Folk.'"

"This one," said I, "is a plague: and I hope that he can hear me say it!"

"They are all tricky and full of their fun. Sometimes they come into houses, but not often."

"Do you know any way of apprising them of what happiness good conduct brings?"

"I do not."

I pondered the question of reforming Gilpin. He was more mischievous than a monkey, and I had an uneasy feeling that he rocked with laughter every time I searched in vain for something that he had taken: and drew himself up with a sense of the power and dignity residing in mountain elves when I came upon a pile of important papers scattered on a rug, or found a missing thimble in a close-locked box. Gilpin soon convinced me that not only could he make things disappear and re-appear without any intermediate stage of half-visibility or half-materialization, he could put one solid through another with a turn of the hand, so to speak, and a wink of the eye. It was a trick that he was fond of. He liked to play with bright shining silver spoons, with scissors, or with a thimble. A belt of mine with a silver buckle caught his fancy. I also had a fancy for that belt. I would place it carefully and circumspectly on a chair at my bedside, and wake in the morning to find that it had disappeared: and I must solace myself with an inferior belt that could not boast of a silver buckle. Later, on opening a chest or a locked drawer, I would find that belt!

It was clear that Gilpin must be disciplined in some way —educated, if that were possible! I tried kindness, and the Coué method of suggestion: "Gilpin," I said, "you could be a joy and delight if you were helpful instead of the mischievous plague that you are!" I repeated firmly every morning: *"Gilpin wishes to be helpful."* But it did not work: good counsel was wasted on that rapscallion! Gilpin felt taller by a foot, and thought of further pranks. I had gone the wrong way to work—a rod in pickle was what Gilpin would respect! I must hit him with something that hurt. But what would hurt an elf? I tried a few things—expedients that would make a ghost wilt and feel sorry for itself. Gilpin thought it a new form of entertainment: he belonged to the faery world, and his body was immune. At last I discovered and perfected a shaft of psychic fire that touched Gilpin. It hurt him quite a lot, and he developed—probably for the first time in his life —a feeling of awe. The threat of this weapon could halt him in mid-most mischief: he paused, hesitated—and was lost! I could command obedience. Now when I go to my library shelf for a book of ballads that should be in place third from the end, and find that book gone, I do not hunt frantically about the room in the hope of coming upon it. I just sink into the most comfortable of my chairs and say: *"Gilpin, bring back that book!"* I give him a few minutes before I saunter to the bookshelf. The book is there!

Gilpin has moods now and then of being helpful. He will plank down a pen or pencil on my writing-gear as an encouragement to work: or at times bring a gardening tool, for he stands by to steal bulbs when I plant daffodils. But for the most part he prefers to make things disappear; or to show his skill in juggling one solid through another.

He became so expert a juggler that I felt proud of him: and as a result, basking in the sunshine of my countenance, he followed me to Normandy when I went there to spend a Summer with Maud Gonne in her house by the sea at Calvados. He did not make known his presence at once. He found opportunity and inspiration on a heavy-coloured evening when Maud Gonne and I sat talking far into the night and then, of a sudden becoming aware of how late it was, hurried to our rooms. I had barely lifted a hair-brush from my dressing-table when Maud Gonne knocked at the door. "Come

100

in," I cried. "I can't, it's locked!" Gilpin had locked it without a sound of key-turning. But she was in no mood to admire Gilpin. "It's those servants," she said, "they have left no drinking-water in my room. Have they left a bottle with you?" (In Calvados the water is undrinkable, and water from mineral springs must be imported.) Yes they had left a bottle with me, but no drinking-glass. "What a shame!" said Maud Gonne. "We must get one." We went downstairs in search of one, but as Maud Gonne did not know where the glasses were kept, and we did not discover them, we had to be content with a china cup which was placed on the table by my bed.

I don't know how long I had been asleep when something cold and hard was pressed between the pillow and my cheek. I put up a hand to feel it, and discovered the missing drinking-tumbler. Gilpin had thought of a new ploy!

Gilpin came home with me, to the relief of that household. His education is progressing: I have trained him to turn somersaults without making a noise.

THE HOUSE AT PASSY

MAUD GONNE'S HOUSE in Passy sits green-shuttered and demure beyond a stone-flagged courtyard and a clipped lawn. A stout oaken door, flanked by a high wall, shuts all view of it from the street. It is a house with a plenitude of beautiful things: carved wood, Russian embroidery, Oriental rugs—all thrown together carelessly. There are mirrors everywhere reaching from floor to ceiling. Maud Gonne likes the effect of light and space that they can give. There are many dogs, large and small: Great Danes, Toy Pomeranians, haughty court-bred Pekinese, and one Persian cat. There is a parrot that curses in Spanish, and a comrade that yells in a language of its own. There are many servants. Everyone speaks French.

The centre of delight in the household is Maud Gonne's son, Shaun McBride, a golden-haired boy of four, gracious and fascinating. My French is very bad, and my pronunciation of it worse—a thing to provoke laughter! But when I tangled myself an hour ago in a more than usual barbarism, Shaun, gravely courteous, merely said: "But it is a language very difficult, the French language."

Iseult, Maud Gonne's adopted daughter, has taken upon herself to instruct Shaun in Art, Poetry, and Literature. She, herself, is being instructed in these branches by William Butler Yeats who is in Paris just now and comes to the house in Passy every day. Iseult, a beautiful dark-eyed dark-haired girl of twelve or thirteen, can hold her own in every discussion. She has a lovely voice, and the Poet is teaching her to chant verse as he thinks it should be chanted. He is desirous of chanting verse to the sound of a plangent string, a note now and then for accompaniment or emphasis. He has in mind an instrument unfamiliar and strange-looking, worthy to be carried in the hand, and yielding a pleasant resonance when plucked by the finger. Not a harp! Not by any means a harp: too many people have exploited the harp!

Maud Gonne is rather in favour of the voice alone. She is working on a play to be produced by The Daughters of Ireland. I have written two lyrics for it: "The Red Sunrise," and "A Lament." These Maud Gonne chants to music that came to her in dream—music out of the faery world.

There is much talk these evenings of The Faery World, and of Astrology and Magic. Since Yeats has an uncle, Mr. Pollexfen, who is a very fine astrologer and has proved his skill in many predictions, the Poet feels that his own studies in astrology have had auspicious tutelage. He has always prided himself on his knowledge of magic: though he is willing to admit that in this respect Macgregor Mathers outdistances him. (Maud Gonne tells me privately that there is no

102

comparison at all—Macgregor Mathers is a really great magician.)

The other night we made enquiry of each other as to whether a man can change the verdict of his horoscope—outwit the stars, challenge destiny. The Poet was certain that it could not be done. Maud Gonne and Iseult seconded him in a half-hearted way. I maintained that man is master of his fate, chiefly, I think, because I was born in a good Presbyterian family and had predestination drilled into my childhood and made hateful to me. My un-gospelled self is inclined to believe that life follows a pattern, conditioned like the pieces of coloured glass in a kaleidoscope.

No description of this household would be complete without mention of Miss Barry O'Delaney who is in and out most of the time as devoted adherent of Maud Gonne, and worshipper of Shaun for whom she has made a toy theatre. Miss Barry O'Delaney has lived long in Paris but is all the more Irish because of that. Exile cannot deprive her of the satisfaction of looking exactly like that portrait of Curran the orator and patriot, treasured in Dublin: Curran about to address an assembly, his face rapt with the thought of his own oratory. Barry O'Delaney acts as secretary to W. B. Yeats when he is in Paris, writes articles for magazines, and is keeping a diary in which she records the sayings and doings of many people with well-known names. Maud Gonne will have the lion's share of it. Yeats, I fear, will not come off so well. Barry O'Delaney thinks that she can turn a verse as skillfully as he, and one with a more Irish twist to it. She has a poor opinion of him as a magician ever since an afternoon when he hypnotized her, and forgot how to bring her out of the trance. "This is a case for Macgregor Mathers," he said contritely. Maud Gonne, however, took the affair in hand, and all ended happily.

Day after day I go to the Louvre with Maud Gonne and Iseult. They want me in especial to see the pictures by Leonardo da Vinci. Those pictures and the Botticelli frescoes at the head of the stairway are a wonder and delight. For the rest, I devote myself to Egyptian sculpture, and the archaic Greek. The smile on those wide-eyed untroubled images holds the attention of Iseult. She bids me remember that this archaic smile found hostel in the Cathedral at Chartres, innocent and subtle, before it captured Leonardo, subtly triumphant and charged with the knowledge of a world not human.

Egyptian sculpture has for me a greater allure: Horus the Hawk, too certain of his godhood to exult in it; heads of Pharaohs in black basalt, calm-lipped; the lion goddess, unconcerned with her worshippers. These have a strength the centuries cannot bite on; the endurance of basalt itself. It seems fitting that the head of Akhenaten, leaning forward as the Dionysos leans weighed upon by mortality, should be of friable honey-coloured stone, strange and uncompanioned among those others: asphodel in the fissure of a sea-cliff!

A stone from Peru, in which a feathered serpent has coiled without breaking the natural shape of the stone, stirs in me a wish to come at night and steal it: perhaps to give it back to Peru.

MAGICIAN

WE ARE ON our way to the house of Macgregor Mathers in Passy. We are walking: Maud Gonne; her cousin, May; and myself. Winter sunshine is bright and cold upon the little street. Maud Gonne says:

"You will like Macgregor, indeed he is Count Macgregor, and you will like his wife. She is young and charming, an artist, and interested in Gaelic folklore."

"I thought it was Egyptian mythology," says the cousin.

"That also, of course. Don't you remember those ritual

104

dances that she and Macgregor resurrected from their studies of Egypt, and their memories of past lives there?"

"I have not forgotten those dances, or the talk they stirred in Paris."

"Oh, they astonished and delighted most people—people that mattered!"

The house, in a quiet side-street, is small and quaint. It is two stories high, and has the air of wishing to be no higher. It sits behind its iron railings, its grass-plot, and its gate, well-contented with itself: satisfied with the days of its life, the sunshine and the shadow.

While Maud Gonne knocks at the door, I go over in my mind the things that I have heard about Macgregor Mathers: he is the head of a secret Occult Society; Rosicrucian Adepts have entrusted him with ritual; he has written noteworthy books on magic; he has restored the obliterated symbols in "The Key of Solomon." Maud Gonne and the Poet regard him with respect and, at times, with astonishment. Iseult says—but Iseult has the most extravagant sagas about him— he is a righter of wrongs, a chastiser of evildoers, a champion of the oppressed! Iseult has a romantic mind.

Macgregor Mathers greets us in the hallway, a tall square-shouldered man with a strong clean-cut face, dark hair, and strange steel-blue eyes. He gives the impression of power, efficiency, and a certain ruthlessness. We go at once to the studio where the countess has a half-finished picture on the easel, a picture of a child reading a book while a strange faery face peers in at a window. Maud Gonne bespeaks it as a picture that she wishes to give to Iseult.

The main room is long and low. From the moment of entrance it takes possession of one, shutting off the world of today. It has an indefinable and potent atmosphere, a light that shows everything clearly yet has the quality of dusk: a motionless quality. The mantelpiece displays the richest collection of Egyptian treasures I have ever seen outside of a museum. A mask of Hathor fascinates me: not only for sake of its beauty, but because, looking at it, I feel certain

105

that a psychic face has many times imposed itself on the stone mask.

Curtains, woven in Egypt, make a background in one corner of the room for a small altar. A flame burns there before an image of the god, Thoth. Macgregor explains that separate hours and days are ruled each one by its own divinity. This day and this hour belong to Thoth. Had we come earlier we would have heard the invocation which Macgregor has instructed himself to chant as he believes it was chanted in Egypt. We talk for a while of Egyptian magic. We agree that it depends largely on the making of mental images and astral vehicles, and on will-power. Finnish and Gaelic magic, on the other hand, aim at a comradeship with Nature and the Earth. Iron, in the *Kalevala Saga*, is addressed as a comrade and bidden to leave a champion unharmed, under penalty of having its secret name revealed. This, however, leads back to Egypt and the threat of Isis to reveal the secret name of Ra.

Maud Gonne's cousin is excited about Apaches. She fears that it is dangerous to walk the streets of Paris. Macgregor, unable to resist such an opportunity, launches into a series of wild fables anent adventures with Apaches. The countess tries to bring back the subject of Gaelic magic—in vain!

As we take leave, I pause in the hallway to contemplate what I suppose to be frescoes in mosaic. They climb to an upper room along the staircase wall, occupying the entire space between the ceiling and the low staircase panelling. They are, apparently, images of Egyptian deities. "I see you are interested in these," says Macgregor Mathers, "I did them myself." "Yes," chimes in the countess, "he was so excited about them that he couldn't stop! He did them all in one night." I step closer to examine them. What I had supposed to be enamel is thin paper of various colours: paper cut in tiny longitudinal pieces and fitted together with the utmost exactitude. Truly a marvellous piece of work.

When we are in the quiet street again, I say to Maud

Gonne, "How can he expect us to believe that he did those mosaics in one night?"

"I think it quite likely that he did."

"But—to cut those strips of paper, sort the colours, glue them into position: to say nothing of designing and drawing the figures—it seems to me impossible!"

"He can do things like that. One time he made up his mind that the Society should have Taro cards. At headquarters he took a packet of white cards, asked a member to mark them, went into an inner room for a little while, and came out with those marked cards. The Taro signs were painted on them. The cards used by the Society are copied from that pack."

I had seen those cards. To produce them at short notice "while you wait" was a feat equalling the mosaics. I begin to think that Iseult's account of Macgregor Mathers may not be so fabulous after all!

THE KILKENNY PLAY

ENTER MRS. O'GRADY with the air of one who has news to impart.

"Could you come up to the cottage on the hillside for a week-end, or a week? There will be just you and me and Standish."

"Of course I'll come. How did you persuade Standish to leave town?"

"Oh, Standish has been paid a compliment and he doesn't know whether he likes it or not."

"What has happened?"

"Well, a group of boys in Antrim, Mr. Bigger's boys, have been studying Irish history and reading books that Standish

107

has written. His book, *The Flight of the Eagle*, all about Red Hugh O'Donnell, is their favourite book. Red Hugh took their fancy because he belongs to the North, and the boys have formed themselves into a Red Hugh Club. They have made themselves bows and arrows, they know how to put up tents." (Here I muttered something about leaden roofs and arquebuses.) "They have to do without them," said Mrs. O'Grady. "Their resources only run to tents."

"Isn't Standish pleased?"

"He's more bewildered than pleased. The boys have come down to Sheestown, Captain Cuffe's place in Kilkenny. They've pitched their tents in a remote part of the estate and announced that they are going to stage Red Hugh as an outdoor play."

"This ought to please Standish."

"It would if it didn't transpire that Standish has to write the play for them. He says nothing will make him sit down and hammer words together for a play. The boys came there to give him pleasure and pay him a compliment. Let them do it!"

"What is your idea of the way out?"

"I think you will have to write the play."

"You know well enough that Elizabethan English is a thing I cannot get my tongue round. It is home-tongue to Standish."

"I think you might get Standish started. Anyhow, somebody has to write a play for those boys."

Soon we found ourselves in the train making for the mountains. Standish maintained a gloomy and aggrieved silence on the subject of the play. But he was voluble on his favourite topic, the need of agriculture in Ireland. Grassland after grassland whirled past the train windows, cattle everywhere! Standish even fell to counting them in a maledictory mood. How the plough would thrive if they were away—those ill-omened cattle! I maintained a sympathetic attitude, Mrs. O'Grady one strictly neutral. I like cattle and grasslands myself, but Standish *had* to write that play.

108

Luxuriously lonely on its hillside the cottage beamed upon us. The wood that stretched away from it was loud with bird-song. Across the narrow valley the austere peak of the Golden Spear thrust skyward in the level afternoon sunlight.

Standish retreated to his room. He said he was going to meditate. Mrs. O'Grady went out to enjoy the sunshine, and I tried my hand at a play. When the first act was written, Standish condescended to listen to it. He was irate.

"What sort of language is this?" he said. "Do you think Elizabethans talked that way?"

"I know they did not. It is my misfortune to be ignorant of the way they talked."

"This won't do at all," said Standish.

"Perhaps if you wrote a scene, even a few lines, I might know how to go on."

"Something has to be done," said Standish, making for the haven of his room.

It became apparent that he was working. He wrote scene after scene, and soon the play, *Red Hugh,* was ready for the young actors.

RED HUGH

THE BOYS PITCHED their tents in the demesne of Captain Otway Cuffe at Sheestown. They lit camp fires, and though their bows and arrows did not procure them deer-meat they had a plenitude of beef and mutton purveyed to them by their host, Otway Cuffe. Standish was at home in those tents. He knew exactly what kind of yew was used in bows, and what the bow should measure from tip to tip. He knew the best way to make camp fires. He could name the moss and heather they gathered. Best of all, he could talk of Red Hugh

109

and of that other illustrious champion, Hugh O'Neill, whose clan-territory stretched into their own homeland.

The boys revered Standish as a historian, a law-giver, a great chieftain out of the past—and perhaps they were not far wrong! They begged him to put all that was possible of the life of Red Hugh into the play. Heedful of this, Standish extemporized and re-modeled scene on scene: now aboard ship, anon in Red Hugh's ancestral castle; in the feast-hall of Battle-Axe McSwiney's stronghold; in the fortress-prison of Dublin Castle. Red Hugh growing up, the well-loved youth, the one choice of his clan; Red Hugh instructed in war-games by his foster-father, the warrior McSwiney; Red Hugh treacherously captured by the English; Red Hugh in prison.

The boys had selected the ruins of the old castle of Shees-town as the place where they would stage the play. A wide arch still spanned what had been a turreted gateway, and one turret reared itself high enough to do duty for Dublin Castle. Once the boys discovered that they could climb the turret and be lowered by a rope, as Red Hugh was when escaping, they felt that everything necessary had fallen to their hands. The builders of the castle had set it firmly on a grassy platform. Behind it stretched the woodlands of Sheestown. A wide grassy sweep in front gave ample room for spectators. It was an easy matter to bring horses to the castle—real live horses for the escape of Red Hugh.

Otway Cuffe, T. W. Rolleston, Stephen Gwynne, and other friends of Standish concerned themselves about a stage setting. How divide scene from scene, without curtains? How depict a ship's cabin, a feast-hall, a prison cell? At last a solution was found. Behind the archway a large white cloth was stretched. Appropriate background scenes were thrown on the cloth by a magic lanthorn. When the lanthorn was turned off, darkness provided the drop-curtain.

The boys, eager to add a crowning glory to their play, begged Standish to take part in it: "We are doing this for you, and we want you to be in it!"

110

"I can't act."

"You can do anything. You made the play, and we want you in it."

"I didn't make a part for myself. I want to sit and watch the play."

"Come with us for only the shortest time, hardly any time at all! We want you with us. Maybe we will never see you again: we have to go back to our own country."

"I suppose I could be a watchman walking round the tower. Yes, there should be a watchman."

"Hurrah!" yelled the boys. "He'll be the watchman!"

He was. Wrapped in a dark cloak and carrying a lanthorn he patrolled the tower, taking care to gaze always in the wrong direction when Red Hugh craned a head from the battlements; muttering complacently: "Not a mouse can stir! *I* am on guard!" at the very moment when Red Hugh and the two O'Neill princes climbed down.

The audience rose with cries of recognition and a thunderous clapping of hands while Standish tried to slip unnoticed to his seat in the grassy amphitheatre.

The play ended with the escape of Red Hugh, and was followed by a pageant representing the triumphant home-welcome accorded by chiefs and clansmen in Tyrconnel. Magnificent horses led by running foot-boys, pipers drawing music from their war-pipes, shield-bearing warriors, bards, historians, shouting children, made sound and brightness among the trees and grassy spaces of the demesne. The audience, cheering and singing, joined the procession.

Cheering and singing they went homeward. The narrow cobbled streets of Kilkenny heard the song of the young patriots:

> *'O welcome us, O welcome us,*
> *'Tis we that bring the Summer in!'*

The tall houses leaning their heads together echoed the singing; the Nore heard it, sliding lazily gray-green between its reeds and meadow pastures; the Cathedral heard it, and

111

the Black Abbey buttressed with stone on stone of age-worn Kilkenny marble. The stars did not listen: they have too marvelous a music of their own.

PEARSE'S SCHOOL, SAINT ENDA'S

ON SATURDAYS, PEARSE assembles his pupils in a lecture-hall, and people who are interested in Pearse's ideas come out and talk to the boys. This Saturday afternoon I am going to talk to them. It will be something about Gaelic Ireland, perhaps some story out of the old sagas. Saint Enda's lies a couple of miles out of Dublin, a fine old Irish country house with gardens, ornamental lawns, and fields about it. A little river runs through the grounds, and there is an artificial ruin. The Eighteenth Century specialized in grottos and artificial ruins. I am met at the entrance gate by Thomas MacDonagh, gorgeous in a saffron kilt and emerald-green brat. We greet each other in Gaelic, and find Pearse waiting at the house-door.

It is a joy to talk to those boys: they have such eager alert faces. One face I remember above the others, a thin clear-cut face with straight dark hair on either side of it and eyes that listen delightedly. I learn that the boy, one of the youngest there, is Norman Reddin. When the talk is over, Pearse shows me through the high-ceilinged rooms of the beautiful old house. In one room he has established a collection of weapons that have lived through hazardous times and high adventures: a cannon-ball from the siege of Limerick; pikes with hand-hammered iron heads that were carried in the '98 Rising; swords and pistols treasured once in mountain caves, or in camps of the "Wild Geese" in France. The boys are allowed to handle these things. And so was I.

We stepped from the house upon a terrace where a path

112

wound among daffodils. "Emmet must have walked here often," said Pearse. "The man who owned this house was his friend." As he spoke, he looked across the slanting meadows to where the line of the Dublin hills met the sky—those hills to which Emmet retreated with the remnant of his pikemen, after the lost battle.

We turned in the direction of the little stream that was singing to itself. Pearse said:

"This little river has kingfishers. The boys are under oath not to frighten the birds. Perhaps we can surprise a kingfisher!"

We walked a good distance, but we did not surprise a kingfisher. Pearse was distressed about it. He fell silent as though he feared that the sound of voices might scare them. They are so blue, those kingfishers; so sudden-darting; so joyous; so flamelike! We did not see one. Butterflies there were a-plenty, and wild flowers by the stream-marge. Padraic Pearse took care not to trample on a wild flower. He has a tenderness for all living things, yet in him is a potency that may shake life to its core as the earth-tremor shakes hills. It is hard to envisage this man, so little concerned with an estimate of himself. He is like a continent vast and unexplored—one never comes to the end of him! He is like a towering ice-crag that keeps eight-ninths of its bulk and its strength in the depths of the sea.

There is no one who can rouse an audience as he can, yet he speaks very simply and without gestures: some fire in the man himself kindles flame in the listeners. His mere presence in a room, though he sit silent, dominates all that goes on. In some strange and subtle fashion everyone who comes in contact with him is overwhelmed for a moment—awed, or uplifted—by his passionate concentration of purpose, his chivalrous generosity, his power of understanding people and things: for a moment, ineradicable, the poorest soul, the most faint-hearted, absolves itself in the selfless consecration that links Padraic Pearse with Hell and Paradise in the abysmal and purgatorial Vision that is Ireland.

113

TEMPLE HILL

WHY DO I always choose an old-fashioned dilapidated house, just because of its charm, and find that I have to repaint and repair it, and refurbish a deserted garden? I live now in a most charming old house furnished with a secret hiding-hole and a ghost. It has tall rooms and long corridors that open off each other, making it possible to go in at one door, traverse several rooms that must be stepped down into, or up into, and come out at another door—far off.

Temple Hill had a riotous and notorious ghost (it still has him) and because of that stood empty and neglected till I fell in love with it and persuaded the skeptical landlord to let me have it at a very low rental provided I undertook to put it in order and live in it. The paper was hanging from the walls, the paint peeling from the woodwork. The landlord did not believe that anyone could live in it—but that was my affair! Paint and paper would do his house no harm.

Maud Gonne, who had given up her house in Coulson Avenue, put in her carved oak furniture and other beautiful things. Miss Fox, who joined in the venture, put in some rugs and other furnishings, and we braved the ghost. He was energetic and angry. He banged on walls and doors, slipped stealthily along corridors, and gave excellent imitations of a drunken or rage-mad man stumbling up the staircase.

Fortunately Bill, the great bull-mastiff, does not howl or recognize these manifestations in any way. He lies in the main hall and seems to be immune to noises. Indeed so immune had the household become that when a drunken burglar stumbled up the stairs and blundered from room to room, he would have passed for the ghost if he had not carried a candle. That betrayed him. The ghost never carried a light. When the burglar had been chased from the house, across the lawn, and over the enclosing wall, I began to wonder what had become of Bill. He was asleep in the basement where Pat and Mary were also asleep. I was indignant about

114

Bill: but Mary, the cook-housekeeper, and her husband, Pat, stoutly took his part averring that big dogs always slept, and if one wanted a guard one had to keep a sharp-eared sharp-voiced terrier to waken the big dog and egg him on the burglar. (Bill will have to snooze, I couldn't stand a sharp-voiced terrier!)

When Maud Gonne came to the house for the first time she knew nothing about the ghost. She arrived at eleven o'clock at night on a jaunting-car and saw only the blackness of trees, a winding drive, and the lighted house. She went to her room almost immediately, but barely had she entered the breakfast-room next morning when she said: "You never told me you had a ghost here."

The ghost, who always devoted himself to the entertainment of any guest that Temple Hill might house, had been more than usually forthcoming.

Maud Gonne said: "After the lights were out in my room, I felt a cold wind on my face. I thought that a window was open, but both were shut. Then I became aware of the ghost. He said that he wanted to show me a secret passage, and immediately I found myself outside the house. We went round one wing and came to a place with high green banks and a large pine tree. The secret passage was there, but I refused to explore it, and immediately I was back in my room. The ghost was there too. He wanted to explain something that I could not understand. I told him that he was wasting time here: he should go forward in the spirit world."

This advice seems to have had some effect. The ghost was quiet during the few weeks of Maud Gonne's stay. He had shown her a tree, a tall sinister tree, that seemed to remember hanged men. The high green banks were as she had described them, but we never discovered the secret passage.

I stumbled on the secret room by accident. Stooping to adjust a rug in the little room off the drawing-room that spied on the roses and apple trees of the walled garden and was used by Eighteenth-Century ladies as a retiring room when they wanted to powder their noses, I chanced on a

115

plank that looked as if it could be moved. Trial proved that it could. The room, entered only from above, is in the thickness of the basement-wall behind the wine cellar. It may yet be useful, for already the basement cellars have heavy cases of ammunition; stacks of rifles and bayonets; and even a few of the heavy Mausers landed at Howth on that day of days when Erskine Childer's yacht, the *Asgard*, swung out of hiding at Lambay Island, stood into the sunshine and the sight of the Dublin hills; and came, light as a sea-gull, to the landing-pier at Howth where hundreds of Volunteers waited to shoulder the rifles and load themselves with ammunition.

The Ulster Volunteers can parade, armed to the teeth, but our Volunteers have to drill in secret and hide their rifles. The O'Rahilly has the task of distributing the weapons stored at Temple Hill. Every now and then a man, or a couple of men, will come to the front door. Confronted with me, for I always answer the front door now, they give a password in Gaelic. When I answer it, they produce a small strip of paper: "Give X so many rifles, etc., etc." Pat, who has an Irishman's delight in handling arms, moves heavy cases about as if they were featherweights. I offered to get him help—trusted patriot help—but he said stubbornly: "I wouldn't trust eye-sight of these cases or a hand-grip on them to anyone but myself."

There was a tense moment a few evenings ago when a large touring car stood in the driveway with two Volunteers in charge. Pat and the Volunteers had loaded it with "stuff." We wished it God-speed, but it refused to move. Everybody tinkered at it earnestly: we daren't use lanthorns. The local constabulary, idle and bored, have constituted themselves the guardians of all disabled cars and sick bicycles. They descend upon one at sight and offer their services, which may vary from real help to useless advice. The trees in the curving driveway hid the car, but a lanthorn and sound of hammering might bring a passing policeman at any moment, eager for a tip. Pat felt strong enough almost to lift that car and

116

shake it. The Volunteers offered prayers and vows to the Virgin. I prayed fervently myself. With a sudden jolt as if it had wakened from sleep the car moved! Everyone wiped sweat out of their eyes: "Luck holds!" we said. "Better the hard start now with night beginning than an easy start an hour ago with the half-light to betray us!"

The derelict garden at Temple Hill had kept one beautiful thing; a patch of the low-growing gentiana acaulis—triumphantly, unbelievably blue! Rose and carnation had succumbed, but this plant, usually hard to establish, had by a miracle survived. I determined to fall in with the humour of the ground and make blue the dominant colour of the garden. It has many patches now of gentiana acaulis and starry territories of gentiana verna, together with bush lupines that can boast of blueness, and the Italian bugloss, blue as lapis lazuli. Roses too it has again and heavy-headed double narcissi, jonquils, and white and purple violets. A blue Persian cat walks daintily from stepping-stone to stepping-stone with a fluffy-haired black Russian, slant and emerald-green of eye, to keep him company.

The lawn has its old trees, the better for the years they have seen. I am establishing cohorts and battalions of daffodils in the grass of the lawn together with blue anemones and the scarlet windflower of the Apennines.

If this old house has luck it may prosper—but who knows? Even the strong bones of the earth maintain themselves but for a season.

THE PROPHECY, 1914

EVERYONE IS PROPHESYING the outcome of the War. Little pamphlets are being sold, pamphlets with predictions by English astrologers, pamphlets with prophecies collected from foreign sources. The English astrologer, Seraphiel, predicts that Germany will lose the war, the Kaiser will lose his kingdom, and the Crown Prince his inheritance. A prophecy by the French mystic, the Curé d'Ars, has been unearthed. After the War of 1870 and the French defeat, he predicted that the Germans would return. They would come close to Paris, but would be defeated, and France would take back the territory she had lost and more than that. There is a vision of Tolstoy's, taken down by his daughter. Tolstoy describes the kindling of war-flames in Europe, and goes on to say: "There will arise a man in Russia who will have great power, and as he commands, so it will be done. He will be a half-Mongol. He will be the Napoleon of Russia."

Our own *Sinn Fein Journal* comes out with a prophecy. It is said to be about two hundred years old, the prophecy of a poor Gaelic-speaking peasant of Antrim. He was a man who wandered about the roads and was thought by the country-folk to have the hand of God on him because his wits were troubled. He went from house to house, and had bed and supper and a welcome offered to him, alike in small cottages and in comfortable farmhouses. One night he came into a friendly farmhouse and said that he had a vision. He wanted it written down because he knew he was going to die. No man can talk with the Great Beings beyond life and not go beyond life himself.

It was a prophecy of wars to come. As printed in *Sinn Fein,* it is long and detailed. It could be fitted into past events, but one part of it seems to be concerned with this 1914 War. The prophecy says: "A war will break out about the time of harvest. The English will be fighting in it and the Irish, and, my grief, Dublin will be burned! The war will be in two parts, the second part rising out of the first, and in this second part the power of England will be broken and she will lose her ships."

Truly a prophecy to welcome! England welcomed it by raiding the Sinn Fein offices and confiscating the printing-press, together with as many copies of the *Sinn Fein Jour-*

nal as she could capture. The patriots welcomed it and retailed it to each other. Was it real or faked? I wondered. It was certainly opportune.

If it were faked, would it have that passage:

"My grief, Dublin will be burned?"

Why should Dublin be burned? Why should a patriot inventor, eager to hearten his fellow-countrymen, invent such a catastrophe? A seer of course does not invent anything: perhaps this very prediction proved authenticity. In any case one could bear it in mind. It was not likely to happen—but if it came to pass, if fire indeed seared Dublin, perhaps the whole prophecy would come to pass: perhaps the power of England would be broken, and her battle-ships destroyed in the second part of the war. That would mean freedom for Ireland!

Was it because I had read this prophecy, printed in full in Arthur Griffith's *Journal,* that I had a vision which came some weeks later? I was standing on the sidewalk near Trinity College waiting for a tram-car. The day was bright and sunny. I was looking idly down the street. Suddenly I became aware of the fact that I was looking at blackened and ruined buildings. As far as my eye traveled down the shaft of Westmoreland Street to O'Connell Street I saw gaping windows and piles of fallen masonry. I saw them clear and distinct in the sunlight. In a few seconds I had shaken myself out of this strangeness. The buildings stood unharmed, and I was waiting for a tram-car.

At the house of Owen MacNeill I recounted this happening. Several people were there, amongst them Madame O'Rahilly, blonde and joyous. Those ruined streets distressed her. She could not shake off the thought of them. She sat silent through the evening's talk.

What threat clutched at her from those gaping fire-scarred walls? Can she—unable to name it, unable to see it clearly— fore-sense disaster to O'Rahilly who moves so gaily now, so arrogantly, in the midst of hazards, countering every thrust

119

of evil-fortune with a smile or a jest? If Dublin burns will the acrid smoke be in his nostrils?

WIND OF CHANGE

THIS HOUSE HAS an uprooted feeling. Rugs are coiled in bales for storage. Waterford and Venetian glass stand in close array, waiting to be swathed and packed. Dust has gathered in the crevices of carved furniture. I am leaving Temple Hill. War-time prices and the general difficulty of living have made it impossible to remain here. But the house will be in safe hands. Mrs. Trench is taking it over. She will keep up the garden and the lawn. Her daughters will have joy in the roses and daffodils: tall beautiful Sive, and her dark-haired sister, Margot.

If stone walls remember—and I think that they do—these walls will remember lamplight and firelight; laughter and the sound of a violin; voices that chanted verse; great bowls of violets; bronze jars with branches of plum blossom; spicy fragrance of pomander and pot-pourri: and, longest of all, perhaps, the spirals of incense smoke that curled before an image of Kwan-Yin, Goddess-Mother of Consolation.

Some hearts will remember firelight and candle-light in the long lofty drawing-room and the good talk that ran and scintillated, that twined and twisted, a living thing, among those who came there so often, that small intimate group skilled in the art of conversation. They will not be utterly forgetful of crowded nights when my sister Elizabeth put on a play, as she did now and then; *How he lied to her husband, The Stronger* or, perhaps, a scene from Shakespeare. Poets, artists, sculptors, dramatists moved from room to room or loitered in the long corridor: many of them lovers of Ire-

120

land, passionate enough to have their names on her bedes-
roll.

In the lawn the almond trees are red-budded. Snowdrops
make a whiteness here and there. Bill, the great bull-mastiff
who has two colours in his smooth coat, gold at the hair
roots and black at the tips, could find places to lie in the sun.
But Bill has realized one of his ambitions. He always wanted
to sit on the front seat of a limousine. He does that now, and
his new owners have given him a massive silver collar. But
the blue Persian, Zoro, and the black Russian, Goblin, have
a premonition of disaster. They are coming to Howth, and
later to the Curraun in County Mayo where there is a cottage
to be had with twenty acres of heather and bogland fronting
on Achill Island and the sea. A Gaelic-speaking village is
close at hand. I can get a shanachie to recite poems of the
Fionn Saga. I can hear, perhaps, a few more adventures of
the Gobhuan Saor and his Son.

I hope to spend a Winter on that sea-verge. A man who
spent a Winter in a milder part of Gaelic Ireland says to me:
"The west coast of Ireland is not fit for human habitation in
Wintertime. The wind is like a keen-edged knife. It never
lets up. Scarcely can a stone wall stand against the wind.
There is not a tree, there is nothing larger than a sloe-bush—
and not even that!" There will, however, be the Winter
colours that I have never seen; there will be Gaelic story-
tellers and poets; there will be the glitter of the wide Atlantic. There will be sound of the sea, and silence, and the
whirr of wings.

IN SPRINGTIME

IT IS STRANGE to be in Dublin again, to see tall houses and
crowded streets after those months of spacious loneliness at

the Curraun, with wide glittering Atlantic waters, the Winter redness of sedge grass on the hillsides, snow upon the summits, sudden swirls of tempest, and the ever-present biting wind. Among the Gaelic-speaking folk of the Curraun, England's war seemed worlds away. I wanted to think of it as little as possible. It had cost me Temple Hill, and exiled me from Dublin for more than a year: just when Volunteers were drilling, when a wind of change was blowing everywhere, when anything might happen!

Something is going to happen on Easter Sunday. On that day there will be a sound of marching feet. Men everywhere are to strike for Ireland's freedom. Eoin MacNeill is to give the signal for the Rising. So much I know: but how much more there is to know! Have cargoes of arms been landed? Have we strong well-equipped outposts beyond Dublin? Will Roger Casement get back in time from Germany? He should be with us when the Flag of Ireland takes the wind. I wonder what flag it will be: the Sunburst on a blue ground; the Harp on a green one, or, perhaps, the Tricolour: green, white, and orange, borne of late in so many processions.

The O'Rahilly, who loves armorial bearings and heraldic designs, talked much of flags with me on those last days at Temple Hill. Should the Sunburst or the Harp have the chief honour? Both go back to the age of the gods. Fionn, son of Uail, had the Sunburst. The Harp takes one's mind to the Harp of the Dagda, Mannanaun's Harp, "the oak of the two greens" that with its music brought Spring, Summer, Autumn, and Winter upon the Earth. We could not choose between them, and O'Rahilly decided to have both. How many rays should the Rising Sun have? Seventeen, because that number carries the meaning: *I am specially appointed.* Should the Harp have seven or nine strings? Nine is the number of a god, the number of the Dagda: but it is also the number shown by a chief when he is defeated and declares in dying that the cause will live. Parnell, in that last fight, returned exactly nine members at the election. He was then mortally ill. Seven might be luckier. O'Rahilly was de-

122

signing those flags when I left Dublin. I wish that I could see him, or have news of the flags.

The Sinn Fein tricolour, green, white and orange, has the colours of Springtime in Ireland: white of the blackthorn blossom; green of the fields; golden flame of the gorse on every hill. It is Springtime now. The windswept heights, the sheltered valleys are flaunting the Sinn Fein colours: yet I think it an ephemeral flag.

Tomorrow is Easter Sunday.

EASTER WEEK, 1916

EASTER SUNDAY—A DAY of uncertainty. Parades, maneuvers, and marches of the Irish Republican Army should have taken place today. We hear they have been called off. What does that mean? They were to be the signal for the Rising. After so much hope and preparation, has the Rising fizzled out? No one seems to know. It is said that Eoin MacNeill himself has called off the maneuvers. A slack, uncertain day filled with rumours.

Easter Monday. The sun is shining, but it seems to be the only brightness. Nothing is happening. It does not seem as if anyone expected anything to happen. Sounds of shots! Everyone tense and alert. Something *is* happening! I hurry from my lodgings in Leinster Road to the Town Hall at Rathmines. People are standing there, wondering. From Rathmines one can see as far as Portobello Bridge. One can see the Portobello barracks where the English Tommies for some time past have been leaning over back-walls and trading rifles, blankets, and other equipment, for bottles of whiskey, pressed on them by eager patriots. There is a stir in the barracks. Soldiers are marching out from the barracks, along the road and across the Canal Bridge, into Dublin City.

123

More and more shots! "Must be a riot of some kind," mutters a bystander. "It's more than that," replies another; "it is a Rising of sorts."

More shots. Farther off now, dull and muffled. News begins to creep along the knot of bystanders. "They say that Pearse is in the General Post Office, that they have taken half the city. That the Volunteers held up a train-load of soldiers. They'll win with the help of God." "It can't be! They can't hold out more than a day, do their best!"

Seumas O'Sullivan and Estella Solomons come up to me as I stand listening with all my ears to every shot, to every rumour. "The telegraph wires are cut! Railway stations are in the hands of the Volunteers," says Seumas. "It is terrible and splendid. If it could only be true that they are rising everywhere in Ireland!"

The trams are not running. No one can get across the Canal Bridge at Portobello. English soldiers are posted there. People who live in Rathmines are turned back from the bridge, and wander aimlessly, telling each other news that they have heard or invented: "The English have a warship in the Bay!" "They are sending gunboats up the Liffey!" "The Irish are rising everywhere, God bless them!"

Easter Tuesday. News is filtering in. Constance de Markievicz, second in command with the Citizen Army, held Saint Stephen's Green Park all Monday. Trenches were dug there, and sharp-shooters exchanged shots with the English soldiers. Pearse, with Tom Clarke, Connolly, and The O'Rahilly, has taken possession of the General Post Office. MacDonagh is in Jacob's Factory. De Valera holds Boland's Mills. No one in Rathmines seems to know what is going on. But soldiers are everywhere: behind barrack walls; behind walls of gardens; on the roofs of houses! Machine guns are sputtering. Rifle shots, rifle volleys puncture the intermission. There is fighting in the streets. How much or how little, no one can guess. But certainly dead bodies are in the streets.

Easter Wednesday. A sound of heavy guns from the river, accompanied by heavy guns from another point; the English

124

are shelling some important position. It must, by the direction, be Liberty Hall.

No one can get into Dublin City across any canal bridge without a pass signed by a British officer. But every little servant girl can get across. She has only to sidle up to one of the "Tommies" marching up and down there with a rifle on his shoulder and a general look of boredom. After a little conversation, she tells him about her sick mother, or something of equal importance, and slips through to town.

My mother's little serving-maid has reason to believe that her sweetheart has come up from the country, and is fighting now side by side with the others, or holding out behind the walls of Jacob's Factory. He may be killed at any moment. She does not grudge him to his country, but she *must* see him! She asks an afternoon off for the attempt, and comes back triumphant with this tale of what happened. At Portobello Bridge there was just one sentry. Young and bored. She told him that she *had* to get into Dublin Town. Her mother was dying, and she was the only child! The Tommy looked round to see if there was an officer anywhere, then he said: "You had better get through while the going is good," and she scuttled across the bridge. On foot she made her way to Jacob's Factory. It was like a beleaguered fortress, right enough! The windows were sand-bagged, except where some patriot defenders were leaning out to take the air. The English Tommies, besiegers of the place, were enjoying a rest. No officer was in charge. Standing, sitting, or lying, they were smoking cigarettes. She explained to them that she wanted to talk to her sweetheart who had come up from the country. "Just bawl out his name," said the Tommies, "and if the fellow is inside, he'll come to the window."

She stepped up to a window, and asked if her sweetheart was in the building. Yes, he was. He could come to the window and talk to her. He came to the window. They had a few words together. Then one of the Tommies said, "Look out now, and get away from here. We're going to fire." They lifted their rifles. The patriots disappeared behind the sand-

125

bags. The Tommies fired—and shot a civilian! Civilians were always on hand, huddled close to the fighting zone. They could not resist such an attraction! Sometimes sympathy with the patriots drew them there, but curiosity, for the most part, was the lure. The little maid returned safely.

Easter Thursday. Every sort of gun is coughing, spitting, and stammering. There is a curfew regulation. Everyone must be indoors at six o'clock. No lights can be shown. Outside, there is plenty of light, for Dublin is burning! The Post Office is burning, and so are other buildings in the heart of Dublin. A red, a blood-red cloud like a pall. The wildest rumours now are flying. *"Whole regiments of English soldiers have been held up, have been annihilated."* These are things one wishes to believe. But with the terrible appearance of truth, other rumours like serpents force themselves into one's consciousness. *"Connolly is wounded and dying. There is no general Rising outside Dublin. Pearse, O'Rahilly, and others have burst out of the flaming Post Office, and have been massacred."*

Easter Friday. Phyllis MacMurdo came to see me. Since she is the niece of General Sir William MacMurdo, and strongly pro-British in sympathy, she is in touch with the military here. She had authentic news: Pearse, Clarke, Connolly, The O'Rahilly, and others are still in the charred and fire-thridded Post Office. They must burn to the bone, or surrender. A small column of the Citizen Army, under Sean Connolly, almost captured Dublin Castle. Emer Moloney and Doctor Kathleen Lynn were with that column when it barricaded itself in the City Hall. They are prisoners now. Sean Connolly is dead. Sheehy-Skeffington, the noted pacifist (who had nothing to do with the Rising), was shot in Portobello Barracks on Wednesday. The English arrested him in O'Connell Street on Tuesday night, when he was trying to stop the looting of the big shops. It was pandemonium there, unchecked and even encouraged by the soldiery. Plateglass splintered the sidewalks; men, women, and children staggered under fur coats, damask armchairs, and bales of

126

silk. Diamond rings and jeweled watches were sold in the street for little more than the price of a drink. Phyllis came to warn me that I must leave Dublin at once. She has information that my name is on the "black list."

I shall stay, but it will be advisable to take my pistol to my father's house (he is pro-British). The ammunition I can hide. Roger Casement is in the hands of the English. They will hang him.

Easter Saturday. Firing has ceased. There is a horrible silence. They are all dead—or it is surrender!

AFTERMATH, 1916

THIS IS SUNDAY, April 30, the Sunday after Easter Sunday. Pearse signed the order to surrender yesterday. It is his own death-warrant, and the death-warrant of those who with him proclaimed the Irish Republic. All the leaders who are not dead will be executed: but the surrender saves the lives of a few young fighters, and ends the slaughter of civilians.

Sentries are still on all canal bridges. No one can go into Dublin Town without a military permit.

It rains, and rains, and rains.

Monday. It rains, and rains! The skies are purple-black. There is a heaviness as of thunder, but no lightning. This is May-Day: I am repeating to myself the Rann of the Four Jewels. There will be no blossom on the blackthorn today.

Tuesday. The rain is torrential!

Wednesday. 'Tis the third of May. England is again triumphant! The sentries are no longer on the bridges. People on foot are crowding into town, crowding across all the canal bridges to see the broken, battered streets, and the smoking ruins of the Post Office. From the windows of tall houses

127

hang red-cross flags, the first that I have ever seen in Dublin. They are red and white: the colours of the New Age.

Newsboys are crying the news! I buy a paper, and lean against a wall to spread it out.

EXECUTIONS

Executed this morning: Patrick H. Pearse, Thomas MacDonagh, Thomas Clarke.

The sun is shining. This is a day of the days of the Festival of Bealtine: the old Celtic festival of the coming of the Gods of Dana, the young eager Gods who took on themselves the burden of heartening and fashioning the Earth. They lost Godhead in the struggle. But strength and beauty showed themselves in the Earth. This is the Festival of Springtime. Gods do not die—nor do heroes!

Everywhere the trees have thrust forth leaf and bud: such a brave greenness, as if Summer had arrived suddenly—out of season! Spring is cold and tardy in Ireland. The rain of Springtime is cold and wind-tormented. Not so the rain with which Ireland took farewell of her lovers. That rain was warm and passionate: the trees have burgeoned because of it.

The story of the Rising comes to one in fragments, in excited whispers, in the scarred machine-gun-pitted houses that stand windowless, yet with a sort of hidden triumph, stonily returning the stares of a crowd: a crowd that has always in the midst of it a hunger and a triumph. "You see that house, Mister?" says a small boy. "They held out there for three days, and there wasn't more than three or four of them in it! The soldiers shelled it. They didn't take it till the last one left, and he was the only one alive! But he's alive yet, Mister. He got off over the back wall, and he's alive. They'll never get him now!"

THROUGH THE EYES OF OTHERS, 1916

THROUGH THE EYES of others I obtain glimpses of happenings in Easter Week. My friend, Maud Joynt, saw the Countess Markievicz, on Easter Monday, walking by the edge of Saint Stephen's Green Park to take command of her battalion. She had a green uniform, a hat with a feather, and knee-breeches. "Something," said my unsympathetic friend, "like a Robert Emmet costume." I can picture her in the morning sunshine, debonair and light of heart, walking jauntily. The Rising, long desired and despaired of, represented to her the liberation of Ireland. She had worked for it, and dreamed of it for years.

The sister of The O'Rahilly said to me: "It is strange what one remembers. I remember the green automobile that O'Rahilly had, and how the door of it swung open where the catch didn't fit properly. On the morning of Easter Monday I saw that car for the last time. Young men were loading it with dynamite outside Headquarters. I said to them, 'Be careful, you must not slam the door!' I went inside. My brother was there; Pearse was there; and Tom Clarke. I said to them: 'Isn't it a shame for you men to start a fight that you can't win! You're taking hundreds and thousands of the young men of Ireland to their death.' My brother looked at me, but he said nothing. Tom Clarke looked at me, and he said nothing: but Pearse said: 'We have to do this, there is no other way.' I went outside. They were putting in the last sticks of dynamite. I said: 'Be careful of the door!' I knew that I would never see the car again, that I would never see any of the leaders again. My brother had tried to call off the Rising. He was going out because the young men of Ireland were going out. If they died he wanted to die with them."

A girl, who had been standing near the Post Office when the Republic was proclaimed, said: "Pearse came out on the steps. Some of the people cheered him, others were sullen. An old woman from the crowd climbed up the steps and kissed his hand. Pearse said a word to her, and went back into the Post Office. There was a silence about the place. The flag of the Republic was flying from the roof. We knew that Pearse and those with him were death-doomed."

A girl who saw the last of The O'Rahilly, said: "He was lying wounded in the narrow laneway by the Post Office. It was a pity to see him, so young and handsome he was! English soldiers were firing into the laneway: fire was eating the walls of the Post Office. We knew that thirst was a torment to him but every one was afraid to go out. After a while the girl that was with me said: 'I can't stand this any longer! I'll chance it.' She took out a cup of water. The O'Rahilly drank it, and died as she knelt beside him. He must have waited for that cup of water."

GREEN ABOVE THE RED, 1916

WITH THE DEATH of Roger Casement, the executions have ended. Sixteen men have died for their part in the Rising. The others are safe in English jails. A small occult society, that worked for years with the object of reaching to the power of the Stone, the Danaan Jewel with which is bound up the Royal Sovereignty of Ireland, was told in the year 1908, that sixteen is the number of the Stone.

It cannot have been a mere coincidence that the Rising took place in the year 1916, and that exactly sixteen men were executed: nor can it have been merely by chance that the surrender was made from the house, number sixteen in Moore Street. Memorial cards have been printed with the names of the sixteen men arranged in the form of a Saint Brigit's Cross: four names to each arm. Since red is the sacred colour, Ireland has the power-symbol in its most spiritual aspect. She has paid a blood-price for it.

130

Padraic H. Pearse, Thomas Clarke, Sean MacDermott, James Connolly, Joseph M. Plunkett, John MacBride, Eamonn Ceannt, Thomas MacDonagh, Michael Mallin, Michael O'Hanrahan, Edward Daly, Con Colbert, William Pearse, Thomas Ceannt, Sean Hueston, and Roger Casement.

Someone was bold enough to plant the Sinn Fein Flag on the blackened and gaping roof of the General Post Office. It hung there for hours, with Hermes to watch it, Hermes the Pathfinder, young and smiling as in the Golden Age of Greece. Bombs and the raging flames had destroyed the other gods which a classic-minded architect had set on the roof of the Post Office. Hermes remains unscathed.

Everywhere among the people there is an awakening— a pride, a joy in the achievement of the undaunted group that attempted the impossible.

"We have lived to see an Irish Republic proclaimed," said Padraic Pearse, "I am satisfied that we have saved Ireland's honour."

It was a poet's Rising. Poets bring offerings now to the dead.

James Stephens lays a green bough for them:

> *"Be green upon their graves, O happy Spring!*
> *For they were young and eager who are dead!"*

Joseph Campbell gives them voice:

> *"If we are dead, it is for the great love we bore the Gael."*

131

To ANYONE WHO has not loved a country more than success, more than life, more than God, the Rising must seem foolishness—yet it is for such a foolishness only that men martyr themselves! What the Rising means to those who regard it as wisdom I am not able to say in words, even to myself. Yet I would wish to say it if I knew how. I would be speaking for others, for thousands of others who worked for it longer, who made sacrifices that I did not make, whose faith, whose prayers, whose passion coloured and upheld it. I would be speaking for the earth of Ireland forced to drink the blood she could not avenge. I would be speaking for the dead who had no thought ever to speak for themselves.

I would be speaking of the splendour of a Vision that triumphed, and triumphs, over suffering and loss, transmuting failure into a spiritual heritage, a great rose of saintship and warrior-deed; a chalice with the wine of immortality.

Eire, the Virgin Mother, holds the chalice and the rose.

THE RETURN, 1917

ONE MORNING, IN the coldness before dawn, the streets of Dublin heard the patter of running feet. Somehow, from the port of Dunleary miles away, word had filtered through that the prisoners taken in the Rising and lodged in English prisons had been landed: landed at that early hour and without warning, to prevent a reception of any kind. But there was going to be a reception. Newsboys, young men, sympathizers of every kind, running on foot brought the news to Dublin. The citizens were trooping to Dunleary on foot.

132

There were no cars at that hour of the morning, no railway trains, and only a few people had autos. But the people were there. They formed a cheering procession and escorted the released prisoners into Dublin. The news spread; folk threw up their windows, flags appeared, from house after house the occupants tumbled into the street, eager for news, eager for a sight of the returned heroes. De Valera was there.

"Where is the Countess Markievicz?" was the cry. "We want the Countess!"

"She is not coming into Dublin till tomorrow. There will be a real reception for the Countess. It takes a day to prepare it. She is the people's Countess, and we will give a proper welcome to her!"

Next day, toward evening, the Countess entered Dublin in the midst of a long procession, with banner after banner and brass band after brass band; with riders on horseback; with running boys waving branches; with lumbering floats drawn by big slow-footed good-natured Clydesdale horses; with trade-guilds carrying emblems; with public notabilities in uniform; with ragged urchins from the slums—a glad and multitudinous company laughing, shouting, and singing.

Upon a float piled high with flowers and greenery the Countess stood, very fair to look on, radiant and slender. Towering beside her was a large Sinn Fein flag: green and orange and white. Small red flags like poppies blossomed everywhere. From a window I could see the River Liffey, curving between its wharves and tall narrow-fronted houses, spanned by bridge upon bridge till lost in the distance. When the Countess crossed the bridge nearest to me, every bridge behind her was a-toss with red flags, and the people were singing *The International*. I had a window over a baker's shop. The woman of the shop knew me. She knew boys who had attended my classes, my talks on Irish history. She said to me: "I want to tell you there wasn't one of the boys that didn't fight in the Rising."

The woman was pale and thin. She had seen too little of the sunlight. The shop was a poor one, scantily furnished:

flies buzzed in it. The woman had not given herself a holiday to join the procession, yet she was more than part of it. She was one of those who made that triumphant pageant possible. For half a lifetime she had spent her few free hours in work for the Irish Cause. She had given with both hands out of her meagre possessions, taking no thought for the morrow. Her man had been in the fighting though he had to rise from a sick-bed to shoulder his rifle. He was free now of the sick-bed and the burden of life.

She did not think that she had done anything noteworthy. She did not think of herself at all.

THE WATER-FALL

I AM STAYING in a farmhouse in County Wicklow, a farmhouse on a hillside. There is no other house for a mile or so, but Nancy Campbell and her husband Joseph Campbell, two poets, come across a hill path to see me and sit talking in the flowering meadow: Austin Clarke rides here from Dublin on a bicycle. There is a high hill road from Dublin and a low flat one by the Plain of Bregia. Austin always comes by the hill road. At times he thinks of returning by the low easy road, but as soon as he catches sight of a mountain peak he decides that he must go home by the hills. He is putting the old tale of the war of gods and demons into epic words. He talks of it with a fine poetic frenzy, walking up and down gesticulating and quoting long passages. It will be a splendid thing when finished, for Austin Clarke can put more of the strangeness one finds in the old literature into swiftly moving words, can achieve a more vivid picture of ancient whirlwind confused happenings than anyone else can achieve. With a crust of bread in his pocket, and not even a pilgrim's staff in his hands, he has climbed nearly

134

every mountain in Ireland: has stumbled upon forgotten causeways where bronze-wheeled chariots once thundered, has lain, night-long, under frosty or benign stars in desolate places where eagles can yet cry to each other, and the peregrine falcon circles unmolested.

Other people come to talk with me at the farmhouse: The Hon. Ethel Macnaghten and her gentle-spoken friend; Sive Trench comes with her sister Margot. Sive belongs to a mountainside. She is tall and beautiful and splendidly alive. Her eyes are coloured like the bronze that shows in a dark mountain-tarn when the sun slants on it. She walks as Emer, the proud wife of Cu-Cullion, might have walked, or Deirdre before the sorrow, that was foretold at birth, overtook her.

I have two rooms at the farmhouse. I am not writing. I am not studying. I watch the colours of the day on the hillside and the changing rhythm of the wind in tree tops. I hear at times the faery trumpets blown from hill to hill, or the sound of a song piped at evening. I am aware that my friendship with the Nature Spirits has progressed. I can ask them to do things. They are very gracious. They do things when they can.

The daughter of the farmhouse has a holiday on one day of every week. On that day we harness the mare and drive to some beautiful place. We have fine weather, as a general rule. But these last days have been full of rain. There is one place that I want very much to see; it is the water-fall in the Powerscourt Estate. I have been talking about it with the farmer's daughter.

"Next week," she says, "on Thursday, we can go."

I ask my friends, the Nature Spirits, for a fine day. They promise it. But Thursday comes and it is still raining. It can rain with great thoroughness and pertinacity in Ireland. It is raining at nine o'clock in the morning, it is raining heavily at eleven. The farmer's daughter says that we must give up our jaunt.

"It will clear," I say confidently, "at twelve o'clock."

135

"It is not the kind of rain that clears," says the farmer's daughter.

I thought that myself, so I went hastily into my room, opened a window, looked at the heavy rainfall, and said to the Nature Spirits:

"You have promised me a fine day."

"We have promised it."

"But this rain," I said.

"We thought you would like water in the water-fall."

That was it. How stupid I had been!

"It will clear, then?" I asked.

"It will clear."

I hurried out to the farmer's daughter.

"It is certain to clear," I said. "Ask your father if we can have the mare."

The mare is a splendid animal, but she can't stand rain She is temperamental, and rain makes her kick and bite.

At twelve o'clock the rain stopped. We harnessed the mare and drove through birch woods with the leaves all gold and the trunks a rain-washed silver; past mountains rich with Autumn bracken, rose and bronze—deeper rose and livelier bronze because rain-soaked.

The sky was a dense purple, smoky-purple of rain clouds. The water-fall was magnificent—a shouting, gesticulating multitude of waters! Not a drop of rain fell. We drove home with sunlight slanting on the wet road.

CEOL SIDHE
(Music of Faerie)

HERE ON THIS HILLSIDE with a farmhouse to supply my needs, and leisure through all the hours of the day to watch the colours of sunlight change and fade in the valley and on the line o̶ ▮▮▮▮▮ I have a chance to listen most intently and ▮▮▮▮▮dly to the Ceol Sidhe, the Faerie Music that so▮▮▮▮eople in lonely places have heard: that I myself have he▮▮ in snatches ever since the power to hear it came to me in Achill Island sixteen years ago. Suddenly and unexpectedly that power came to me. How often before its advent someone, Margeret O'Grady, perhaps, or Æ, had said: "There is a flute note! A lad is playing the flute in the faerie hill. Listen!" But I was deaf. I had of course heard fiddlers and pipers play music that reputedly came from the faerie world: melodies and rhythmic dance measures. I knew that the Gaelic song "Cailin deas cruidhte na mbo" (The pretty girl of the milking of the cows) is set to an air that a priest overheard at twilight in passing a faerie hill— heard and remembered. I believed in faerie music, but belief was with me, at that time, an act of faith.

The Gaelic-speaking people, who are familiar with this music, have named it Ceol Sidhe which may be translated "Music of the Faerie Hills" or "Music of the Faeries," since sidhe (shee) means both a sacred hill and the divinity connected with it. The older people still use the title given in our ancient sagas to those divinities: "Folk of the Gods of Dana."

The music as I first heard it was orchestral and of amazing richness and complexity. Here on the hillside I have heard snatches of song and little lilting airs, but have always been aware of an orchestral background. I find, too, that by concentrating on any phase of the music I am aware of it almost to the exclusion of the rest. On this account I have been able, to a certain extent, to analyse the sound. There is in this music a heavy rhythmic beat, a great basic sound which I have named "The Anvil Beat." There is a myriad-tongued litany; there are voices that call on fixed notes; there are also voices that wrangle and seem to shout aimlessly: clamorous, clangorous voices that do not repeat a rhythm on one note, yet the turmoil they make resolves itself into harmony with the whole. Even so the strident and blurred noises of a great city, heard from some height or some angle, might

137

resolve themselves to a tapestry of ███████████ ground for a clarion melody. This faerie musi████████████ he sound of every instrument used in a great orc██████ nd the sound of many, many instruments that no orc█ stra possesses. It has singing voices in it sweeter than human: and always it has a little running crest of melody like foam on a sea-wave or moon-gilding on the edge of a cloud. All these sounds, and sounds more indefinable, are going on at the same time: undertones and overtones to a great main melody; to a lilted air, a snatch of song; or the resonance of a swung bell.

I have made notes in my diary of this music as I heard it, and shall set down here some extracts:

MUSIC OF THE SIDHE AT BAHANAS ON THE SIDE OF MAULIN MOUNTAIN ENNISKERRY AUGUST 1917

This district begins at Glen Cullen and extends by Lough Bray to Djouce Mountain (I do not know how much farther) and is full of the most beautiful music. On Monday, 20, it was specially loud and varied. I tried to isolate the districts and listen to each separately. The valley below with the pine woods had a music like bells and like very sweet harp strings, with a recurring melody in a sort of three-beat time. Crone Wood had a high austere note as of reed instruments. When I listened for Djouce I heard as it were the most unimaginably beautiful human voice singing.

On the evening of Wednesday, 22 (about ten o'clock Irish time) I heard music so loud and so like what human-made instruments could produce that I got out of bed and went to the landing of my room to listen if perchance any instrument were in the house. I leaned out of my window, but finding I lost the music that way I concluded that it was music of the Sidhe, and going back to bed composed myself to listen. The music grew in volume, and then it seemed that a procession of musicians passed close to the house. They had bagpipes and cymbals and tinkling instruments like the little steel triangles used by orchestras. They had several musical instruments that I do not know. The tune

138

was full of the maddest joy, with strong recurring rhythms. It could have been reproduced by a piper had he heard it.

On Thursday, 23, there was a strong wind, and for a long time I could only hear the swish of it in the trees. Suddenly, behind a strong gust of wind, the music broke out: shrill as of fifes at first, then swelling to a great volume with instruments that I cannot liken to any used on this earth: instruments, some of them, that the musicians blew through. The music was very wild and un-human in character.

Friday, 24. The wind still high, but the music of the most delicate tinkling rhythms, as of silver branches shaken till they sounded like bells, waves of sound breaking into a spray of a thousand colours.

Saturday, 25. Comparatively silent. Faint, isolated sounds, if one listened intently.

Monday, 27 Aug. I woke and heard wonderful music at 1.30 A.M. Irish time. It came on with a certain monotony, like long slow-moving waves. On the crest of each wave there was a running melody, and as spray curling on a wave-top takes one's eye this caught one's ear: but the whole wave was an intricacy of sound, closely knit as the water of a wave is, and yet little more than a splendour of silence.

Tuesday, 28. Very high wind and rain. At night a great burst of music like the clashing of innumerable cymbals. This changed to the sound of bells with clashings intermixed. Then a curious melody obtruded itself in which there was a dominant high note as high as the highest note on a piano, but with a tone and volume such as no instrument that I know of could produce. I heard also a music as of stricken anvils, as if a myriad smiths hammered out a music. The wind came in very strong gusts, breaking and silencing the music. In the wind there was a clamour of shouting and singing voices. It was difficult to hear anything but those voices, though I was aware that the music went on. After a while I found myself listening to a vast litany with chants and responses. If every blade of grass had a share in the responses it would not have seemed strange to me, so multitudinous were the responses. At times I caught the words but they were in a language that I do not understand. Several times I heard the word "Abaktha."

Thursday, 30. I woke before dawn and heard delicate intricate rhythms with the most exquisite melodies interwoven. A myriad, myriad instruments produced this music. I was able on it to approach the Mountain, Djouce. The music and Djouce became one Being—not music, not anything that can be told in words.

Friday, 31. At darkfall heard a melody with a strongly marked third beat which was emphasized by an instrument like a muffled drum. What instrument produced the melody I do not know. If drops of water could be made to produce sounds, as harp strings do, they might give such notes.

4 Oct. 1917. I heard noteworthy music at darkfall last night. There was a gusty wind. I had been aware of a wandering music all day. At darkfall great trumpets sounded as if mountain called to mountain. Against this clarion urgency a swirl of many-sounded music broke like starry fire mingling with —engulfing—the trumpet sound, and subsiding. As the swirl subsided, the trumpets re-asserted themselves, but only for a moment. Again and again the swirling music broke against them: and each swirl was a wonder to hear, and each swirl differed in beauty from its fellows. This music; the Long Waves (which I described some pages back); and the music of Djouce (which I could not describe) make the three most wonderful things that I have heard, so far, on this hillside. As I write, at twenty past seven P. M. it is dusk, and a lovely pulsing all-pervading faint music is going on outside. I am, however, too tired to listen.

17 Oct. Last night I was aware of Gregorian chants, and many voices singing. The sound increased in volume and the rhythms became very intricate. Men's and boys' voices rose in what was more like Palestrina music than anything I can think of. The voices chanted words, or phrases, and I caught some. These were chanted by different groups. Thus while deep voices chanted, a marvelous swirl of high sweet voices

140

rose, with an interval between: in such a fashion that it was almost a harp-string accompaniment to the singing. Also there were sweet high-sounding percussion instruments. No description can do justice to this music: the intricacy; the beauty; the changing rhythms; the way in which a sound is echoed and re-echoed with undertones and overtones.

10 Nov. Before daybreak I heard again the Dawn Music in great complexity. Many of the sounds were produced by voices crying on notes. A deep-voiced Gregorian chant served as background for a thousand other sounds, a silence as it were, a darkness on which these showed as stars show in the blackness of the sky. Indeed a sky of stars might serve for symbol of these multitudinous sounds: but they are more diverse than stars.

I ceased to write in my diary concerning this music on the twelfth of February, 1918, but the music had not ceased. I am convinced that this music is everywhere and that it goes on all the time. It seems to occur or fall silent only because the human receptivity is sharpened, blurred, or obliterated.

VOICE FROM AMERICA

I AM BACK IN DUBLIN AGAIN, LODGING IN rooms within sight and sound of a church. The church has a cracked bell. I wish I were out of reach of it! Probably the strange music that I heard surging everywhere on the Wicklow hillside surges here also. At night sometimes I catch faint echoes of it. Daytime is perturbed by news of ambushes, by the rattle of lorry-cars filled with Black and Tans, and by the sight of men in tin hats at every street-corner. The house of Doctor Kathleen Lynn, who battled so successfully against the deadly "Black Influenza," is close by. I see something of Kathleen Lynn though she is a very busy woman, occupied with patients, occupied also in the furtherance of various political and national affairs: affairs that took her not so long ago under gun-fire and into prison, and may take her again.

Dublin is filled with excursions and war alarums. There is fighting in the streets, and news of fighting in streets all over Ireland. Patriots have been murdered in their homes. Dail Eirann has declared a state of war to exist between Ireland and England. Officials of the foreign government have been ambushed. The Irish Volunteers are under arms. There is hope that America may intervene: the House of Representatives passed by a majority of 261 to 41 the following resolution:

"That it is the earnest hope of the Congress of the United States of America that the Peace Conference now sitting at Paris and passing upon the rights of the various people will

142

favourably consider the claims of Ireland to self-determination."

"The Friends of Irish Freedom" have sent a delegation to Paris to interview President Wilson, and the delegation is coming to Ireland to see things for itself. The purpose of its visit is thus defined:

"To obtain for the delegates selected by the people of Ireland a hearing at the Peace Conference, and to place before the Conference, if that hearing be not given, the case of Ireland, her insistence upon her right of Self-Determination and to international recognition of the Republican form of government established by her people."

The American delegation will certainly see things.

THE LORD MAYOR'S RECEPTION
May 9, 1919

THE LORD MAYOR of Dublin is giving a reception tonight in the Mansion House. We are all invited. De Valera will speak. Other patriots will be there. Doctor Kathleen Lynn has asked me to go with her. We start in her motor-car. Soon we form part of a procession. Other cars are going to the Mansion House too. But in Saint Stephen's Green we come to an untimely and sudden halt. Something has happened. We get wind of it from the newsboys who crowd around the car, knowing that Doctor Lynn is a patriot. "They are looking for two men," whispers a newsboy. "The Black and Tans are hunting for two of our men. They have blocked the lower end of Dawson Street and they're at the upper end of it now." We could see for ourselves that they were at the upper end. Tanks were lumbering along. Lorries filled with Black and Tans, their fingers on their rifle triggers, jolted to the barrier. The Mansion House is in Dawson Street. It is plain

143

that no one will get there. What about the American Delegation—the specially invited American Delegation? They will not get there, but they will, with their own eyes, witness the tyranny of the English soldiers in Dublin.

To the sound of a brass band, the American Delegation comes upon the scene, its handsome conveyance decorated with American flags, and crowded with Americans. When the array of tanks and guns brings it to a halt, Doctor Kathleen Lynn leaves her own car and goes across to explain matters to the Americans. Meanwhile, a ruthless and hurried house-to-house search is in progress on Dawson Street. Tanks are nosing up and down; officers shouting commands; companies of soldiers obstructing each other in an effort to be efficient. Presently the newsboys, who always know everything, dart here and there with the news: "They didn't get a hair of their heads. The boys escaped."

A whisper is spreading like stone-circles widening in water. The names of the wanted men—Michael Collins and Robert Barton! The news runs through the crowd, and to add to the jubilation the newsboys flourish their newspapers and yell:

"ANOTHER BRITISH VICTORY"

At last the armored cars, the tanks and the searchlights depart. The barrier is withdrawn, the crowd surges towards the Mansion House, and like a wave that falls back from a cliff takes possession of Dawson Street. The Mansion House can admit only invited guests: it is packed to capacity. The multitude will wait till De Valera comes out to speak to them.

At times I look from a window in the Mansion House. The crowd is there, solid and determined. De Valera sends Lieutenant after Lieutenant to speak from a balcony; to advise the people to go home. They are obdurate. At last he comes out. I hear his speech, as with Kathleen Lynn I thread my way along the street.

"My friends, there is nothing I could say to you that you

144

do not know already. It is late. We are all tired. I say good night, and wish you a safe journey home."

A BLAST OF STRONG LANGUAGE

It is a long idle holiday that I am having in this guest-house of the Nuns of Saint Joseph—a spacious country house standing in considerable grounds: a house given to the nuns by a woman who had found little happiness in it. The convent is near by, and the sisters have the conduct of the guest-house and the care of the grounds for their chief business. The Reverend Mother is trying to husband the hay harvest at present with the help of three seasoned men well-versed in the art of escaping work. I don't know how she ever came to employ them, unless it were out of sheer goodness of heart and a desire to give sinners a chance to repent. Every morning the three veterans line up under her window to receive directions for the day. The ringleader answers cheerfully and readily for himself and his comrades. He is an old tar who was discharged by his captain for what he himself describes as: "a blast of strong language!" If the Reverend Mother could gird up her long robes and superintend operations there would be some work done—as it is, those three go about matters in a leisurely fashion: it takes two hours to capture the work-horse.

The country hereabouts has low wooded hills, river meadows, and ample-foliaged trees, many of them horse-chestnuts. These take colours of rose and amber and pale yellow: an opulent tapestry against the austere skies of Autumn, and the somnolent blue of the mist-soaked hills. I spend much of my time in the grounds where I have discovered a tree that rests its branches on the grass and forms a thick green tent with the tree-trunk for ridge-pole. It is a spacious

145

Peter Pan house. While the sun is high and hot I recline there at my ease.

It is almost a mile from the house to the big entrance gate: outside the gate is a winding country road with a fallen tree-trunk by the side of it where one may sit and "admire the colours of the day." I admire them at all hours, but just about sunset is the loveliest hour. Sometimes Norah Heneberry sits by me. She is a native Gaelic speaker, and like her brother, the Reverend Doctor Heneberry, an authority on the ancient Gaelic music and traditional singing. She has a beautiful voice, and sings keenes and ballads in the traditional manner. It is a joy to talk with her. She knows old histories, has stored in memory many curious and almost obsolete customs, and takes a lively interest in the efforts being made to revive the National Spirit.

Curraghmore, the beautiful demesne of the Marquis of Waterford, is not far off. Although it is open to the public, Norah Heneberry and I seem to be the only people who care to walk under the ancient trees there, or sit by the deep pool that the river makes. These far-stretching territories, the grass here, the trees, the water-worn stones, have been unmolested for centuries, but battle-shout and weapon-clang made turmoil enough when the clan O'Flaherty defended their ancestral lands for the last time. Oliver Cromwell, with better weapons and with steel-corseleted soldiers, loosed destruction here. The O'Flahertys were utterly defeated and forced to such refuge as broken men may find: but Cromwell, with unwonted generosity, declared that if the daughter of the slain chief would choose a husband from among his men he would give the lands to that man. She chose a tall trooper named Beresford. He was a man who bettered his fortune. A Beresford today is the Marquis of Waterford, another Beresford has command in the English fleet. Stories gather about this family. It is known to be under a curse. No one who bears the title will die in his bed, the country-folk say: and no one has, since a Beresford flogged the widow's son to death. The lad was an only son and the widow

146

was poor. A Beresford flogged him to death in the troublous times in an effort to extort from him the names of patriot comrades. There was no redress. The widow cursed the murderer and his heirs after the Gaelic fashion. The Curse works. The flogging Beresford died bloodily, another was slain in a duel, another was thrown from his horse. Every Beresford that held the title has died by violence. The present Marquis is not yet of full age. His father was found dead in the shallow river that flows through the domain. The boy, the peasants say, will be the last Marquis. They bear him no ill-will. His father was popular. They just believe in the Curse.

Norah Heneberry tells me that there is an ancient ritual of cursing. The person who invokes the curse must be deeply injured and deprived of justice. Such a person must bring witnesses, declare the accusation, and cite the accused, who may or may not be present. The wronged person kneels with both knees bared on the earth and invokes earth, air, fire and water and the Supreme Lord. The curse, which is always quite definite, is declared aloud. This method of righting a wrong is still resorted to and is much feared.

Norah Heneberry knows of a curse which fulfilled itself so recently that old folk remember it. A man who kept a tavern accused his servant-boy of stealing five pounds from the till. As thieving was then a capital offence the boy was hanged. After his death the money was found. The mother, by the old ritual, cursed the inn-keeper: declaring that he would lose house, land, and gear, and die ragged and poverty-stricken in a ditch. His cattle died. His wealth dispersed itself. He lost everything. But the Curse clung to him closer than his rags. He died by the roadside in a ditch.

When Sir Walter Scott in his ballad: "The Eve of Saint John," tells of a woman who talks with a dead lover and wears for her lifetime the mark of his hand-clasp on her wrist, he is using a widely-known incident in the Beresford family. The Countess wakened one night to see a man, who had once been a suitor, seated by her bedside. Startled, she cried out: "How could *you* possibly be here?" He answered: "I

147

am free to go everywhere now." He was dead. They talked through the night, and she said: "How shall I know that I have not dreamed this?" "I will throw the bed-curtains over the canopy," he said. "That is not enough," said she, "I could have done as much in my sleep." "Reach me your hand," said he. "Your wrist will have the mark of my fingers in the morning." It had. They seem to have talked of many things, but two only remain in the popular memory. He told the Countess the date of her death-day: and gave a date, 1917, which would, he said, usher in an event of great importance and good fortune for humanity.

As a child, I knew Scott's ballad and this story. I used to repeat the date, 1917, to myself, and wonder what would happen.

KNOWLEDGE FROM THE OLD TIMES

I WISH I HAD time and strength to go among the Commeragh hill-folk and make friends with them. Norah Heneberry has been telling me such interesting things about them. They practice magic, and even yet on May Eve the farmers sit up all night to keep evil-disposed persons from stealing milk and butter from the cows. I asked her how the witches do it. This is how they do it! The witch must plait a rope of hemp, bring it into the byre, and fasten it for a few seconds to the udder of the cow. She must milk some drops of milk on the rope. Then she can take it home, and every day in the year she can milk from it the milk of that cow.

"Does the farmer always have to stay up all night on every May Eve to watch his cow?" I asked.

"That is the best thing to do, but he might tie a bunch of rowan berries to the cow's tail; or get a wise man to put a protection on the cow. Farmers have to be wary, for witches

148

and warlocks can take the harvest from a field. And that happened to one of our own fields."

"This is something I never heard of. Tell me about it."

"We had potatoes planted there. The potatoes scarcely made a pretense of growing. They were very weak and poor. We thought someone was taking the strength from the field. We were certain of it when we began to dig the potatoes because we saw the eggs. We began to dig up the eggs."

"Eggs!" cried L "What do you mean by eggs?"

"Just hen eggs. The person who wants to take the produce from a field must bury an egg in every ninth row of the furrows; must come when the crop is being planted and contrive, unnoticed, to bury the eggs. Then that person can take strength and increase from the field and add it to a crop in their own field. But it must be a crop of the same kind as the one that is being stolen. When we got the eggs, we thought we knew where our potatoes went. You should have seen the poor little things we dug out of the ground—small as marbles!"

"What did you do?"

"Oh, we knew what to do! We made a fire and took care to have some blackthorn branches in it and some stalks of the potatoes. Then we threw the eggs on the fire. They burst with a loud noise. In a little while after that a neighbour woman came running in a state of great distress. 'Put out that fire!' she said. 'If you've any heart left in you, put out that fire! It's burning me to the bone.' We put out the fire. We knew it would be a lesson to her. She was the woman whom we all along suspected."

There is Gaelic up there in the Commeragh hills. The people are not particularly ashamed of their magic. They do not call it a work of the devil: they call it knowledge from the old times.

EVENING

THE SKY IS SOMBRE; it is the colour of ashes with a tongue of flame in the West. The hill-road between its glimmering stone walls is empty. The long pasture-meadow slanting from the road burns with dull fire—not green, not any colour that daylight knows; the beech trees at the foot of it smoulder a sullen amber and red, but the river is coldly patterned in tarnished silver.

A peasant lad strides, whistling, in the pastures; it is his way of calling home the cows. He seems giant-big, but the cows have grown small. They are redder and whiter than cows of the daylight. They are moving half-heartedly towards the shed in a corner of the field. The herdsboy moves with them scarce urging them. A white calf and a red one gallop together. A black kid, trim as a roebuck, holds himself defiantly; he stands till the last cow has straggled into the shed, then with a sudden caper he bounds and leaps and sidles the whole length of the long meadow.

"O Michael, look! Look at him running—look!"

It is a woman with a shawl over her head, speaking to her child. There are people on the hill-road: a quaint family group—the woman stately and mysterious in the half-light; her man, long-limbed and lithe, with a length of tree-sapling on his shoulder; and between them, upon a sleek, small donkey, little barefoot Michael holding by the mane. He turns his head to look at the black kid and laughs softly. The little ass patters along delicately; it is not burdened by its rider. The woman does not speak again. After Michael's laughter there is only the sound of footsteps growing fainter and fainter.

Did that other Mother, traveling out of Egypt with the Child, ever say to Him: "Look! Look!" when some long-eared goat sidled and capered at twilight in a way-side pasture? Did He ever look and laugh softly and shyly?

The black kid has reached the cattle-shed and leaped in,

150

the herdsboy has gone home. Nothing moves now in the wide, slanting meadow: colour burns low in it and in the ragged trees, but the river is still patterned in silver. There is no wind, and all the faint noises of the dusk, half heard, uniting with each other make silence. But there is someone on the road. Surely it is a faery child out of the elf-mounds that comes with such an ecstasy of motion! His feet scarce touch the roadway, his hands, his arms are stretched out as though he wanted them to be wings. His small, slender body, buoyant as flame, seems to have drawn to itself the passionate beauty of the sunset.

"Ardan! O Ardan, wait—wait for me!" It is a child's voice shrill with entreaty and command, but the changeling child in front does not pause, does not slacken speed for an instant.

"Ardan!"

Following his voice, slowly and heavily he comes into sight, a lad of eight or nine—or perhaps he is older, for hardship and scant meals stunt the children of the poor. He is carrying a sack bulkier than himself, the mouth of it gathered with both hands above his shoulder; it is crammed with branches and chips of tree-trunks and just clears the ground as he shuffles along. Behind him comes a smaller lad, also burdened, but his sack is not stuffed to bursting—it contains, by the look of it, a couple of long pieces of wood, and drapes itself limply round them. Such as it is, the boy finds it too heavy; he drags one foot as he walks; his stockings have slipped and wrinkled about his ankles, but he has not the heart to pull them up. His face is twisted in an effort to keep from crying. Suddenly he stops and strips the sacking from the wood. Which to throw away? They are equally hateful.

"Ardan, Ardan, wait!"

The boy with the big sack breaks into a halting run, but has to stop and shift the burden higher on his shoulders. A sob bursts from the smaller lad.

"Shaun! Shaun, I'm going to throw it away—I am!"

Shaun turns, the awkward, overheavy sack tripping him; he had filled it like that for himself; he had put together a

151

light load for his brother; he had given the youngest nothing to carry—and now, when they are nearing home—

"You are not!"

His voice rings like a hero-call; so might Cuchulain have shouted to his comrades had they spoken of going back from the face of the enemy.

"You are not!"

Virtue passes out of him with the words. The younger boy straightens himself. He sees Shaun with the load he has taken, and the hero-will revives in him; he also can endure. He twists the sacking on the wood nonchalantly, shoulders the burden, as one whom small things do not gall, and steps out valiantly. Shaun waits; they go on together, and the dusk that has taken Ardan takes them also.

EXCURSIONS AND ALARUMS

MY HOLIDAY AT THE nuns' guest-house has ended. I am in Dublin again, engaged in furthering the publication of my book of verse, *The Rose of Heaven*, for which Maud Gonne has made decorations in black and white. Colm O'Loughlin, who does such beautiful work, has undertaken the printing and publishing of the book.

There is a passionate surge of expectancy, an urgency of combat and martyrdom, a tireless springing of hopeless hope in this city of old pillared houses and crooked streets. Every day brings news of some daring ambuscade; or of the death sentence on some young patriot. Poetry is little needed at a time when life itself has reached a lyric ecstasy, an epic splendour of achievement. An art more in keeping seems to be Mia Cranwill's work in metal, enamel, and semi-precious stones. Hammered copper has a martial clang in it: perdurable crystal, gold that keeps its brilliance unclouded,

152

and platinum, that diamond-hard metal, whiter than silver at one angle, dark as a starless night at another, can be fitly wrought to symbolize a spiritual triumph, or enshrine a relic. Indeed this play of life and death bestows upon what touches it a poignant and subtle beauty. This is well seen in the stained-glass work of Harry Clarke: it glints in the delicate prose of Michael Gillacrist, and lends intensity to Estella Solomon's etchings. This city, with its hazards, its fantasy, its artists, its seers, its young men armed, takes the mind back to medieval Florence, passionate city of the red lilies, but in this city the lilies are white: unearthly Annunciation lilies of a Dream—the apotheosis of Ireland!

This Dream that so many have died for—that so many have lived for, renouncing all less delight—this Dream, at once a purification and an ensoulment, daily becomes more vivid, more compelling: the chapels are crowded with suppliants, the executioners have their hands full, the blood-stained stones are not silent in the streets.

O Rose, dark Rose, when wilt thou blossom red?
"I blossom now, a splendour for the dead."

A RAID

IT IS ELEVEN O'CLOCK at night in the tall, highly respectable house where a highly respectable and pro-British colonel's daughter has leased some rooms to highly respectable tenants. It is a quiet, decorous residence-house. I have the garret rooms. Considering how highly respectable they are, they have a neglected appearance. The furniture is battered and the carpets long past their use. But I like this place because from the windows I can see the line of Dublin hills, and the city streets are close by where life and idealism is passionately surging.

153

The folk in this house are abed, and the lights are quenched. Suddenly there is a rattle and a clatter and a great hooting of horns. Tanks! Yes, it must be tanks! It is a raid—a raid going past this house.

But it does not go past!

The tanks halt, and presently there is the sound of a door bursting in. Soldiers have come by the lane at the back of the house, and have burst in the kitchen door. They might as easily have commanded admittance by the front door, but the other way is dramatic and amusing. Outside, searchlights are playing. The whole sky is lit by the searchlights. And by the way of sound accompaniment a few shots are being fired.

It is a raid on this house, of all impossible happenings!

I have a little store of ammunition, but it is well and carefully hidden. I await the arrival of the soldiers. I can hear them going through the lower rooms of the house. They seem slow in coming to the attic. At last a step approaches. It is the officer in charge, carrying a pistol and a searchlight. He halts outside the door and says courteously that he must search the room. I say that I hope he will do so. He is very half-hearted about it. He just flashes the searchlight around the room and departs with an apology for troubling me.

I wonder what has sweetened and softened the temper of the search-party. Later I find out. They began with my landlady's room, and discovered over her mantelpiece a large framed photograph of Lord Kitchener, together with photos of her father and his military friends.

Amid a torrential and indignant protest, they began to search her trunks—and found more evidence of loyalty to the British Empire! By this time they were thoroughly daunted. They had mistaken the house, it was evident. (They had indeed mistaken the house. The raid was meant for one lower down the street.) The search in other rooms was only a matter of form, undertaken by the officer himself. When it was over, he collected his men, who had managed meanwhile to collect a bottle of whiskey and were in a tolerant mood. Without more ado, they bundled into their armoured cars and turned off their searchlights, which all this while had been dazzling the midnight with prodigality and effectiveness.

They did not raid the house farther down the street which might have rewarded such an attention. They went back to barracks, wondering, no doubt, whether there would be an enquiry into this outrage on a respectable pro-British residence.

ESCAPE

It is sunday morning. Mia Cranwill and I are lounging by the window of her flat. We are looking idly at the jaunting-cars and the automobiles drifting past. Presently a large handsome touring-car comes to a standstill. We recognize it at once. It belongs to Andrew Woods. His wife is with him, and they climb the stairs to the flat.

"Would you like an adventure?" asks Mrs. Woods. "It might be a little dangerous, but it would help the Cause."

"An adventure sounds good."

"It is like this," says Mrs. Woods, "two of our young captains have broken jail. They've managed to take cover in Dublin. They are just now at the house of a friend, and we want to drive them out into the country where they can join the fighters. The best way to do it is to take them openly in the touring-car, but we must make it look like a family excursion, and we want you two to give colour."

We donned our best Sunday clothes and our gayest hats, and set out in the car for the hiding-place of the captains. One was tall and dark-eyed, the other slender and blonde. They were eager to start at once, and soon we were all sitting in the car, laughing and chatting together. We took the main road out of Dublin going south. Other citizens were going south in cars and trying to forget that a war was on. Every now and then we encountered lorries and patrol-cars, but we kept up a good face on things. No one stopped us. At last we came to Enniscorthy and drew up before the somewhat conspicuous house of a well-known patriot, folk-lorist, and collector of old and rare books.

So far it had been a great success. There was nothing now to be done but give the captains a good supper, let them rest until dusk, and then slip away through the country roads to where their comrades were.

It all seemed so fine that the young captains, who had been cramped in hiding-places, proposed to take a little stroll through the town. They came back in a few minutes with terrible news. A detachment of Black and Tans had just descended on the market-place. They were making a house-to-house search of Enniscorthy. What was to be done? They would surely come to the house that harboured us.

"To think," said Mrs. Woods, "that we brought them all this distance just to be dragged out and shot."

"We might try to take them back by the way we came," said Mr. Woods.

"That's useless," said his wife. "They must have a cordon completely around the town."

"All the same," said I, "it is the only chance."

"But there's another thing," said Mrs. Woods. "They'll ask what big car came to this house, who owned it, and why it went hurriedly away when the soldiers arrived."

"I have an idea," I said. "You must all start off in the car and leave me. I'll say that your car brought me to this house because I wished to consult its master about the folk-lore of a book I am writing. But hurry now, hurry off!"

The car swung away, and we waited in some perturbation for the search-party. It never came. Instead, a well-wisher came in to say that the soldiers were gone. They had searched a few houses, with the officer standing in the market-square, watch in hand. He was timing himself for some appointment.

156

In a little while he lifted his eyes from the watch-face and gave the order to "Fall in." The men scrambled into the lorries and drove away, followed by the muttered curses of the populace.

I had settled down to a discussion of folk-lore and the idea of staying all night in Enniscorthy, when the big car swung back, and three joyous people came up to announce that the roads had not been blocked: without a single maladventure they had brought the young captains to a part of the country that they knew well.

It was a successful break-prison and escape.

CURFEW-EPISODE

I LOOK FROM A WINDOW. It is dusk, it is past curfew. Curfew means that at six o'clock lights go out everywhere. If a light shows in a window, a Black and Tan fires, haphazard, at it. If anyone is on the street, that person is arrested.

The window is open, the room behind me is dark. I hear the tramp of soldiers. They come to a halt in the gateway alcove just below the window. I cautiously lean over the sill and look out. Yes! Several soldiers, Black and Tans. I can see them quite plainly in the light of the street-lamp. They have two prisoners with them, Republicans, Patriots. The soldiers are smoking cigarettes. The two prisoners are standing close to each other. Nothing happens for a while.

The soldiers stand idle, smoking and talking. They are waiting for an officer of some kind who apparently is taking his ease in an inn, or elsewhere. Presently he approaches. The soldiers straighten their shoulders. He arrives. An order is shouted: "Fall in!"

They fall in, two and two, the prisoners in the middle of the column.

"March!"

They move with echoing steps on the deserted sidewalk. Now they are close to the mouth of a little lane, dark and crooked. The soldiers pass it, heads erect, in fine marching order, but the two prisoners dart into it like trout into a rock-fissure.

Instantly the night is alive with shots. The bereaved soldiers crowd and jostle up the narrow lane, firing as they run. Soldiers far off discharge their rifles. Other soldiers, in the distance, answer them: soldiers from behind walls, soldiers from house-tops. It is a danger to all night-walking cats!

There is a lull now, with a stray shot or two. Soldiers straggle out of the lane. They have lost the prisoners.

ADVENTURES

SEATED BY THE FIRESIDE of a Dublin house, a young captain of the Irish Republican Army is recounting adventures:

"Mountains are strange things. One time a queer thing happened to myself when I was out with 'The Boys' in Donegal. We had word that the English were coming, indeed that they were everywhere with machine-guns. We scattered over mountain and bogland, going like foxes that run solitary. I was coming down Blue Stack and thinking that after three days without sleep or food I would find a farmhouse with something good to eat and a place to lie down secure for a while. It was the afternoon. And as I came down the mountainside I spotted the English soldiers. There was a lot of them. I hoped they hadn't seen me. I turned and began to go up the mountain. I was praying hard to the Virgin, and maybe to the mountain itself.

That mountain could put out a mist, a cloud-mist that covered it like a mantle close and heavy. No one that knew

158

anything would climb that mountain when the mist was there. The mountain was dangerous. It had treacherous bits of green morass, and here and there it went down in precipices. But I was not afraid of the mist. I was glad when suddenly like a soft rain it came all about me, for it was my one hope of escape. After a while I didn't know where I was, but it was borne in on me that I must stop—I must sit down! I sat down, and found my back against a great pillar-stone. I leaned there and went to sleep.

When I wakened, I saw that I was not alone. Men that I could see dimly in the mist were walking round me. I thought at first that the English soldiers had climbed the mountain, and I was done for! But they didn't close in. I noticed that they were very big, almost giant-tall. They had a friendly feeling. I said to myself: 'These are either Spirits of the Mountain, or souls of the dead that died for Ireland. They are guarding me.' I leaned against the pillar-stone and went to sleep.

It was broad daylight when I wakened. I got to my feet and felt as light and airy as if I had been sleeping on a bed of goose feathers. I wasn't hungry. I wasn't tired. A few steps in front of me the mountain went down sheer in a precipice. I could make some sense out of that adventure, but a thing happened to me that I can't make sense out of.

I was coming from Galway on my motor-bike with a message for Dublin Headquarters. I had my side-car, and a friend of mine was sitting in it. We were going along pretty fast on one of those white roads that wind for miles without a house or a human being. The light was failing a bit, but in front of us we could see standing out against the sky, at a crossroads we were coming to, a very tall woman. She was dressed in black. It was a queer long garment that she had, with hanging sleeves, and her two arms were stretched out cross-fashion as if to stop us. We stopped. She had nothing on her head. Her hair was gray and lank. There wasn't a soul or a house in sight.

'What can we do for you?' I said to the woman.

159

'I expected my friends,' she said. 'I waited here for them. They have not come. It may be that you will help me.'

'What do you want of us?' I asked her.

'If you would take me to Athlone, my house is there.'

I thought to myself: 'Maybe she's out of a mad-house.' But she looked sane enough. My friend climbed out of the side-car and got up behind me. The woman got into the side-car. We were smoking. I offered her a cigarette. I did not think she would take it, but she did. She said, 'I want a match.' I gave her a couple of matches. She put up the matches and the cigarette, and said, 'Maybe they will be useful.'

We tore along the roads. It was between ten and eleven o'clock, and dark enough, when we got to the town of Athlone. 'Where is your house?' I asked the woman. 'My house is a little farther on,' she said, 'beyond the town.' We went on, and presently we came to a rusted and broken iron gate hanging loose on its hinges between two stone pillars that might have had stone lions or eagles on them years ago. It looked like the entrance to a big manor house, but by the look of it nobody had been there for a long while. 'My house is up beyond,' said the woman. 'Let me off at this gate!' 'I won't do anything of the kind,' said myself, 'I said I would take you to the house, and I'm going to do it!' We swung through the rusted gate and up a rutted avenue. 'Are you sure,' I said to the woman, 'that this *is* your house?' 'It is my house, and my friends expect me.' After a bit we swung out on a terrace and there was the house! A big house, black against the sky. Not a chink of light anywhere. Not a dog to bark. Not a sound. 'Is this the house?' I said. 'I think there is no one here.' 'My friends are in it,' said the woman. 'They expect me.'

I knocked at that door loud enough to wake the dead. There wasn't a yip from a dog, or a sound of any kind. I knocked again, and this was loud enough to waken anyone within half a mile of the house. Not a sound, not a yip!

'I suppose the place has windows,' I said. It had. After a

while I broke an entrance. I got through the window and struck a couple of matches. I was in a bedroom richly furnished, but with everything in disorder. As I was about to strike my third match I caught sight of an electric fixture. That gave me a queer sort of feeling, for it's not a thing you'd expect to see in a country house: even if that house was well set up, and far from being the God-forsaken blot on the night that this one was! I turned on the electric light. The furniture was handsome. The high chest of drawers had the drawers pulled open. Silken dresses, and articles of every kind, were thrown on chairs and on the floor. Someone had ransacked that room in a hurry! It was a woman's room, and very handsome.

I went into the hall, the large hall of a country-house. It had electric fixtures. I turned on the lights. The hall door had a chain across it, and was securely locked. I opened it. My comrade and the woman were standing on the doorstep. She came inside. So did my friend.

On either hand from the hall a door opened into a spacious room. She turned to go into one at the right-hand side. 'We will leave you here,' I said. 'Oh, no,' she said, 'you must come with me into the room and have a drink.' Well, my comrade and I thought a drink would not be out of place. We went into the room. It had electric lights. She walked about from cupboard to cupboard, opening doors. She said: 'The wine ought to be here.' We said: 'Never mind it now! But are you *sure* that this is your house? We'll take you farther on if you want us to.' 'This *is* my house,' she said, 'and I am expected.' Again she began searching for the wine.

I thought I heard some kind of faint sound in the hall. I went out there and down the length of it. At the end there was a room with the door half open. Light was coming from it. I went down there and looked into the room. It was a bedroom, richly furnished like the other one. On a splendid bed a man and woman were lying. They were young and handsome. They were both dead.

I turned and ran for the front door. 'Come along,' I yelled

161

to my comrade, 'let's get out of this house!' We got out. And the wind behind didn't overtake us for a couple of miles. That's all I know. My friend here will tell you the same thing.

We promised each other we would go back some time and try to find that house. But I had lots of things to keep me busy—work for Headquarters and for Ireland! Up to this time I haven't been able to search for the house."

THE TRUCE, 1921

A TRUCE HAS BEEN PROCLAIMED between the army of the Irish Republic and the forces of the British Empire. The English Prime Minister, obeying the wish of King George, has asked Eamon de Valera to consider ways and means of agreement. The ways and means are somewhat difficult to find, but the military truce is for the present effective: no more ambuscades, no more burning villages, no curfew, no rattle of musketry in the streets. Sinn Fein flags display themselves; soldiers of the Republic pass in military formation; hunted men come out of hiding. The country heaves a sigh of relief: but there is a sense of bewilderment, of unreality, as of something encountered in dream.

The Irish leaders are wary, and have made it clear that this is no victory: it is rather a time to maintain discipline, to be on guard, keen-eyed and unrelaxed.

In order to further a close sympathy and intercourse with the young captains at distant points and with Cumann-na-mBan, the women's auxiliaries, Headquarters in Dublin is selecting emissaries to travel in various districts; give news; and learn on the spot of local conditions. It is possible to do this, for the first time in a long while, since roads are being cleared of barricades, and trains are running. Mainly through the good offices of Erskine Childers, I am being sent to a

162

district in the South-West. It is a lovely Gaelic part of Ireland. I shall talk with many hardy and resourceful patriots. I shall have a chance to gather folk-lore: a chance to hear traditional singing. I am going to Kerry.

GOOD FOLK

THE HILLS ARE very green and the place is very faery-haunted. It is a country that stretches into the unspoiled Atlantic. There is nothing but the hotel where I am staying (a primitive inn with a landlady who speaks Gaelic). There is nothing but that inn to mar the countryside—that inn and the O'Connell house at Derrynane. The O'Connell house is like a palm tree in a northern forest. It has many windows, and fuchsias grow against its walls. It has a garden with flowers unknown to these hills and lowlands breathed upon by the sea.

I am walking on the green hillside: it has delicate fine grass pranked with little flowers, mauve and ivory-white. The sea is making a faint sound in the distance. There is nobody for miles, but I am not alone. Five or six elves of the hillside are trotting beside me. They are about the size of a child twelve years old. Their heads are large for the size of their bodies. They have pointed ears, round eyes, and an engaging grin. They are going to show me anything worth seeing on the hillside. I see many wild flowers, but they say that isn't much. They know something really fine. They conduct me to it. It is a great stone thrusting from the greenness and against it a cotoneaster is growing, with multitudinous red berries on its branches. The elves display it with delight. There is nothing like it on the hillside. I haven't the heart to tell them I have seen cotoneasters before—in gardens. I show a proper astonishment and joy. I say, "Let us take some of these berries and plant them in other parts of the mountain."

The elves smile from ear to ear. I take some berries and they troop after me. We plant them in different places.

We have come a considerable distance, and I begin to feel that I must turn back. I don't want to turn back. The elves don't want to either. I shouldn't call them elves, because I know what the Gaelic-speaking people call them. They call them the "Good Folk," the "Daoine Maithe," less with an idea of their goodness than with an idea of suggesting what they ought to be. Well, the Good Folk don't want to go back either. We stand in a group and consider matters.

"If I could make a circle," I say, "if I could, by going on, find a way across to the inn, I need not turn back."

They assure me there is a way. We proceed to follow it. Apparently it does lead back. But suddenly we come on a marsh. It is one of those soft places with masses of sphagnum moss, green as an emerald, rose-red and amber-ivory in places, but everywhere treacherous. I am taken aback and deeply grieved. Never before had the Daoine Maithe deceived me. I know they play tricks on people, but they are friends of mine.

"Do you understand," I say to them with emphasis, "that I cannot walk in places where my feet sink, whatever you folk can do?"

"You can walk here," they say.

"You are sure?" I ask.

"We are sure."

"Well, then, show me the stepping-stones."

I went forward. I couldn't see a path, but always I found a stepping-stone, so I came safely out of the bog. My friends left me when I reached the high-road. I have never been back there, but if I were to go tomorrow they would usher me to any cotoneaster that sprang from that sowing.

164

TRADITIONAL SINGING

I HAD BEEN DRIVING all day in a jaunting-car, always with something new and beautiful to see: stretches of the ocean at one time, deep glens at another. The young captain who drove me had many stories of places that we passed. At one place he said: "There was a terrible spirit used to haunt this road. It was the spirit of a woman that died with the evil heart in her not worn out. She used to kill people on this road. No one could pass this way at all after dusk. At last there came a priest who had power. He went out to try that power on the spirit. They say that he wrestled with the evil thing all night: but, anyway, he got the victory. There was nothing in the morning but a lump of jelly." "A *lump of jelly!*" I said to myself, remembering a book of travels I had read in which the author states that she and her family rented a house in Cairo and found it haunted by an evil spirit. Their Arab servant undertook to wrestle with it, and in the morning triumphantly showed them what looked like a lump of jelly. What a field for investigation if one had time and method!

We seemed to drive endlessly: through violet dusk, purple dusk, and finally blackness of night. We were due to attend a meeting in a hall that stood on a lonely part of the sea coast. It had been built by the Hon. Albinia Broderick to serve as a hospital but was now in the possession of soldiers of the Republic. Presently we saw the glitter of it like a great low-hung star in the blackness of night. There was nothing but standing room, and scarcely that, when we got there. I had to address the meeting, and when it ended, one of the men said: "We know that you care about traditional singing. We have many singers here, and we will sing for you."

A lad of eighteen with a beautiful tenor voice began a ballad. The sea, close outside, sent wave after wave up a beach of loose stones and dragged wave after wave back with a rattle of shaken pebbles: a wild and fierce accompaniment to the song, itself wild and fierce. Singer after singer followed the first, standing half in light, half in darkness where a kerosene lamp swung from a rafter in the centre of the room. The young captain who had brought me to the meeting (he is one of the most famous singers in Kerry) sang the song that Thomas Costello made, almost three hundred years ago, about the girl who died for love of him, MacDermott's daughter, Una:

"*A Una bhan, a bhlaith na ndlaoidh omra*"

Beautiful that song is in the Gaelic, both words and air, beautiful too in the English that Douglas Hyde has put upon it:

"*O fair Una, thou blossom of the amber locks,*"

I shall not soon forget that night.

THE BOAT OF THE DEAD

I HAVE BEEN LISTENING to a Gaelic story-teller, a red-bearded, blue-eyed shanachie from Devenish Island. He has Kerry Irish and knows many of the traditional stories. He prides himself, however, on his knowledge of Irish history. One could question the accuracy of the history. It has already been questioned by the son of the house. An altercation results—a fine chance for me to acquire a Gaelic vocabulary, since they adorn the argument with gorgeous imagery and splendid-sounding outlandish oaths. With a view to restoring calm I seize the first lull to suggest that the shanachie tell of some strange happening on the Island. We would all—the son, the woman of the house, and myself—be glad to listen.

"The queerest happening," says the shanachie, "was the

166

time the boat came in from nowhere. Most of the folk had gone across to the mainland for Mass. Myself was the only one left in the house. I did not go across because I had a feeling of weakness that day, but my mind was on the mainland. I was thinking of my uncle maybe on his death-bed there, for a heavy sickness had gripped him. I was sitting out in whatever sunshine there was to be got when I heard the sound of a boat coming into the little cove. Must be a big boat, I thought, for it had about four men rowing it. I went down to see what folk were in it. The boat was full of people, but there was only one man that I knew in it, and that man was my uncle. 'Get into the boat,' said the man that had the tiller. 'We have come a long way for you.' But my uncle stood up in the boat and motioned me to keep off. 'Don't put foot in the boat,' said he, 'or you'll never put foot on the Island again. And bid us begone now, and turn your face to your own house-door.'

"There was a fear came on me, and I did as my uncle bade. I could hear the boat pushing off, but I did not turn my head to look at it. I had a fear on me. I sat in the sun and recited the Rosary till the folk came back. They had bad news when they came back. My uncle was dead."

This sets all of us ferreting in our minds for strange happenings. The son of the house recounts a tale of a piglike human-headed animal that lurks on a lonely road to waylay the solitary venturer after dusk-fall. I speak of a Kelpie in the swirl of a mountain-torrent in Skye, a Kelpie that can be heard crying on starless nights. I hope to hear in return a tale of a Kerry Water-horse, but the woman of the house is growing apprehensive. She says that it is dangerous to talk overmuch of these things after darkfall: we might draw down the other world on ourselves. It would be better to sing some heartening songs. The idea of heartening songs pleases me well. The son of the house is one of the best singers in Kerry. By all means let us have songs! Let us have: *The Fair Hills of Ireland:*

167

"Curled he is and ringleted, and plaited to the knee,
Each captain that comes sailing across the Irish sea.
And oh, the fair hills of Ireland!"

Oh, the fair hills of Ireland! fairer, surely, because the Folk
of the Gods of Dana have not forsaken them.

THE KINGDOM OF KERRY

So JOYOUSLY AND graciously this kingdom of Kerry slants
to the sea, reaching out long fingers to the Atlantic, widening river-mouths to take a tidal surge of saltness: so pranked
it is with happy flowers all pied in white and rose and
purple and scarlet that I am loath to take leave of it. But
inexorably the hour draws on when I must return to the
highly respectable garret of my highly respectable landlady.

I have traveled over many mountain-roads. I have spoken
with many people. I have seen sunshine and rain-puddle in
many a crooked street. Everywhere I have found bravery
and greatness of heart. These people of Kerry are not only
keen and experienced fighting stock: they have shown that
they can organize for peace as well as for war. In out-of-the-
way places Sinn Fein Courts have been established; shrewd
judgments have been handed down; just settlements have
been made. I shall long remember these people of Kerry,
these straight-limbed handsome Iberian Celts: their stout-
heartedness, their resourcefulness, their pride and bravery,
their singing voices—Kerry itself is a song in my heart:

A song of how the heron flies,
Of how the osprey stoops and cries
And the sea-gull slants at will.

Since today I have an hour of idleness I have chosen to
168

spend it, alone, on a tongue of land that runs, treeless and venturous, into the sea. The Atlantic water spreads and laps softly in the reedy inlet: it is of a marvelous blueness—blueness that seems infinite and indestructible—and the sky matches it. The reeds and flowering grasses are a frail, a crumbling barrier. Sky and sea in one's consciousness engulf the land: engulf the sense of self and separateness. There is no past in this one moment, and no hereafter: neither time that was, nor time that shall be.

VOX POPULI

THIS GARRET ROOM, the fourth story of a tall old-fashioned Dublin house, has several advantages. Craning above comrade roofs it looks across neglected down-trodden fields to the Dublin hills strung out against the sky. They have a light powdering of untimely snow. I can lean from my window and watch them, bright or shadowed with the changing hours. Townward I can see the curve of the street that winds to the cathedral. I can hear the noise of that street, a confused myriad-throated clamour, a surge of sound, a voice behind the transitory pavement noises that come up here—noises of passing feet and passing vehicles. Hope and fear and anguish and triumph throb and cry in that many-throated insistent voice. It is the people's voice, the voice of the crowded poor quarter of Dublin, the fiercely patriotic quarter of Dublin. People there have been welded together by suffering, by a common endeavour: caught up in a fiery ecstasy.

Going about the poverty-bitten unlovely business of life, unhelped, unpitied, in that narrow street are people who have surged out towards the sound of pistol-shots, to give a young fighter a chance to escape. They have trudged, foot-

169

sore, to Mountjoy: to kneel by the prison wall, while men within waited for the hangman. Tears ran down their faces as they knelt there, praying aloud, reciting the Rosary; fingering prayer-beads that dead men had fingered—the sky stark above them, the white pitiful candles blinking in the cold dawn.

I think of the people whom I interviewed in Kerry: their kindliness; their devotion.

"We want something to come out of our victory that will be good for all alike. We have found comrades in unthought-of places: we would not have the least one cheated of a share!"

I remember that young girl who was head of Cumann-na-mBan in a remote village. She had the violet-blue eyes and the rich dark hair of the Iberian Celts. She had a free-from-worldly-entanglements Madonna face, all innocent in red and white, yet she was chief adviser of the young fighters, "The Boys," and as brave in the face of danger as any one of them. After a successful ambush, which she had helped to plan, "The Boys" hurried to her:

"The Black and Tans are coming to shoot up the town and burn it house by house. What things under your roof do you value most? We'll carry them out for you."

"You will take nothing from my house. Let it burn with all it has! This is no place for you, with the Black and Tans on your heels. You belong to Ireland—away with you!"

From the street comes a sound of martial music and measured steps: young men are marching there with Sinn Fein flags. They are wearing the uniform of the Irish Republican Army. They are carrying rifles. They are singing as they march.

There is a joyousness in the air though the year is declining. We have all of us the hope of victory in our hearts. If we triumph now in this struggle of wills with England—and there seems a good chance of it—seven centuries of disaster triumph with us: Hugh O'Neill, the Great Earl, triumphs,

170

unregretful of the lost battle and the long exile; Parnell triumphs, and all the dead.

The young men are still passing. They are still singing. I cannot hear the words of the song, but I remember the words of Padraic Pearse:

"We are young today as men were young when to be a young man was to be a hero . . . We are about to attempt impossible things, for we know that it is only impossible things that are worth doing."

THE BETRAYAL
December 6, 1921

NEWS, LIKE A THUNDER-CLAP, came this morning: "An Agreement has been signed with England." It came obscurely by rumour and the Press. No one knew what to think, or believe. How could an Agreement be signed when De Valera was in Limerick, and the Delegates—who are bound to consult him before signing anything—were in London? What shamefaced and stealthy announcement is this of a signing that should have had the good-will wish of all Ireland: that should have been announced by the President of the Republic?

I hurried to Doctor Kathleen Lynn. She—who had been hurrying to others—had, like those others, no explanation: nothing but perplexity, ignorance, and foreboding.

Now when the evening papers are being cried in the streets there is news at last—astounding news! The Irish Delegates, the leaders whom we trusted, Arthur Griffith and Michael Collins, have signed away the Sovereignty of Ireland.

171

Our Country is to acknowledge herself part of the British Empire, and members of our Parliament must take an oath of allegiance to the King of England.

De Valera is in town. He is to speak at the Dante Commemoration to be held in the Mansion House tonight. Surely he will repudiate this infamy! He has always warned us that we might have to face resumption of the war with all the suffering that it brings. He knows, as Tom Clarke knew—as all our martyrs knew—that suffering is not what destroys a nation. It is the loss of honour that destroys. We have suffered and survived for seven hundred years, but in all that time we could hold our heads high. We could claim a proud comradeship with other peoples that endured—in our prayers we remembered them! Our sorrowful years linked us to the sorrows of the world.

We are armed. This Rising has carried us nearer to victory than any Rising before it: and now, to placate an Empire that has robbed and tortured, and then maligned us, we are to swear away our birthright and take upon ourselves in return the burden of her crimes!

May God forbid it.

DIES IRAE

ONE THOUGHT LAST night the blackest of nights—black and treason-sodden—but there was hope that De Valera would repudiate the oath. He has not spoken. Last night he presided at the Dante Commemoration Meeting in the Mansion House. He must have had the news that even the street boys knew—yet he said nothing!

Today no word has come from him. This night, this Wednesday night, is blacker still.

I cannot stay in the house. I do not want to talk to any-
172

one—I must go somewhere—anywhere, on foot through the streets. I must walk—and walk—and walk. My mind is on fire, yet I cannot think: I know that I am muttering to myself as I walk.

The crowded houses are black against the sky—the Dublin hills, if I could see them, would be black tonight. House after house is shuttered. But here is a house lit up—a house not sorrowful, one indeed that is holding festival. It has voices and laughter. Someone is drawing from a violin the notes of a Viennese air:

> *Where slim green willows hide me*
> *And wild white violets grow*
> *My Love stood once beside me:*
> *But that was long ago.*

> *Silver in swirl or shallow*
> *The singing waters glide,*
> *How light my heart would follow*
> *Were my Love by my side!*

The trees by the canal are very black. They are leafless against the stars.

MOON-FLAME

THESE NIGHTS I HURRY from street to alley-way and from alley-way to street again till I am worn out, yet I cannot sleep. Last night I flung out of bed and raged about my room like a new-caught beast. The moon made a sinister light in my attic, for the blind had not been drawn on the window. Padding aimlessly from wall to wall, with instinct enough to save myself from tables and chairs, I became aware of the mirror. It irked me to think of the mirror. I would have to avoid it. Ever

173

since I could remember I had been afraid to look in a mirror after dusk: when I had to pass one I carefully turned my eyes away. I feared that if I looked in it, without the security at least of candlelight, I might not see my own face: I might see instead some demon-thing, frightful and unforgettable.

Padding aimlessly, I avoided the mirror: but it bit more and more into my consciousness. At last I said to myself: "I will look into the mirror tonight—nothing matters tonight!" I came close to the mirror and looked squarely into it. The mirror reflected nothing of the room. Filled with pale light that was motionless, it showed the face of an unearthly Being: a delicate strange face, pale as though it had known only moonlight, a face that leaned upon a slender neck as the sculptured Dionysius leans forward, as the sculptured Akhenaten leans in the gallery of the Louvre. The eyelids drooped heavily upon eyes, that if they looked at anything, looked at it spread below: far down, as fields are spread below the moon-crescent. The hair, fanned prodigally on either side of the face as though a wind from nowhere blew upon it—or rather as if it moved of its own volition—was thread by thread like silver flame. One corner of the mouth curved in a still and secret smile.

"I must be crazed," I said to myself. "This is some trick of moonlight—some fantasy of my own face!" I moved my head, I moved my eyes and lips, but in the mirror that unearthly face leaned sideways with drooped lids unlifted, with faint smile unperturbed.

Awed by it, intent upon it, I remembered that as a child I treasured such a face with no word spoken of it for years. Where had I seen it? That I never knew!

I said to myself: "Now I will keep vigil—now that I see it again! My eyes shall cling to it: I must not lose a moment, hours shall not out-wear me." So I thought, staring wide-eyed upon it. The face maintained its still perfection; its awareness of the unseen cosmos, and of me; its subtle and mysterious smile. It endured—I could not endure! That beauty, faint and strange as light beneath a sea-wave, weighed too heavily on me.

Immortal beauty devours the heart. The sight of it, at first a keen and lovely ecstasy, at the end pierces like a sword. I crept away without a backward look. I saw it for the last time untarnished—as it would always be—beauty unobscured by youth, unmarred by age.

THE TREATY

Eamon de Valera, as President of the Irish Republic, has repudiated the Treaty. We thank God for that, though it is a sad enough thanksgiving. Arthur Griffith, with Michael Collins and a considerable following, is standing by the Treaty. The fight goes on in the Dail, but it will not end there! Words, arguments, impassioned oratory—it will take more than words to decide this issue, there is blood and bitterness of death in it.

It is said that several of the army chiefs urged De Valera to arrest the members of the Delegation, charge them with treason, and take a high hand at once, but the President wished to give his old colleagues a chance to explain their conduct. He believed that he could get some clauses in the Treaty altered, and so avoid a resumption of the war with England. He has never flinched from the position that he took up at the beginning of the negotiations. He will not flinch. We know that, but day by day it becomes apparent that the gulf widens, and no policy of sweet reasonableness can bridge it.

There is a deadness in the air: a deadness, too, in many a heart. What draws on bodes no good to us, but we cannot escape it. Whichever way the dice fall, we lose!

175

Was it chance, or a twist of the World-Controller's kaleidoscope, that brought me face to face with Madame O'Rahilly at a crowded street-corner? She said to me: "When I see these streets, I think on your vision of the ruined and burnt houses: and how it all came true in the Easter Rising." "I keep thinking of that 1914 vision, myself," I said, "the Easter Week devastations did not entirely exhaust its potency. The ruin that I saw spread farther northward on O'Connell Street. More houses, I fear, will topple—blackened by fire." "Do not say it," cried Madame O'Rahilly, "we have suffered enough!"

The Dail has accepted the Treaty: "under duress."

RESURGENCE
Spring of 1922

THESE WEEKS AND MONTHS, spun out in argument, while Eamon de Valera carried the fight in the Dail and elsewhere against the Treaty, have been leaden-weighted. Now a clear voice rings out repudiating the action of the Dail and proclaiming afresh the sovereign rights of Ireland. It is Rory O'Connor, with almost the whole of the Republican Army behind him, and the support of Liam Mellowes, Sean Russell, James O'Donovan, Liam Lynch, Earnan O'Malley, Thomas Maguire, Liam Pilkington, Michael Kilroy, Oscar Traynor, Andrew McDonnell and other Brigade Commandants.

It is fitting that Rory O'Connor, wounded in the 1916 fighting, should lead in this resurgence. Comrade and friend of Joseph Mary Plunkett, he has worked for years in Ireland's cause. He is standing now for what Pearse stood for, and Thomas Clarke—for what they died for with all those others, Ireland's lovers. It is a re-affirmation of the sovereignty of

176

Ireland, of sacrosanct values, of sanctions that break life but may not themselves be broken.

Rory O'Connor's name brings to mind that other Rory O'Connor, the last Royal Sovereign, the High King of Ireland, who strove so valiantly to oust the English devastators of his country more than seven hundred years ago. That King held in 1168, for the last time, the great Festival, or Fair of Taillten, with its contests of song; its horse-races; its foreign merchantmen; its bards, and shanachies, and princes. From the long ridge of the Sacred Mounds, looking towards Aide's Hill, he could see that concourse: the chariots, the tents, the blazoned banners, the stallions splendid with gold and enamel, jewelling the plain for seven miles. Many times that plain had lent itself to noble companies, for the Festival goes back and back to an unremembered beginning, presided over by gods and demi-gods—The Festival of Ollamh Fodhla; Tailtiu; and Lugh: the Sun, the Earth, and the Fashioner of the World.

It was full flood tide of Fortune with Roderic O'Connor, upholder of an ancient magnificence. The years to come brought him defeat, and a bitter death-draught. May better luck await today's contestant.

The winds of March today are brave and joyous-hearted. They troop from hill to hill, riotous among gold-empanoplied gorse and starry-shaken spoil of blackthorn branches. The March winds lift Rory's banner. O Eire, who foldest the mountains with their trees and their crystal well-heads in thy Mantle, thou whose reward is the death-gift, call us again to the quest from which no one of thy lovers turns back!

THE ROYAL SOVEREIGNTY OF IRELAND, 1922

WHEN RORY O'CONNOR spoke out that day in March with no uncertain voice, declaring that the young soldiers of the Irish Republican Army stood firm for the Royal Sovereignty of Ireland, many hearts were gladdened. The shame of the officially accepted "Oath" was lifted. The March sky had sunshine in it. Now it is early July, Rory O'Connor is in prison, with other young captains and comrades. The Four Courts, dome and pillars, is a cinder-heap. Tall houses in O'Connell Street have toppled to ruin. Cathal Brugha is dead, refusing surrender.

It had all gone happily enough at first. Even when Rory O'Connor took possession of the Four Courts and placed the upholders of Ireland's Sovereignty under the protection of The Virgin, and Brigit of the Mantle, no one thought that war between brother and brother would come of it.

A heavy sound of cannonading in the dark of early morning—a continuous ominous sound. Field guns! I had not heard them give tongue since the English pounded Liberty Hall in the week of the Rising. What could the English be pounding now? I asked myself that question as I hurried along a Dublin street. I asked it of a friend whom I encountered, and had for reply, "It is not the English, it is the 'Treaty Makers,' battering Rory O'Connor in the Four Courts." "But the guns?" "They got them from the English!"

All that day, Wednesday, 28 June, and all that night the guns boomed. They boomed day and night on Thursday, but as it drew towards noon on Friday there was silence. I stood with Mia Cranwill in the window of her flat. It looked in the direction of the Four Courts. We spoke of the men there, and even as we talked a black pillar of smoke shot up into the sky, and spread domelike. The ground muttered and shook. Denser and denser grew the mushrooming blackness.

178

It was without flame, but darting through it, with a white glint where light caught them, were what seemed to be myriads of white birds. But they could not be birds. The Four Courts had blown up. Only death could be there, and what survived death. Were those white birds, or supersensual flames—souls escaping?

It was not till next day that we learned what those white flying things were—pages from the books, the history-matrix records stored in the Four Courts. They fell to earth miles away, torn pages, fragments of parchments judged worthy, once, to be engrossed and empowered with seals and signatures.

The fight shifted to O'Connell Street where Headquarters of the Irish Republican Army had been established. Cathal Brugha was there, as were De Valera, Austin Stack, and other leaders with the Dublin Brigade commanded by Oscar Traynor. Tunneling from house to house they had reached the Hammond Hotel. They knew that Rory O'Connor, Liam Mellowes, Joseph McKelvey, Richard Barrett and a hundred good fighting men had escaped the destruction of the Four Courts, and were prisoners in Mountjoy. They knew that the Country was rising. They knew that they could do nothing but hold out for a while, with surrender or death at the end. They held out for five days, and surrendered only when the walls fell in and flame licked about their feet.

Cathal Brugha did not surrender. He is dead.

Like fire the civil war spurts and rages from town to town, from countryside to countryside. The Feast of the Lughnassa draws on. Fires were lit on the sacred hills of Ireland at this Festival in token that Lugh the Sun-God was wedded to the Royal Sovereignty of Ireland. Those were joy-fires: our fires hiss and flicker embittered with blood.

179

THE BRIGHT RING OF DAY

O Rose, dark Rose, when wilt thou blossom red?
I blossom now—a splendour for the dead!

Rose, dost thou lean towards dawn, or turn away?
Night's whitest star burns on the rim of day.

Rose, art thou pale or red for pride or shame?
I am the pure perpetual ashless Flame.

DUST TO DUST
August, 1922

DUBLIN, TODAY, IS a muted city with open apprehensive mouth that astonishment makes dumb. The shops, big and small, are rigorously shuttered. The trams are not running. The people are standing vacant-eyed on the sidewalks. They are waiting for a funeral cortège to pass—the burial pageant of Arthur Griffith.

Scarcely has the City had time to whisper to itself: *"Arthur Griffith is dead!"* so sudden, so unexpected has been that death. It bursts in a thunder-clap of consternation upon the pro-British and the Unionists. Arthur Griffith had become their bulwark. They felt that he was on the side of "law and order" as Britain understands it. They pinned their hopes on him. Now anything may happen: they have their doubts of Michael Collins.

To those others who had waited, wet-eyed and silent, in the long line of mourners outside that chamber where Cathal Brugha lay in state this death seems like the flash of an avenging sword.

180

Maker of Sinn Fein—and Un-maker—Arthur Griffith was a fighter and wore the scars of conflict. Through the long hard struggle for Irish freedom he had been staunch. He had borne himself valorously. He had chosen poverty and obscurity rather than the success he might have had as a brilliant journalist. He had asked nothing for himself. When he went as negotiator to England he went as our strong man, one who could take buffets and keep his eyes open, one whom Lloyd George could not tangle in his nets. But the web clung to him, so silken-soft it scarcely seemed a menace. It brought him down—Arthur Griffith the iron-jawed, the incorruptible! We thought that if all the world yielded, this man would not yield: yet he led the way in surrender—and the others followed. Erskine Childers, alone, clear-eyed, held out. But he was not a member of the Delegation.

The cortège is passing—priests and soldiers. Soldiers are fitting: Arthur Griffith fought against the British in the Boer War—he was no priest's man! Michael Collins and Richard Mulcahy walk side by side. Dignitaries of the army follow, two and two. Richard Mulcahy limps as he walks. His thin face looks tired. Michael Collins tramps sturdily forward. His face is grim. In all the adventures of an adventurous life he could not have foreseen this one. When the heavy guns, so eagerly pressed upon him by the British, opened fire on the Four Courts he could not have divined, beyond that hurtlement, the sputter of rifle-fire that brought death to his friend, Harry Boland.

It is a leaden-footed and sad procession: and leaden-sad indeed and heavy-footed were the days between Arthur Griffith's return with "The Treaty" and this day; days when De Valera, who never flinched from his position, tried hard to maintain unity and force an honorable peace—and tried in vain; days when windows rattled to the reverberation of the guns battering the Four Courts; days when prison yards —no longer in British hands—were crowded, and overcrowded, with Irishmen whose only crime was championing their country. To such a pass had this dead man's belief in

181

the righteousness of his action, and his stubbornness to stand by it, brought all of us—the brave fighting, the high hopes, the close-knit comradeship!

That Arthur Griffith should have overstepped the authority delegated to him is not so strange. He had been used to call no man his master. He trusted his own judgment and settled matters with a battle-axe as became one of the Viking breed. Fate made him the henchman of a chieftain in whose subtle mind the Byzantine angels could have pirouetted unhampered on the point of a pin. It is possible that through all these months of aftermath he failed to comprehend the difference—the ominous and tragic difference—between De Valera's ultimate concession, and his own. We are puppets in the hands of Destiny. From birth, this day, and this end, awaited Arthur Griffith.

God rest his soul.

BLACK FRIDAY
December 8, 1922

I WONDER WHY I feel so disconsolate this morning. Perhaps it is because the clouds are so lowering and the sky so heavy. I don't feel that I want to do anything and yet I can't sit still. For some days now I have had the flat of my friend, R. B., to myself. She is absent from Dublin, and I have the use of her flat until she returns. It is a cheery place with long windows looking on a street where there is always something to see. But I don't want to look out of the windows. Everything that happens is hateful.

I move restlessly about the living-room. It is meticulously in order: the woodwork polished. The silver shining on the Sheraton sideboard, the chairs placed where they ought to be. (Mrs. Smith, my friend's invaluable charwoman, is a

182

disciplinarian in such matters. She comes every morning, gives me my breakfast, and regiments the furniture.) I re-arrange a few things half-heartedly. There are books, but I can't read. I can't even go downstairs and get a newspaper. I fling myself into the largest of the armchairs, one that a few days ago had pistols stuffed between the seat and the back. They are hidden more securely now. In fact, the flat is an arsenal. Under the floor there are Thompson machine-guns, in the false back of a cupboard there are most impor-tant papers. In hiding places, ammunition.

It is wonderful how that heavy gloom outside and inside weighs upon one. There is a knock at the door. Someone on this dull day has climbed the flight of stairs and traversed the corridor leading to my door. I open the door. An officer of the Free State Army and eight privates are crowded there. Each one of the soldiers has a rifle on his shoulder with a bayonet fixed in it. The officer has a pistol in his hand. They all look gloomy and the officer is shamefaced.

"We have to search the flat," he says. "Information has been received that men on the run are being harboured here."

"I think there has been a mistake," I say. "There are no men harboured here. But as this flat is in a public building, it is possible that men have been noticed going in and out."

"We have to search the flat," says the officer.

"I shall be glad to show you over it," I say. "I make only one request. Do not break open drawers or cupboards. I have keys and will open everything."

The raiding party begins with the living-room. The officer lines his eight men at one end of the room, standing at at-tention, and begins to search the Sheraton sideboard. The silver forks and spoons are neatly arranged. The glass is spot-less. The officer begins to think that some mistake has been made. This does not look like a room where emergency beds house hunted patriots. There must be a mistake he thinks. It has happened many times that wrong information has led to the raid of a house, and complaints from a house wrong-

183

fully raided get raiding parties into trouble. He hesitates, he looks round the room. When his back was turned he had been aware that the men were sniggering to each other. They are quite certain that a mistake has been made.

"I must search the whole flat," says the officer.

"I think you will see that a mistake has been made, but since you are here, I would like you to search the flat. You will then be able to make a full report, and everyone will be satisfied."

The officer searches the armchairs. He puts his hand into the very place where an automatic had been, and finds nothing. He pulls out drawers full of flounced silks and lace. There is nothing there but very feminine underclothes. He is getting red in the face and the men are enjoying it more and more. "There is another room," says the officer, straightening himself.

"Yes, it is a kitchen and bedroom. I would like you to search it."

He opens cupboards. They are full of china cups and saucers and painted plates. He opens canisters—tea, sugar and coffee!

"That is sufficient," says the officer. "I want to see the wardrobe."

The wardrobe is full of women's garments. The shoes he unearths are small and dainty. He is thoroughly tired of the whole business, but he turns out the contents of every trunk. It's going to be a thorough search. At last he is satisfied.

"I want you to sign a paper to the effect that nothing has been stolen or damaged by my men in the course of this investigation."

"I shall have pleasure in doing so."

They go down two or three steps and are about to leave the flat when the officer catches sight of a large trunk in the bathroom.

"What's in that trunk?" he says with a gleam of hope in his eyes.

"Only cardboard boxes and brown paper. Please open it.

184

It is not locked." He opens it. It contains nothing but card-board boxes and brown paper.

In this very bathroom I had suggested a hiding-place for arms. I note with satisfaction that he does not even look at the place. It has, however, nothing but emptiness.

At last they are gone. I return to the living-room and fling myself into the largest armchair. I ought to feel pleased. In all probability this house will not be raided again. But I am more and more depressed. I wander about the room, lifting things aimlessly and laying them down. A newsboy is crying in the streets:

"Special! Special! Extra-special!"

I rouse myself sufficiently to run downstairs and purchase a newspaper. All across the front page is the devastating news:

EXECUTION OF THE FOUR
IRISH REPUBLICAN LEADERS

Rory O'Connor, Liam Mellowes, Richard Barrett and Joseph MacKelvey had been shot at dawn! Shot within the walls that should have been a safeguard to them, for they were prisoners of war. No wonder the sky was lowering and black. No wonder the Free State officer was shamefaced. No wonder that the day was sick with gloom. This is not a treachery of the English Government. It is the work of Irish-men, some of whom had worked and fought in company with these murdered men.

Black Rose that is Eire, Rose yet to blossom red, you are strangely red today—strangely black!

THE MONSTRANCE

FROM A GRAY WIND-SWEPT or rainy street Mia Cranwill's workshop is a joyous haven: warm and spacious and motley-

185

coloured and prodigal of things to look at and touch. The furnace for enamelling, at the far end, draws one inescapably. What has it between its jaws: ring, pendant, or boss? Trays of semi-precious stones tempt one to finger moss-agates, chalcedony, rose-carnelian, opal-matrix, turquoise, and lapis lazuli. Pinned on the walls are designs in colour for casket and for reliquary in hammered metal: for chalice and processional cross—things such as create a wonderment in the treasuries of cathedrals, crowded with the munificence of centuries.

It was a great moment when Mia Cranwill learned that she was to fashion a Monstrance, the gift of Mr. Leahy, for Monsignor Roger's Church of Saint Patrick, in San Francisco. The work would take years, but she could put into it something of the passionate beauty of the Rising; something of the hard endurance of the men who died; something of the faith that renews itself through sorrow and loss in the Ireland that she loves. The Monstrance was to be hand-wrought in gold, silver, and platinum, and enriched with tracery and enamels. Mia resolved to use, wherever possible, enamel à jour (enamel without a back). This would add to the labour and difficulty of the work, but would give when light touched it a jeweled effect as of stained glass.

What shape should the Monstrance have? This was a question which Mia debated with herself. Should it be triangular, pyramid-shaped, like those medieval Monstrances that have a flamelike beauty? Should it be rayed and circular, like images we make of the sun? Mia decided that it should be rayed and circular. It should also embody the cross. By using the cross that the Celts used she has been able to keep the radiant sunflower shape: keeping it as a transfiguration and glory of the cross. Upon the two arms, and upon the upright she is blazoning the traditional symbols of the Four Evangelists: the Bull, the Eagle, the Lion, and the Angel-Man. Models for these she found in illumined pages of the *Book of Kells* where these significators have kept for more than a thousand years their hues of lapis and emerald, and their burnished gold.

These are, indeed, long-memoried images. They have walked among gods in Egypt. They were graven upon stone in Babylon and Nineveh. They glitter in the zodiac, and impart an ancestral magnificence to that Vision which descended upon Ezekiel by the river Chebar in the years of his captivity when he beheld the glory of the God of Israel enthroned above a firmament supported by stupendous "Living Creatures," four-fold of wing, and of aspect: having for countenance the similitude of a Bull, of an Eagle, of a Lion, and of a Man.

"As for the likeness of the living creatures, their appearance was like burning coals of fire—and the fire was bright, and out of the fire went forth lightning.

And the living creatures ran and returned as the appearance of a flash of lightning.

And the likeness of the firmament upon the heads of the living creature was as the colour of the terrible crystal, stretched forth over their heads above.

And under the firmament were their wings straight, the one towards the other; every one had two, which covered on this side, and every one had two, which covered on that side, their bodies.

And when they went, I heard the noise of their wings, like the noise of great waters, as the voice of the Almighty, the voice of speech, as the noise of an host."

Much suffering, a burning pride of race, and a tumultuously aspirant faith, enabled Ezekiel to behold this Vision. We also have attained to a Vision: purchased with much the same merchandise. It has taken possession of us. It will not be gainsaid. Creative and flagellant it urges and strengthens today the devout hands of this Irish craftsman. Hour by hour Mia Cranwill labours on the Monstrance. It is tall. It is magnificently proportioned. It is joyously flowered with carmine of the rose and purple of the grapevine: and marvellously

187

enhanced with traceries in gold, silver, and platinum. The tabernacle for the Host, glorious in the midst of it, is closed-in by one huge flawless crystal from an Irish mountain.

This Monstrance, so strong, so simple, so intricate, so high-hearted in its proclamation of the triumph of the Lord of Life, comes to one with a shock of delight. It has the colour of frozen snow: it glitters opalescent. As it is beautiful, may it be perdurable.

TALK OF MANY THINGS

I ALWAYS LIKE TO VISIT Kathleen O'Brennan's rooms. They have a colourful strangeness, a way of reminding one of half a dozen things at once. Green silken arras covers one wall, and Zulu spears vie with curved swords of Damascus, upon another. Perhaps the sight I most enjoy, however, is the clock outside her door. One sees it as one climbs the staircase, and is saved the labour of knocking. The clock says on its wide face: *Will return at*—and marks the hour! No one else has a clock like that: perhaps it is an American innovation, for Kathleen has lectured in America. This afternoon she is giving a reception in honour of a handsome young American, Chester Alan Arthur—grandson of President Arthur—who has come to this country mindful that it cradled his ancestors, and has found relatives in County Antrim. Southern Ireland, however, holds his heart: being a poet, he is already pledged to the Irish Cause. He wants to throw up his whole career, and work for Ireland.

Some of us try to dissuade him. We know what work for Ireland means. It is an obligation with us, but, perhaps, he ought to hold fast to his career as an architect. He is determined, however, to see things in Ireland. He will have a house here, if Charlotte Wilson, the girl he is to marry in a

188

few weeks, is willing to risk life in a country where ambushes, raids, and bomb explosions enliven the hours by day and night. He is renouncing his English name, "Chester," in favour of a Celtic name that has long been in his family: "Gavin."

Kathleen O'Brennan goes from group to group—a crowd delights her! She always has half a hundred projects on hand: she knows everything, and everybody; she goes everywhere, and appears to be in Paris, New York, and Berne almost simultaneously. She thinks that I would make a success as a lecturer in America, and urges me to venture it. America seems to me very big and far off.

TARA

IT IS AN EXPEDITION to Tara of the Kings that is dashing along the road from Dublin. It consists of two autos. The leading one, a bright yellow roadster flying two Sinn Fein flags, is piloted by the Countess Markievicz. At top speed it ricochets from bump to bump of a road made for horse vehicles. The expedition was organized by Gavin Arthur whose Irish ancestry claimed him as soon as he set foot in the country. The second car belongs to him. His young and brilliant wife, Charlotte, is at the wheel repeating, bump for bump, the career of the yellow car in front. Beside her sits the young poet, Lyle Donaghy, somewhat pensive and a little sullen. He hasn't had any breakfast! But that is his own fault. The back seat holds Gavin and myself. We are exchanging views on Irish history and legend, with pauses to remonstrate with Charlotte on the pace of the car and the frequency of the bumps. Charlotte is unsympathetic. When a most immoderate jolt makes us hit the roof with our heads in no gentle fashion and we both exclaim loudly, she says: "It

189

won't hurt your brains! If you had any you'd know that I must hang on to that yellow chariot—how else can we get to Tara?"

Gavin and I resume our discussion. Lyle Donaghy sits silent. This is due to a lack of sustenance and Charlotte's sense of discipline. Gavin had arranged that the expedition would start at a given hour. His car would call at Lyle Donaghy's rooms in Trinity College, and find the poet all equipped and breakfasted. Instead we found him in bed. Gavin routed him out and hurried him to the car, suggesting as we started that Lyle should get a sandwich or two from the lunch basket. "Nothing of the sort!" said Charlotte, "If we have to do without the starting-time, he can do without his breakfast. It will sharpen his brain!"

The car in front, every now and then, lets out a joyous blast of its motor-horn; sunshine flecks the road with tree-shadow; the rich pasture land in green undulations whirls by. Consoled, placated, well-advised we progress from bump to bump.

Tara is a desolation. One has to trace laboriously the foundations of the great banquet-hall, and speculate as to where other palaces may have been. The fossed mounds that in other places mark the sites of kingly houses are not here. The grassland has not even the quietude of lapsed centuries: it shows wounds where ill-advised enthusiasts have been digging for the Ark of the Covenant! A statue of Saint Patrick, very big and from an artistic point of view very unworthy to be where it is, has the air of bestowing with lifted hand an unsought-for benediction on what Patrick's successors laid waste with bell-stroke and with cursing. "I think," said the Countess, "that a charge of dynamite would do this statue good." "They would only put up an uglier one," I say gloomily. "Dynamite," says Charlotte, thriftily, "is a thing we can't afford to waste."

We fell to talking of the Stone of Destiny, the Lia Fail, in ancient times one of the Royal Treasures of Tara. On this Stone, according to an old chronicle, the high-kings of Ireland took the oath to their people. When a true and destined king stood with both feet upon the Stone it gave out a deep sound of approval. It roared. Where is the Lia Fail? Tradition, trustworthy or untrustworthy, maintained that Scottish kings borrowed the Stone, and kept it. Kings of Scotland were crowned at Scone, standing with both feet upon the Lia Fail, until Edward the First of England raided Scotland and took the Stone to London. There it was fastened into the Coronation Chair, and English kings were crowned on it. A prophecy, that went from mouth to mouth, *"Where the Stone goes, Gaelic kings will follow,"* fulfilled itself when James the Sixth of Scotland was crowned upon the Stone, as James the First of England.

"If we could get that Stone," said the Countess, "the Royal Sovereignty might come back to Ireland."

"Why can't you get it, Constance?" asked Gavin. "The Irish captains have managed more difficult adventures. Anyone can see the Stone, touch it even, in the Coronation Chair at Westminster Abbey."

"We have planned many raids on it," the Countess answered, "but the place is well-guarded, and the Stone is heavy."

I thought, as I listened, of raids planned by Maud Gonne and by Emer Moloney. I called to mind a day, years ago, when I chanced into Æ's house, and found Æ and Yeats discussing plans for the kidnapping of the Stone. Yeats had a bunch of grapes in his hand, and between mouthfuls detailed an elaborate plan of action. Æ was a bit doubtful of its success. I was more than doubtful (we had not then young captains of the Irish Republican Army to rely on). I said that if the Stone possessed the Royal Sovereignty we might, if we could make a strong enough spiritual centre, occultly transport that power to Ireland. The Stone must follow. Something to this effect I said now, but the Countess and Gavin held fast to the idea that the Stone itself was the thing to get. "Just think of the consternation in England!" said Gavin. "And the joy in Ireland!" said the Countess. "Yes, but how

191

to get it across the water?" "We might take it up to Scotland and hide it there for a while!" Gavin detailed plans. He had given much thought to the abduction of the Stone. The Countess, who had also given much thought to the abduction of the Stone, detailed plans. While they argued the sun slanted westward.

I watched the shadows lengthen on the ruined and desecrated ridges that mark the palace-sites of Tara. Once, sitting idle as I sat, Margaret O'Grady saw Tara as it had been: its flags, its battle-standards and its painted palaces. She saw the people moving about. She heard a sound of trumpets blown. She saw the horses and the horse-boys. Tara must keep many memories, but I could not surprise one. Instead, I turned my mind upon descriptions in old sagas. The palace doors were of red yew, elaborately carved. The roofs were thatched in bright colours. The walls inside had plates of beaten copper with designs of birds, eyed with red carbuncles. How gay must Tara have been when the poets and story-tellers, the princes, the druids, the kings of all Ireland, assembled there for the week of the Samhain Festival! Could they have thought, when Cormac gave the house-warming of the great feast-hall, that grass would grow so thickly underfoot there? For centuries the grass has grown and withered: even as it has grown and withered for centuries on the graves of kings and saints at Clonmacnoise. Grass renews itself. The Dream that held Ireland's lovers, renews itself. From ruin and disaster it struggles back to the light: it burgeons a-fresh.

The sunshine seemed brighter when we left Tara. As the cars bumped and thundered along the road we felt happier.

"Why don't we do this oftener?" said the Countess. "We could have many days like this."

"Yes, why don't we?" said all the rest of us. "Let us go again very soon—very soon!"

I knew that I would never visit Tara again.

THE SMITH'S WIFE

A CLEAR CALM DAY in November: it is the week of the Festival of Samhain, and some of us are celebrating it by a pilgrimage to the river Boyne. This river in ancient times had offerings made to it because it is the river of the Goddess Aunya. We have brought some flowers and are throwing petals on the water. It is a slow-moving, beautiful river, the river Boyne. It moves among flat meadows where the iris spreads itself in battalions that are bearded with gold in Summertime. It moves among rushes heavy-headed with bronze. Standing there, we could see one of the great mounds. Gavin pointed it out. "How like it is to a hill that the Earth herself has builded," he said, "and how green. That mound has never been opened! What a shame to have a mill on it and call it Millmount!" "I know what it is called in the ancient sagas," I said. "It is the Mound of the Smith's Wife." "What smith?" asked Gavin. "Why Cullion, to be sure—the Smith whose hound Cu-Cullion was—Cullion, the Shaper of the World, the God, Mannanaun himself!" "We could name his wife then," said Gavin. "Yes, his wife is Aunya, or Fand, the Goddess Mother of the World who gives her name to the Boyne." We stood there, with the water lapping slowly, the Countess Markievicz, Gavin, and I. Had we been able to revivify the past, what processions we might have seen, what strange ceremonies! The Boyne must remember these, perhaps regretfully. Dead folk a-plenty must remember, remembering the pride of life.

"In the Catholic Church this is the Festival of the Dead," said Gavin. "Do you think the dead can see into our world?"

"I think that they can," said the Countess. "A strange thing happened once to me. You know my cottage on the Dublin hillside?" (We knew it well. She had been most generous in lending it to poets and artists. Padraic Colum had spent weeks there, writing ballads and trying to capture a cricket which annoyed him by its constant shrill piping.) "It was like

193

this," said the Countess, "I was crossing over a mountain-field to the cottage, and thinking to myself how heavy the barred gate of that field would be. I had to unfasten it, swing it open, and put it in place again! But when I came to the gate, a man stepped forward and opened it for me. I thanked him, and he answered in Gaelic. It wasn't till I had gone a few paces on my way that I began to think how strange this was! How strangely, too, the man was dressed. He had on a short jacket of white flannel, and his trousers were of blue homespun. On the Aran Islands one sees a dress like that, but not on the Dublin hills. I turned back. The gate was securely closed. There was no man in sight anywhere, and all the hill-side was clear in view! It must be two hundred years since men wore handwoven cloth, and spoke Gaelic on that hillside."

With a sudden movement Constance de Markievicz flung upon the waters all the roses that she held, saying:

"In memory of the dead who died for Ireland!"

There was silence for a while, except for the little song that the Boyne made. We watched rose-petals drifting. The sun was very bright. There was an air from the sea, and ships were leaning out under sail from the river-mouth. A fish leaped, silvered in the sunshine, and vanished.

IPHIGENIA IN TAURIS

LENNOX ROBINSON HAS OFFERED the grounds of his house at Killiney for the staging of a Greek play, *Iphigenia in Tauris*. They are well suited. The house is on a cliffside about two hundred feet above the sea-washed strand. Those herdsmen, and the messenger, who spied upon the Greek ship, and spied upon the young warriors who stepped ashore from it,

194

can clamber among rocks and scale the cliff to arrive most convincingly breathless with the import of their news. There is some stone-work too that will serve for altar and temple walls. For a background there is the circle of Killiney Bay with the pointed mountains that earn for it a comparison with the Bay of Naples. In front of the house there is a flat grassy space, excellent for the stage. Facing this green sward, and the mountains and sea-line beyond it, the ground rises gently in what is almost one side of an amphitheatre. This slope has been planted with apple trees. The trees are in blossom. It is a day in Springtime. Seated on the grass and moss among the apple trees is an invited audience. George Russell is leaning against a tree trunk. Seumas O'Sullivan, the poet, sits beside Estella Solomons, the artist. Yeats is in a patch of sunlight. Everywhere one looks one sees people that one knows. Yeats has arranged for the goddess, Athena, to have a gold mask.

My sister is playing Iphigenia. There were predictions that it would be impossible to play against such a background—the glittering sea, the wide expanse of sky, the magnificent sweep of coastline. But Elizabeth played against it, standing with scarce a gesture. She drew height and splendour to herself even in the presence of those mountains—perhaps because of them! Her beautiful voice going from cadence to cadence in the long lines of Euripides seemed part of the golden air. She was more than the exiled princess of Mycenæ lamenting the downfall of a kingdom and the death of a brother, sole pillar of a ruined house. She was Humanity itself caught in the brightness and glitter and cruelty of life; sport of the gods, yet daring to nurse a will antagonistic to theirs: daring, bewildered and unconvinced, to question destiny—without hope of an answer!

The purple of the sea behind Elizabeth deepened itself in the long archaic garment that clung about her; the sun-shafts glittered on the bronze of her hair and on her golden over-dress. From the strand and the rocky clefts and inlets, far

195

below, came a clashing of waves: a murmur as of multitudinous voices. Was not the sun Apollo once? Was not the sea Poseidon?

The sense of beauty and tragedy that remained after the play somewhat hushed the talk. People crowded about Elizabeth, but she disentangled herself. My brother, Morogh, was but a few months dead. Elizabeth loved him more than she loved anybody. She had no heart for compliments. The grief in Iphigenia's lament for Orestes was not a conjured grief.

This is, perhaps, the last time that I shall see my sister, Elizabeth, draw with the magic of her personality and her genius a whole audience into the greatness of a great play. I am going soon to America, to lecture there. Who knows whether I shall return across the waters?

A DAY IN OCTOBER, 1925

WE ARE A SMALL party on this cloud-threatening day, already sodden with rain: Maud Gonne, Miss Barry O'Delaney, and myself, in Maud Gonne's auto. A young soldier of the Irish Republican Army is driving us. We are bound for a cottage high among the hills where Iseult Gonne lives with her husband, Francis Stuart. It is a farewell visit, for I am leaving Ireland in a few days to lecture in America.

The auto jolting through wet ruts turns in at the entrance to Powerscourt Demesne. I am glad of that, I shall have a chance to see for the last time the great avenue of Chilean pines, planted years ago by a Viscount Powerscourt who had a fondness for exotic trees. They are planted methodically, a certain distance apart, cone-bearing tree by catkin-bearing tree, male alternating with female, in one of the rarest and most beautiful stretches of the demesne. Perfect in symmetry, each one maintaining its individuality by a slight

196

difference, they stand darkly splendid this morning against the rainy sky. They like rain those Chilean trees: this wet Ireland has nourished them well. Many times when I was staying at a farmhouse a few miles off, I came to visit these trees. I have seen them with a great flush of rhododendron blossom surging away to the ridge that touches the skyline and shelters them from the storm. I have seen them with the first greenness and the frail half-reluctant flower-petals of Springtime about their feet. Always they maintain an austere magnificence. Rain drips from them but a whiteness is spreading in the sky.

Iseult and Francis have shaken the dust of cities from their shoestrings: heights give inspiration and security from the herd! The auto climbs to their sanctuary by muddy lane after muddy lane: it climbs slowly with a sense of thwart, and charges along like a maddened bull whenever it can see ahead of itself for a short distance. With loud snorts and pants it breasts the last hill-slant. We have arrived! Here one sees nothing but grass and bracken, rounded hilltops, a stone-walled hollow, and two solid stone cottages amply thatched. One is a dwelling-place, the other serves as writing-room and studio for Francis. (As a matter of fact, Iseult does whatever writing is done at present, she is working on the articles which Yeats admires so much and which she signs "Maurice Gonne.") Francis has fallen into a mood of silence, and spends his hours in meditation except when he rouses himself to paint some figures on the whitewashed walls of the cottage that is particularly his own. So far he has a horse, a wheel emblem, and several flowers. He disentangles himself graciously from the higher existence and comes forward with Iseult to welcome us.

I think to myself how handsome these two are: Francis tall and blonde with amber eyes, Iseult also tall and so richly brunette. Maud Gonne painted her once holding an iris blossom. But though the fleur-de-lis might symbolize her slender poise of body, she needs a flower more compellent to image forth her passionate changes of mood, her

197

tragic exaltation, her dream-fast silences: some flower that can sway in the wind and be flame-red.

We go into the cottage that serves as living-room, and sit by a turf fire, talking of everything and nothing while three wild rabbits, captured by Iseult, hop round our feet and play with each other. Both Francis and Iseult are enthusiastic about their hill-fastness. Francis is planning a herb-garden in this hollow of the hills: he has carried stones to make a well-head, and transplanted spearmint and wild thyme with other spices. Iseult has coaxed some red carnations into blossom. We go to inspect the garden. There is a wild-rose bush by the wall, but the heavy-headed carnations, rain-bowed, make a blood-red splendour that drowns all paler blossoms. Iseult gathers a lavish armful for me, but as I hold them she says: "You must have rue also: these are too red!" Rue has a bitter fragrance.

As we jolt along the muddy trails that descend to the city, I wonder what Miss Barry O'Delaney will note in her diary; she has made up her mind to chronicle every worthwhile saying. There have been few today I fear: I wish the talk had been less discursive. She should have been present a year ago when Iseult, Francis, Austin Clarke, and I sat ensconced on cushions that we had heaped by the hearth in Maud Gonne's drawing-room at Saint Stephen's Green. The tall Georgian room was dark behind us; and we talked, Heaven knows why, of the moon.

"The moon is lovely beyond everything else that the sky has!" said Iseult. "All poets love the moon." "I am sure of that," said Francis. Had he not written:

> "Stoop down one night and try to break my heart!
> Did ever you leave poet quite so whole?
> Hush! Hush! Thou couldst not do it, for thou art
> Too close—my very soul."

"For myself," said Austin Clarke, "I am no lover of the moon. I hold with the ancient Celts that the moon is a young man. He is disgruntled and sallow. He has a brazen counte-

nance, bitter and hard." "I see the moon most often helmed in
brass," I said, "but when the mask is off, the moon is white."
"The moon is always white except when she is blue, or rose-
colour or honey-yellow," said Iseult. Francis agreed with
her. I thought of Yeats: "The moon like a pale rose." These
lovers had looked upon her unmasked face.

"O Lady of all the poems in the world."

Dusk is closing in, and the clouds descend in a gentle driz-
zle. It has rained so constantly all these days that one can't
even feel any gladness in the grass. There is nothing to look
at. I have seen Iseult and Francis in all probability for the
last time. I call to mind the first time that I ever saw Iseult,
when Maud Gonne brought her, a child, to Dublin. In the
little back garden of the house on Coulson Avenue that
adjoined George Russell's, Iseult sat on the top of the divid-
ing-wall. Beside her sat Brian Russell, young as herself, and
on the wall between them was a pile of snails in their brown
shells. "Iseult," said Maud Gonne, coming upon the scene,
"why have you gathered those messy things?" "Because they
are good for the agriculture," said Iseult with her French
voice. "No!" thundered Brian Russell, "they are not good for
agriculture—they are bad!" "But the French farmers sell
snails—the French farmers are wise, and snails are good!" "I
tell you they are *bad*—BAD!" reiterated young Brian. Iseult
administered a smart slap on the face, and descended from
the wall.

I remember Iseult dancing at twilight on the long flat
Normandy sands at Calvados—the flat sands and the flat sea-
bitten meadows deserted save for a little stir of wind from
the sea. Iseult, with hair outblown, dancing a fantasy of her
own composition. Minnelouse, her black Persian cat, dancing
opposite with plumy tail erect and serious-minded orange
eyes.

Iseult, woman-grown and passionate to marry Francis,
eloping with him against the wishes of her people who
thought that he had little to offer beyond his tawny beauty

and his poet-songs. Wise Iseult, how much rue have you gathered for yourself?

Street lamps now, and houses with lit windows; blank walls; shopfronts; the shabby down-at-heel old parts of Dublin. Bits of dirty paper swirl about the street—sad exchange for the October gold in the country laneways. I lift my armful of crimson blossoms. The rue is safely there. One does not need to husband it ever. It takes care of itself.

VALE

It is farewell now, a long and lasting farewell,
To the Land that nurtured me,
Mother and goddess.

A wood that I loved will remember:
A mountain that looks seaward will not forget me.

I shall not forget the last greenness,
Nor two sea-hawks circling, circling,
In the pale morning sky.

Book Two
AMERICA

THE LIONESS

How could I know, America,
Hearing you praised for bigness,
For opulence alone,
As a calf is praised for the market,
How could I know you a land
Lean-ribbed and austere,
Splendid as a lioness
Golden-eyed and languorously alert?

PORTRAIT OF ELLA YOUNG
BY ANSEL EASTON ADAMS

HAIL AMERICA

*E*LEVEN YEARS AGO WHEN I THOUGHT I HAD settled down to enjoy Temple Hill, the beautiful house that I had renovated, and the garden I had reclaimed, a gypsy came to the door. "Put a piece of silver in my hand with good-will," she said, "and I will tell your fortune." I put a piece of silver in her hand. She said: "You think you will live here pleasantly for a long while, but you will leave it in a short time very suddenly. You will cross the Big Water and in the country beyond it you will have more luck than ever you had here. You will end your days across the water."

Within three months I had to leave Temple Hill owing to conditions set up by the 1914 War—a war that had not started, or even threatened, when the gypsy spoke. That was eleven years ago.

The chance in America came at last unexpectedly. The well-known manager, Mr. William Feakins of New York, decided to arrange a lecture tour for me in the East and Middle West, so I find myself in New York. The city shows itself auspicious, its towered skyline fantastic and delicate, its multitudinous sharp outlines, its dazzle of sunlight on glass.

It was a joy to be rid of the steamer. Tramp steamers and freighters had endeared themselves to me and I fancied I should like the voyage, but the well-equipped, indeed over-equipped, liner on which I traveled was not a boat—it was a big hotel! With a blare of dance music it churned across the Atlantic, shedding garbage and ashes on every wave that lifted a head within reach. When it berthed itself triumphantly, I caught sight of a bronzed and bearded man who seemed to be looking for someone. It was Mr. de Lima who came from Mr. Feakins' office to welcome me and tell me of arrangements. Columbia University was to have my first lecture.

At the crowded end of the lecture, quite a group of Irish people came to talk with me. Mary McSweeney was there, and Joseph McGarrity, and Merriam Golden who insisted that we all come to her apartment. It was a very real bit of Ireland. We found ourselves talking of banshees and faery cavalcades. Mary McSweeney thought we should talk of something more serious, yet she ended by telling the best faery adventure of the evening. Joseph McGarrity, big, broad-shouldered, and over six feet tall, brought a sense of power and bigness into the apartment. He was known to have aided, abetted, and counseled the Irish leaders; he had lavished a fortune on the Cause: but we could not persuade him to talk of the part he had played over and over again—of the part he was then playing—in Irish affairs.

"Never mind about that," he said, with his big genial smile, "I know a good Irish faery story. One early morning in Ireland my mother called me to the door: I was a young lad at the time. '*Step softly*,' she said, '*and I will show you something.*' We came out on a grassy field that was beaded with the dew, and there by the side of a thorn tree were footprints plain in the dew-wet grass. They were the smallest footprints, too small to belong to the smallest child: they began for no reason, and went nowhere—just footprints, with the stretch of the field undisturbed and silvery before and behind them. I never forgot that morning. '*It is a lucky thing*,' said my mother, '*to see the faery footprints.*'"

I think it must be a lucky thing to hear about them from Roger Casement's friend, the friend too and adviser of Liam Mellowes: the man whose house welcomed and sheltered Eamon de Valera when, escaped from an English prison, he made his way to America.

204

SALOME DANCING

I WAS SO ANXIOUS to get my first glimpse of America, my first sight of New York City, that I resented it when officials came on board and sent the passengers below deck to hunt for passports and other papers. Afterwards I felt glad of the interruption because, when I came on deck again, the liner was gliding smoothly past a group of giant buildings that thrust starkly from the water, sky-devouring, incredible—the City of New York! It was early morning. A light mist—a cloud in fact—lay on the water, and the towered magnificence of the city rose above the cloud.

It is a city that one could not imagine—the strength of it, the fantastic beauty, the inhuman quality that it has! It might be a city built in a single night by Djinns, or by Afreets: strange as those fabulous cities that sprang into being at the word of a magician, and vanished at a word into thin air, leaving only the bruit of them to perplex and astonish humanity.

I have seen this city crouching with its canyons under the stars: cold moonlight whitening one cliffside, shadow blackening the other. I have seen it a-glint with sunlight that does not warm the thought of it, as sunlight warms in one's mind the thought of other cities. It is born without father or mother. It reminds one of nothing save itself. But yes, at night when Fifth Avenue glitters with lights that wink and change colour like jewels I am reminded of a picture that I looked at many times in Paris, Gustav Moreau's painting of Salome dancing before Herod: Salome, her naked body scaled with jewels, beautifully inhuman, dancing snakelike, with bare feet soundless on the tessellated floor.

Salome danced for the head of a prophet—the head of one man on a lordly dish. For what dance-price does this city cover her naked splendour with jewels?

BLIZZARD

THERE IS A BLIZZARD outside. Such fine snow, like powder. I have never seen snow like that. Snow in Ireland falls in large slowly-descending flakes. I want to feel what this fine snow is like. It is a thing not to be missed! I hurry into an overcoat, and catch a bus which arrives with such an opportune suddenness that I have scarcely a chance to experience the blizzard. But I shall be changing buses presently. This is New York and I am going to the Metropolitan Museum of Art.

I am out in the street now.

The blizzard is terrible. It chokes one's eyes and ears and nose. It blots out the sky and the sky-reaching New York houses. It whirls itself and whirls me. I can scarcely stand. Presently a stalwart Irish policeman comes up. "Where do you want to go?" he enquires. "To the Museum," I shout.

"My God," he mutters, "she wants to go to the Museum on a day like this!" Then regaining his composure and his official manner, he says: "You're in the wrong place for the bus, Madam, you must cross here."

He grips me with a huge hand and shunts me, not unkindly, across the street to the place where I ought to be standing.

The Museum is warm and full of colour, remote from blizzards. But almost the first thing that catches my eye is Rodin's "Storm," the Storm-Spirit leaning out of a block of marble and blowing the hurricane from jubilant lips. White cold marble here, and cold white snow outside!

Memory comes to me of white hard sunlight and a warm room with closed windows and paneled walls. Rodin's studio in Paris. Maud Gonne had taken me and the poet Yeats to visit Rodin. Through streets of old Paris we came to a noble-looking mansion that had been a nunnery in the days of Richelieu, and still seemed worthy to house a king's daughter

206

as abbess. Our footsteps echoed all too loudly on the black and white marble pavement of the vestibule.

We entered a long room, high-ceilinged, paneled in wood, and lit by three French windows opening on a formal garden in the French style. Rodin was chiseling at a block of marble without a model of any kind. He was doing it, as we used to say when children, "out of his own head." So did Michelangelo chisel. Beneath his feet as he worked was a rich Oriental rug. Save for it the floor was bare and highly polished. Marble groups saw themselves reflected in it. Rodin was broad-shouldered, bronzed, bearded, and had the air of a man who spent a good deal of time in the open country. He received us graciously, and explained that the marble he was working at would be a rapture of Sainte Therese.

We gazed at it solemnly.

It looked like anything and nothing! I felt that it might shape itself into an Assyrian bull, or crouching faun—but scarcely into a saint! Yet who knows what form a spirit torn free of the body, delirious with ecstasy, would shape for itself?

The room was full of Rodin's sculptures. He led us from one to the other talking of them, and gesticulating as he talked. He invited us for a week-end at Meudon, and said finally:

"But you must see my pictures in the other room, my sketches. They are my great works."

The other room opened off the first. It was tall and paneled in wood. The sketches hung in a line from wall to wall. When I had contemplated two or three of them, I looked into the garden. Yeats went reverently from sketch to sketch. Maud Gonne joined me at the window. "There is one thing I know about Rodin," I said to her. "He is mad, brutally and sensually mad. Perhaps it will never break out, but it shows in those sketches." "It does break out," she said. "He has at times to be shut away. He is dangerous."

As we re-crossed the room where Rodin worked, a beautiful lady came in with her arms filled with red roses "for the Master."

We left him chiseling.

TAWNY LIONESS

I THINK MYSELF LUCKY that I have come to this country in the Autumn. I say Autumn rather than Fall because I like the sound of the word, Autumn. It is a country that would be beautiful at any time, and I find myself wishing that I could see it in the Spring. If I can see it only once, I choose to see it now, as I do, in the Fall. It seems to me that Autumn is the really austere season. Everything burns into a glory of colour and disappears. The green splendour of Spring degenerates into lushness, the leaves are tarnished with dust, but the flaming reds and yellows, the pale gold, the rose colour, the splendid purple-red of these trees will swirl with the wind, will have one splendid moment of sailing in the blueness of the sky, one moment of motion beyond anything that a leaf could dream of. The forests will stand bare, beautiful in bareness, against the sky. They will not be dead, they will not be even asleep heavily. They will be dreaming of Springtime, furtively pushing buds into symmetry, steadying the sap in their veins for the riot of Spring.

I have seen this country for the first time at an austere season. But it would always be austere because it is passionate. The earth burns with a colour of orange, with the colour of red, burns with a purple blackness, shows its ribs of stone, coloured, blanched, carved into fantasy. Its trees branch out with a delicate precision. Its cypress trees spring like flame. I love those cypress trees. In them the very passion of the earth springs upward, lifting itself with a song.

208

This country is a lioness, tawny, alert, passionate, austere, a beautiful, splendid—perhaps terrible—thing!

NEW CANAAN

THIS TRIM CONNECTICUT village with its wooden houses painted white, this village with snow upon its pathways and an elm tree here and there, does not remind me of an Irish village, but the people who live here, poets and writers, form a group that prompts memories of a group that I used to know in Ireland. I am a guest in the house of Padraic and Molly Colum. They used to have a house in Ireland to which poets, writers, patriots and other interesting people came. Once a week folk came to that house to sit by the fire: to sit on a long bench carved with Celtic symbols which made a handsome strangeness in the room. It wasn't overcomfortable to sit on, but the beauty of it lured adventurers. When Molly and Padraic set out for America there was grief in Dublin. Light no longer beckoned from that house; the lilac bush at the threshold might flower in Springtime as once when Roger Casement stopped to praise it, but no such poet-lover would halt by it again.

Here in New Canaan, Padraic and Molly have a two-story wooden house, painted white. It looks very trim and neat. So do the other two-story white-painted houses that sit here at discreet distances from each other. To the house of Padraic and Molly people drop in of an evening for talk with the casual joyousness with which people drop in for talk in Ireland. They are people whose names have sounded in my ears before their advent: Elinor Wylie, William Rose Benét, Van Wyck Brooks, and others tongued by fame already. The talk is of anything and everything. We persuaded Elinor

Wylie to recite poem on poem. Indeed, everyone recites poems: Padraic even reads some by James Stephens so that he may not be absent from the gathering. William Rose Benét has a poem about a whale that we make him say over on more nights than one, as we make Elinor Wylie say over that series of sonnets with the wild peach trees in it and the slant stone-walled field.

The beauty of Elinor Wylie, the strange arresting quality of the woman, delights me. She is like a note on a violin. She is like those cypress trees that thrust upward with such a singleness of purpose, such an intensity of passion, from the passionate earth of New England. She is like flame that sings. She moves and changes mood with the subtle grace of a panther—unpredictable, untamed.

Folk say that, pantherlike, she strikes out with claws at times, but I am sure the occasion warrants it. I shall always remember her with delight, I shall always be glad that at the beginning of my adventures in America I met with her. Salutation, Golden Panther, Lady of the Passionate Heart, austerely beautiful as the Land itself!

WOLVES

THESE NIGHTS IN the house of Molly and Padraic are almost like nights in Ireland. There is the same feeling of comradeship. Someone recites a poem—or tells of a mountain: ideas rise in one's mind like coloured bubbles; something that belongs to no one person, but is born of the group, flashes and flames and scintillates, sustained by each in turn as the feathered ball is sustained by the shuttle-bat.

Some nights ago the talk turned on folklore, ghosts, and strange happenings. Two people from Canada brought a Northern magic into the circle. They were man and wife, young and interesting: traveling for the first time in the United States. The man told of a strange experience. I set it down here:

"As a boy I lived in Canada in a little town that had a forest close to it. Wolves were in the forest. People talked about them. I had a great love for wolves, but the wolves stayed in the forest and only the hunters saw them. I wanted to see wolves—not one wolf only, but many wolves. They did come down one night into the town—to disturb a dead woman in the graveyard! It made a great stir in the place, for the woman had been murdered, and the man who murdered her broke jail that night and escaped. The wolves dug at the grave of the woman till they left the coffin-boards uncovered. There was a horror in the town about the wolves. But I hoped that they would come again. I stole into the graveyard and waited to see them. They did not come again for a year. Then they came again to the graveyard and dug the grave of the woman till the coffin-boards showed. It was on the anniversary of their first coming. The man who broke jail was never captured.

"It is a strange story, the story of the murder. The woman was young and much thought-of in the town. She was engaged to be married to the man who murdered her. He shot her in a fit of jealousy. Everyone said he had no cause, and it's likely he came to that opinion himself. When the wolves made a second devastation, the family of the woman put a vault of brick over her grave. The wolves never came again.

"Years after that, a wolf—and a strange wolf too—came close to me. I was about fifteen or sixteen years old and was earning a little money by taking care of a school. It was a small country school near a forest. I used to sweep it out, clean the blackboards and do anything else that needed to be done. I did it at night because I wanted to have the hours of the day to myself. There was a lonely feeling about the school. I always used to lock the doors when I went in there, and draw the curtains on the windows. I shut the door of every room as I went into it.

211

"One night I was rubbing chalk off the blackboard when I heard a noise in the corridor. Something was moving there and dragging a heavy chain. As it came nearer I could hear its footfalls—soft padding footfalls. It was an animal of some kind. I was glad the door was shut. When it came to the door, it stood there snuffing, and scratching with its claws. It was a big animal, too big to be a dog. I knew that it was a wolf. The door opened slowly until it was wide open. There was darkness outside—an empty darkness! Nothing stood in the doorway, and yet I knew that a giant wolf stood there. I could not bear to stay in the room. I knew that I would go mad if I did not take my strength in my hands and walk out through the door to the corridor. I walked out through the door and through the corridor. Nothing touched me. There was not a whimper, not a snuffle. I ran all the way home. In the morning I said to myself, 'I must go back to that school. The doors must be standing open.' Yet strangely, I had the key to the entrance door in my pocket. It was broad daylight when I went to the school. The entrance door was locked. The door into the schoolroom was locked. The key was on the inside of the door. I had to climb in through a window. That is the whole of the adventure."

But is that the whole of the adventure? I asked myself as I listened. Why did the wolves dig open only one grave, dig it open again on the anniversary, and never after that? Why did the phantom wolf come to the boy who loved wolves? Was it seeking help and sympathy? Did his desperate courage give courage to a creature hard beset and in need of help? Could one put the story of it together? Evidently, we are in touch with a werewolf. What is a werewolf? A werewolf is a person who loves wolves, who loves the strangeness of a forest at night, who wants to run with a pack—a joyous free company rejoicing in the same things as himself! At night many people have the power of freeing themselves from their physical bodies and going at will in whatever shape they choose. The werewolf chooses to leave his phys-

212

ical body sunk in deep slumber, chooses to slip away and run with the wolves. Unless he is a criminal he does not wish to kill people. He wants the feeling of power that the leader of a wolf-pack has, for when the man-wolf runs with a pack he is always the leader: he is something more than a wolf—he is super-wolf! The man who was jailed had perhaps in his lifetime never broken out to run with the wolves. But in some other life he knew how to get free, and when free he ran with the wolves. Cooped up in prison, expecting a death-sentence, regretting, perhaps, the murder of a woman he had loved, desperate for freedom, he slipped back to a forgotten usetude. He ran with the wolves that night. Leader of the pack, he led them to the churchyard. They dug the grave so that he could see the coffin-board. Perhaps he wanted to see the face of the dead woman.

That night he broke out of prison and escaped. On the anniversary of that night his mind went back to the agony of it. Again, perhaps unconsciously, he ran with the wolves. Again they dug the grave that he might see the coffin-boards.

Did that man find himself, finally, free of the body—deprived of what is often a cave of refuge—find himself naked in the astral world, afraid to go forward, fearful of condemnation from those who were strong enough to help him, helpers who might turn in horror from a werewolf? Did he seek help from someone who loved wolves—someone who understood how joyous it might be to run at night with the dark shadows of the forest trees; under the light of stars, under the benediction of the moon? Did he seek help from one young and courageous, strong enough to go forward, strong enough perhaps, to strike a chain from him—someone who would not condemn the super-wolf?

This is a story of Canada, Canada with its giant mountains, its dark forests, its slow-moving mysterious waters darkly-coloured or translucent as the emerald, its cold strange magic: strange with the strangeness of the North, cold as wind-bitten snowdrifts. Canada under the Northern Stars.

KALEIDOSCOPE

FROM DAY TO DAY life changes pattern with kaleidoscopic colour and completeness. Now it is a journey to the Middle West and lectures there: again it is a stay in Boston, the town so quaint and charming, the people so well worth knowing. I see Thoreau's lake with sleety skies above it and sleety ice upon it and a great quietness. I see Emerson's house; and the house of "Jo" in *Little Women;* Longfellow's house; and the house of Amy Lowell. I snatch time to lecture in Washington, D. C. I admire the monuments, the marble and the granite—alas, the cherry trees are not in blossom! Piloted by Molly Colum, I find myself motoring along roads in Connecticut—roads with glimpses of purple-red forests and heavy-pounding gray-green seas.

I am at Vassar College, Poughkeepsie, where I lecture. There is a carnival on the ice, a whirl of changing lights and graceful, swift-moving forms. A Vassar student who has forsworn the delight of skating in order to make me feel a welcome guest, is conducting me between the dark hemlock trees and the glinting joy-fires. She has the charm and distinction that seem to be common to all the students at Vassar. I am told that they are chosen because of their brilliant precollege careers: one might imagine they were chosen simply for their beauty. I feel as I look at them that here I acquaint myself with a type of girlhood purely American—a type as native to the country as its cypress trees, distinct and finely moulded as its flowers.

These slender gracious-moving damsels, dark-eyed for the most part and dusky-haired, have a shy grace as of woodland creatures, a sudden way of showing themselves for a moment as wild creatures have. I talked with one about forests, the joy of climbing trees, and the green light that comes through high-up branches. We exchanged views on the subject, and all at once she said: "I must show you what I carry about with me for luck." She took from her pocket a catkin, a

214

willow catkin, soft of fur and silvery: where the stalk had grown, it had what looked like eyes. I stroked it with my finger-tips and said: "I must show you what I carry about." I took from my pocket a stone that came from a quarry in Wales, a flint stone of a gold colour with a splash of ebon-black. It had been polished to a lovely smoothness, but not shaped or cut. It looked like a frog sitting meditative and happy. We introduced the mascots, and they well-wished each other.

Snow lies thick and stubborn on the streets of New York. I have persuaded Martha Beckwith to come to the city for a few days. I want her to meet some of my Irish friends who, on their part, are eager to acquaint themselves with the author of those books on Hawaiian folklore, the holder of the Vassar Chair in Mythology. The star of Russia is in the ascendant just now. Boris Artzybasheff is showing us New York. We are on our way to a Russian restaurant run by Cossack chieftains, and Boris Artzybasheff has promised to order the meal in Russian. The moon is high, and fortunately it is late for traffic. Boris Artzybasheff sits supreme in his own car: he is urging it from ice-hummock to ice-hummock as if it were a three-horse snow-sledge in the wilds of Siberia. We bump and say a prayer—and bump again! Boris Artzybasheff is talking of Russian poetry, and takes his hands off the wheel to gesticulate. We become momentarily more aware of the untrammeled scope of Russian genius. He has such a vivid magic that all at once the snow is Russian and the city is not New York. We only need a few wolves—and if a traffic cop catches sight of us he will play the part at once and devour our hopes of ever reaching that restaurant.

We do reach it, however, proclaimed far off by a prodigal-ity of sound and colour—a vivid sun among smaller satellites! The softly-moving foreign folk who thread their way from table to table carrying dishes are Cossacks such as I had hoped to see—slender, lithe, and golden-eyed. Cossacks such as these descended once on Dublin in horse-show week. Their horsemanship quenched the glory of Irish achievements, and cheering crowds watched them night after night ride madly through blazing straw-fires and balance themselves in pyramids that circus-riders never dared. They were even a greater joy when they went on foot through Dublin streets or leaped on the running board of tram-cars, catlike in their soft doeskin boots, their purple mantles swinging in the wind, a touch of fierceness in their furred head-gear matching their untamed eyes.

Boris Artzybasheff is illustrating my book, *The Wonder-Smith and His Son.* He wants to do pictures in colour, he feels that he could disport himself in colour because the book has djinns and pookas in it—but we have to be content with black and white! He shows me a wonderful Russian book with coloured pictures—and I lose my heart again to that country!

Bertha L. Gunterman, who accepted *The Wonder-Smith* for Messrs. Longmans, Green and Co. shares in this Russian and Celtic enthusiasm for Water-Spirits and Masters of Magic. She is eager to have as many illustrations as possible. I am glad of this. I have a fondness for *The Wonder-Smith;* perhaps because I did not invent the stories in the book. I gathered them through twenty-five years of searching, and put a thread of prose round them. Padraic Colum, himself a folklorist, was one of the first well-wishers of the saga: indeed my book owes to his good-offices its American debut. It is only the other day that Miss Gunterman said:

"Did Padraic Colum ever tell you of that afternoon at a library meeting in Atlantic City; how he and I forgot everything round us and finally everyone was gone but we two, and he still telling me the story of the Gubbaum as you had written it. That was my first introduction to the book, and made me hold on to the Ms. even after months had gone by."

Ireland and the Irish make a stir in New York. Joseph McGarrity is giving a party; a poet himself, a magic-master of words, he is eager to show Martha Beckwith some Irish poets and let her hear songs in Gaelic that she may compare them with songs she has listened to in her native Hawaii.

216

We hear songs in Gaelic, songs in the old traditional manner, we hear poets recite, we hear the lilt of the fiddle and the drone of war-pipes. Jest and repartee is bandied about, toasts are drunk, Irish dancers move with well-tutored nimble feet to such music as I have heard in Kerry, music such as Joseph McGarrity listened to in his native Tyrone, years ago, when he little thought that he would live to make name and fortune in the "New Island," live to be founder of the Clan-na-Gael, prompter of many a shrewd venture, supporter of every vital movement planned or accomplished in Ireland or America during half a lifetime. We left the house to the sound of song and music. I carry with me a confused memory of people that I have known or wished to know, of Shaw Desmond's witty sallies, of Joseph Campbell's poems, of Mary McSweeney's biting wisdom, of joyous voices and laughter.

I sit for a while in my hotel room, the lights darkened, un-eager for anything—not even for a new turn of the kaleidoscope. Outside, like the beat of mighty wings, like the swirl of flame, I am aware of the city: strong, triumphant, unscarred by the wounds that have humbled other cities, uplifting itself always more proudly, thrusting skyward, the while its talons clutch the solid rock. It seems to promise with every pulse-beat all the kingdoms of the world. The sound of it is like a song: a song that I have not listened to elsewhere, yet faintly threading through it I hear the lilt of an Irish fiddle, the far-off moan of the sea on lonely islands.

FRINGE OF DAY

I'VE HAD A GORGEOUS time in New York. I'm leaving it for California. I decide to spend my last afternoon with the river Hudson: the river that was the first thing in this immense new country that I could make friends with. There is snow everywhere. The river is frozen. I know there will be a splendid sunset on this last evening.

There is just one way to see the river: I must sit on the top of a bus. I put on my warmest clothes and get a seat well in front. The cold cuts like a knife but I am warmed by the colour in the sky: flame-rose. It is a clear cold blue sky, feathered with vermilion and rose. The Palisades are dark against it, but the river sheeted with ice throws back the light. Here and there the ice is broken, and pools of water are emerald-green; flame-rose, gold, and lapis lazuli. It is not like any world that I have known. The ice and snow have a quality that one would not get in Switzerland or in Ireland— a clear, hard brilliancy.

The sunset flames and burns: burns in the icy pools, and in the icy sky. The wind bites. The intense and painful cold grows keener and keener. It is a cold that burns. It penetrates mind and body, lifting me beyond myself. I am ice and flame like the river, like the sky. It is farewell. I have seen Salome dancing—perhaps for the last time.

JOURNEY

I CAREFULLY STUDIED train routes to California and selected the one I thought would have most desert scenery: to reassure myself, however, I consulted the conductor: "Scenery," he said, "you took the wrong road for it—there's nothing along this track but desert and you'll soon be tired of it." I do not tire of it. I like the thought of it spreading for miles and miles. I sit by the window eager to miss no sun-dwarfed tree, no sun-drenched, wind-defying desert blossom.

My Pullman car has a comfortable emptiness, but there are two people, man and wife, who seem bored with the scenery and the magazines. I know they want to talk to me,

218

and succeed in avoiding a conversation for a day or two. At last they break silence; they are missionaries who have spent many years in Africa. "Missionaries!" I think ruefully, "what have I let myself in for!" but I soon become interested when, learning that I am from Ireland, they begin to talk of Roger Casement:

"He lived in our part of Africa. We saw him often and had the highest opinion of him. What a pity he came to such an end!"

"What do you mean by 'such an end'?" I ask hotly. "Roger Casement died for his country. He lived for it too: there is scarcely a little village in Gaelic Ireland but can show you a school he has founded; a hall that he has given for folk to gather in; or a fishing-boat that he has helped a stranded fisherman to own. Roger Casement is well loved in Ireland!"

"He was ready to help in every good work in Africa," says the missionary woman.

"We are glad to have this news of him," says her husband. "We thought him a man that stood out among men. He was looked up to by everyone!"

These missionaries are evidently well-meaning folk. We talk of Africa and of Ireland in friendly fashion for such time as their journey keeps them on the train—and all the time the train is hurrying to Grand Canyon! I am stopping over to see it. Have I not prayed: *O Gods, Fates, whatever you are that throw the dice, let me not leave America without sight of the Grand Canyon!*

My heart rejoiced in the Grand Canyon but I have no words to tell of it—words in the face of that Marvel are dead leaves whirled on the wind; bat-cries in a measureless abyss!

A wind, icy-lipped, patrols the canyon edge. Crisp underfoot a powdering of snow whitens the ground but the incense cedars lift unburdened branches, darkly green against a sky blue as ice-water. People move about in twos and threes. I keep away from them. Waiting for a sunset, I try to make friends with two bobcats who are in a large open-air cage that has even a tree for each of them to climb. They

219

regard me with haughty indifference, and I go finally in search of the sunset. A girl comes hurriedly off a passing train. She stands beside me to watch the sunset. Something prompts me to say to her: "Do you like cats?" "I love them," she replies. "I'll show you some nice ones," say I.

We went to look at the bobcats, proudly royal, their tufted ears flat on their lean-jowled heads. Each one was almost as large as a small lynx. One of them came up to the rail and eyed us reluctantly. Without a moment's hesitation the girl put her hands through the bars, caught him on each side of his face and rubbed him affectionately and familiarly. "My God!" ejaculated the owner who was idling near by. "Those cats won't stand for that! Nobody has handled them." But the cat liked it. And stranger still, his mate, the she-cat, the supercilious and aloof one, sidled over and put a furry face close to the bars. The girl, a hand on either tawny cheek, rubbed it with enthusiasm and vigour. The prince and princess half decided to purr, but the owner, thanking heaven for a lucky escape, came up, and the cats retreated to their trees.

In the train once more, I shift from seat to seat in an effort to look out of both windows at once. The wide and splendid country flows past, it would seem of its own volition, as a river flows. I watch it till it is too dark to see anything.

There is so much music, such a sweet and subtle music, that I wake from a much-desired snatch of slumber in the rocking Pullman. I look out of the window: moonlight everywhere, moonlight so gracious that it actually seems to warm the earth it touches. Little trees, each perfectly shaped, each standing apart from its fellows, go past in patterns and processions. It is the Arizona desert—singing, making music to itself—and the desert is red: even in moonlight the earth of it is rose-red. I am glad that it stretches so endlessly.

COUNTRY BRONZED BY THE SUN

WHEN I THOUGHT OF AMERICA AS A CHILD I thought of the Falls of Niagara and of California—but chiefly of California! California was a wild country full of Indians who went about scalping people. Also it was full of cowboys and mining camps and gold-diggers and gold mines. As I grew up, this picture was somewhat modified. Bret Harte's stories and Joaquin Miller's poems, tales of giant trees and deserts, mingled in my mind. Mrs. Colbert, my California manager, had arranged a series of lectures for me in California. She expected to meet me in San Francisco, but by a piece of good luck I made a mistake about trains and landed in Pasadena, just as the sky was turning gold behind the snow-peaks of the mountains there. It was the month of March, early March, and I had come from Boston where snow-plows were busy on the streets. This California was a surprise. It had orange orchards and roses and palm trees. Exotic flowers made a spicy fragrance in the hotel gardens. Spanish musicians were playing Spanish love-songs. In the streets little children called to each other with soft musical voices: they called to each other in Spanish.

All day I had seen parched sand; treeless, grassless mountains—mountains sculptured by wind and storm—arid as bronze and coloured like copper when fire has touched it. This sudden-blossoming land seemed unreal. The languorous air, moist with the spray of fountains and heavy with the perfume of orange and jasmin, had a strangeness as if it had wandered in the cloistered gardens of some fabulous island.

I watched the sunset flame behind the snow-sheathed mountains—they, too, seemed unreal.

I knew as I steamed away in the early morning that never again would I see this California, this mirage which existed only for me—existed by virtue alone of journey, mishap, and illusion.

SAN FRANCISCO

MY MANAGER AND I are driving through the streets of San Francisco. I have entered the city twice, once from the Bay, by road, and again from Burlingame, really the best way to enter San Francisco. One approaches it by a wide avenue between rows of giant eucalyptus trees while fugitive, at bends and turns of the road, the city shows itself with an ever-new change of face. Journey's end—the city where one is aware of tall buildings jutting from a labyrinth of streets, of water widespread, and friendly encompassing hills.

As we drive, my manager, Jessica Colbert, says to me: "There are two people in San Francisco that I hope you will meet, one is Albert Bender who has given a whole roomful of Chinese porcelain, together with carved stones and ancient bronzes, to the Museum; the other is Noël Sullivan who has helped many writers and musicians, and has a great following. Each of these throws open a beautiful house and entertains royally; each of them is known among friends and admirers as: 'The Prince of San Francisco.'"

I think to myself as the car speeds along that I know a third Prince of San Francisco, one whom speedily I mean to see. It is Monsignor John Rogers, much loved in Ireland where he has given many artists their first, and in some cases, their only chance; well known in Gaelic districts as an enthusiast for the old music, the traditional singing; gratefully

222

remembered by the fighting men as an augmenter of their meagre and heavily burdened war-chest.

I found him at the Presbytery adjoining his Church of Saint Patrick. He was little changed since I had seen him last in Mia Cranwill's studio in Dublin: his silver hair, his kindly clear-cut ascetic face, his slender figure, his air of youthfulness unweighed upon by the years. We talked of Ireland: of artists he knew there, of patriots living and dead that were friends of his. He was eager to learn how the Monstrance that Mia Cranwill had in hand for his church was progressing: how had it looked when I saw it last?

He knew Mia Cranwill's studio as well as I did: the room with its enamelling-furnace, the sheets of metal: silver, red-gold, green-gold, platinum, and copper; the precious and semi-precious stones that one might handle, the designs pinned on the walls. The Monstrance had taken shape nobly when I saw it last. It stood splendid in gold and silver and platinum with rich enameled insets and that fine interlacing that only Mia Cranwill and centuries-dead Celtic metal-workers could accomplish. In her mind as she worked Mia Cranwill had a thought of the sixteen men executed in 1916 for the part they bore in the Irish Rising. Four symbols that in the *Book of Kells* represented the Four Evangelists: the Lion; the Eagle; the Bull; and the Angel-Man, were being fashioned, to represent the Evangelists indeed, but with a thought of these who had died for their country. An im-mense Irish crystal in the centre made a chamber for the Host. The enamel used in the symbols would be clear-set, that is without a backing—a thing difficult to do, but before I left some lovely pieces of it had emerged from the furnace.

Monsignor crossed in the sunshine to show me the church—well known to me by reputation—the church with its stained glass that had episodes from Irish sagas; its marble from Connemara; its hammered candlesticks from Mia Cranwill's studio. Much work was yet unfinished in the church: the floor was to have the ancient fish symbol; there were carved

223

designs to be thought of; there was marble and perhaps black oak to be brought from Ireland.

This day that I visit Monsignor is a day to mark with a red letter.

BOY WITH A FLUTE

As a child when I thought of how Oliver Goldsmith wandered through the length and breadth of France, just playing his flute and finding that people showered coins on him and begged him to sit by their hearth-fire and share their bread and cheese, I wished that I could be a boy with a flute and go all over Europe without needing a penny-piece. Now I am really doing something of this same thing. My manager, Jessica Colbert, gets engagements for me up and down the coast, and as she has no one else to manage at the moment she drives me in her Buick from place to place.

We go to out-of-the-way hamlets where a nobler-minded celebrity would not think of picking up a lecture. We go there just because the countryside is handsome, or has wild flowers in it, or a lake—or any good excuse for gladdening our eyes. When there is no lecture on hand we spend days among the giant trees, or make friends with Yosemite bears. Jessica does not need money. She has a private income: I am content to make little more than what pays her expenses and mine, provided I can see every day new mountains, new fields and byways, new colours on the wind-nurtured ridge of the world. We park by the roadside to watch San Antonio, ermined in snow, turn rose against a pale snow-glimmering sky at sundown: we lean on cliff-edges to peer into sacrosanct bays, untrodden because inaccessible. We have time to listen to the meadow lark; time to hail Shasta mirrored whitely in her tree-fringed lake.

Goldsmith must have felt anxious at times when he drew near a village and wondered what kind of musical taste the people had. He must have watched the faces of his audience (when he got a stubborn lot) and tried tune after tune. I am fast becoming a quick-change artist. I know that at all costs I must hold my audience. What Padraic Colum once called "dead knowledge" will not do it. My lectures must be living things born of the moment, taking form and substance from my listeners as well as from myself. At times I can picture beforehand the folk who will crowd the hall—but not always! I remember almost ruefully the care with which I got together a discourse on the Greek view of Fate; the Norse; and the Celtic one, to be delivered before the teaching Sisters of a convent school, and the students in the advanced classes —girls of eighteen or nineteen.

When I entered the hall, the nuns were seated, decorous and gracious, the girls of the advanced classes were there, but what else did I see to my consternation—row on row of the youngest pupils of the Academy: all seated in front, bright-eyed and expectant as young birds. The Sister conducting me said: "We had to let the children come in, they loved your fairy stories so much last time. They just had to come." On the platform, with those eager faces in front of me, I had to reconstruct my lecture even as I began to mouth the opening sentences.

What on earth did I say to those children last time? What stories could I grab by an ear and drag into what I fondly hoped was going to be a scholarly discourse? It took quick thinking, but I grabbed a few stories, and shunted out a few quotations and analyses. Everyone was pleased, including myself.

CHICAGO

YEARS AGO THERE DWELT in Chicago a man who cherished the dream that his city could be beautiful, throned at the verge of wide slow-lapsing waters. He made drawings and plans to this end, but while he lived no one took note. He died. The dream, left houseless, sought other fosterers—and found them! Proudly, by the waters, today Chicago lifts herself, embellished with marble: munificent in art-galleries and museums. Ugly buildings crowded the lakeshore. They were yanked out ruthlessly, and replaced by water-gardens and grassy stretches with trees and companies of iris. But the Lake, mindful of an ancient affront—or, perhaps, merely out of boredom or wilfulness—is banking sand upon its eastern shore, and thrusting sturdily against the stone barriers on its western one. Slowly the Lake is moving westward. It has heard, mayhap, of California!

I have a chance to make friends with the Lake, since I am here on a lecture-tour that will last some weeks. I shall see several places in the vicinity of Chicago, and already I have experienced "the infinite variety" of its weather. I am staying at a hotel on Michigan Boulevard, and when I have nothing else to do, I walk where I can see the skyscrapers that like giraffes or palm trees lift their heads above the meaner herd, the poorer jungle, of shops and warehouses. On my right hand, as I walk—if I walk far enough—there is a wide clear stretch of sky. Yesterday, walking far enough, I was aware that the sky was darkening with a fury as sudden and capricious as any that the Lake can boast of. I came to a standstill: and as I pondered the wisdom or foolishness of going on, or turning back, something—was it a sound unheard, a flash of invisible light—something made me turn towards the expanse of free sky.

At that moment the heavens opened, and in a splendour of ethereal light the storm-lords showed themselves: leaning upon the wind, lashing the stallions of the whirlwind. They

226

had the brightness of the sun and the cold strangeness of stars. Immense, in the immensity of the heavens, they moved with a speed so swift that it seemed motionless. Their out-blown hair was writhing flame. Their countenances annihilated space.

Unable to endure the vision, I turned and almost ran to my hotel. Before I reached it, the storm broke. Luckily I was close to a shop, and took refuge in the doorway. Never have I seen such a storm! The rain fell in torrents; in sheets; in waterspouts; so stricken through by lightning that it fell as molten silver, and again as burning gold. The sky, that was like a great hollow shield, flamed from horizon to horizon: rose-incandescent—incandescent green and amethyst, as the storm changed mood. I could have wished that storm to last, but all of a sudden the rain ceased and the veils were torn from the firmament.

I walked home through sunlit streets.

HALCYON

THIS COUNTRYSIDE HAS a subtle beauty of its own, stretching in sandy undulations to the sea with a peaked and isolated hill here and there and ranges of mountains in every direction. I have a small cottage near the Halcyon Temple. It is the guest-cottage belonging to John and Agnes Varian, and stands near their two-storied building. I have persuaded them to rent it to me and I am working hard at my book: *The Tangle-Coated Horse*. John Varian is working at an epic poem which deals with the birth of worlds and cosmogonies: it has Celtic gods with well-known names and gods that he has invented. Henry Cowell, the young and gifted composer, has written music for some of the more lyrical passages, and John Varian sings them with a convincing heartiness. He

227

has made a giant harp—but like the Harp of the Dagda no one can play on it. John Varian knows some folk that I know in Ireland. He is a cousin of Dora Sigerson, the poet.

The cottages that stand about in little gardens belong to the Temple Members who have come to build a new order here at the bidding of a Master—they live simply and have a simple and earnest faith in their mission.

This is a place where one can write. I have a grove of apricot trees close to my cottage, and all about me is John Varian's garden where things grow as they please. He works intermittently at his epic. One line of it delights me:

"The word Lir uttered in the void
Flowered into suns, and seeded into sleep."

SYMPHONY

The Tangle-Coated Horse is taking shape. Sometimes when I feel in a good mood I work through all the hours of the day, either in the porch of my cottage or in the eucalyptus grove that stands on a nearby hill. The tall straight-stemmed trees of that grove have delicately-contoured heads that move gently, their leaves a-shiver, when no wind is a-foot by my porch. If my eyes stray in idleness to them I am enmeshed: I snatch an orange and a few biscuits, a pencil and a supply of paper and journey to those trees—equipped till sundown.

When I have no inclination for work there are many things to do. I can pick my way across a thin stream, a walnut plantation, and a scantly grassed field to the great stretch of the Waller Franklin Seed Farm, that flat Halcyon valley laid out by the acre in delphiniums, poppies, hollyhocks, pansies, veronicas, and all the flowers one can think of. When I have pleased myself with the Oriental carpet spread

228

wide by the low-growing veronicas all intermingled purple, scarlet, rose and violet, I lose myself in a forest of delphiniums marvellously blue. Those flowers, whenever I lose myself among them, produce an effect hard to analyze. Austerely erect, they are at once an Advent—an Annunciation!

Is it because blueness of the sea is horizontal, and blueness of the sky has a flatness in it that this blueness spiring from the earth is so magical? Wild hyacinths are spilled like blue lake-water in Irish woods; lupines gladden with brocaded splendour the rounded hills and slant Halcyon meadows; star gentians and the chaliced gentians shame with blueness the pale glacial streams of Switzerland, the sun-bleached skies. Why should such a prodigality of blueness leave me unperturbed, and these delphiniums stir bewilderment in me? The answer lies, I am convinced, in the perpendicular position of the blue: it is more than unexpected—it is a reversal!

Rossetti makes use of such a reversal in that early water-colour which shows a meeting between Dante and Beatrice. With two attendant damsels Beatrice, *"that Ladye of whom my soul is enamoured,"* salutes the Poet, graciously unveiling her face. Behind her a sad-coloured wood with closely-woven branches shuts out the sky all in a dark greenness. Dante is robed in black, but a deep rich blue proclaims that Beatrice with her ladies has come from a lordlier dwelling-place than earth affords—a lovelier land. Her unveiled face, the blue she brings with her, should make a joyance, and would do so were it not for the wood which occupies the place of the sky and shows perpendicular lines for horizontal—greenness, for blue! This double reversal imparts to the picture a sense of tragedy and fate. One knows that only for a moment Beatrice will show her face—the wood will hide her. She will not come again.

A phalanx of rose-red hollyhocks beckons, but I go from the delphiniums to a world of salpiglossis with colours so varied and subtle that each flower is a new delight. They

229

have a fragrance faint and clinging, these flowers that are at one moment chalices turned sideways to spill sweetness, and the next a myriad butterflies about to take wing.

It is dusk when I return. The electric-light bulb is too large for my small cottage: it makes too harsh a brilliance. I sit in the twilight and listen to the frog orchestra in Mary Elliott's pond. It is a pond so artfully contrived by Mary Elliott and her husband that it seems to have occurred naturally. Mary Elliott has tamed the goldfish till they swim into her hand. The tree-frogs, emerald and amber, know her voice. She has even persuaded the silver-winged falcons to forget their wildness and alight on her lawn where rose bushes that have been allowed to grow ungoverned lean heavy with blossom.

If I had energy enough to go out tonight I might see the white owls that live in a cypress hedge not far off. I am too lazy to go out. I go to bed. The frog symphony continues.

FARDORACA

Do NOT SKIP this chapter: it is about a very noble cat. He limped into my garden one day at Halcyon, a starved black cat pursued by a mockingbird who swooped over him and tried to pluck hairs from his thin black coat. The mocking-bird felt that he was defending his young family which had dispersed itself among the trees of the garden. He swooped low over the cat, swooped beside him, swooped past him, plucking hairs and trying to wound him in the head. The cat did not defend himself. He limped painfully to a low-growing bush and took cover beneath it.

I said to myself. "This cat has come to the end of good living: a lethal-chamber is the place for this cat." Cautiously I approached the bush. The cat sat there. He did not ask for

230

food or drink though it was plain that he had starved for many a day. He did not try to propitiate me, he made no complaint of his misfortunes. He gathered a sombre dignity to himself and sat there. His eyes were amber with a yellow fire in them like the fire in a cairngorm stone. He regarded me as a temple-cat in Egypt may have regarded the populace. I offered him food. He approached it slowly, pausing to acknowledge the gift as an aristocrat should. He made a show of not caring whether he had anything to eat or not, then ate slowly and daintily. I understood that he was a cat in a million and invited him to my house. I gave him a Gaelic name, Fardoraca, and set about improving his condition.

He was indeed a Royal Cat, though his hair from long-continued want of food was coming out in patches, and he limped on three legs. He grew stronger day by day and in a while he marked out a territory for himself, a district to which he thought my house was entitled as demesne land. At the frontier of it he would sit like a sphinx with his eyes on the far horizon. The mockingbird saw that the cat had gotten a protector and devoted his attention to newcomers, but a young and insolent neighbor cat, golden and lithe as a panther, would come swaggering into Fardoraca's territory. Fardoraca, weak and wounded (one hind foot had been wrenched in a trap and two nails torn from it), knew that he could not drive out this cat, twice as young, twice as weighty, twice as big as himself, and he would steal away when he saw the yellow cat in the distance. I chased the intruder. But Fardoraca was nursing his strength for a fight, and I came by chance upon the first phase of it: the Combat of Wills. Fardoraca and the golden cat were seated opposite and close to each other, their front paws tucked under them, their bodies tense, the eyes of each cat fixed on the eyes of the other. Whichever cat made his opponent get up and move away would be victor in this contest. I watched for a long while. Not a hair of either cat stirred. Will in either was steadfast. The world had narrowed to this conflict. Suddenly the yellow cat shrank into himself as though some power that he had projected had given way. Very slowly and stiffly he rose to his feet, backing from Fardoraca, who did not move. Slowly and stiffly he backed from the presence of Fardoraca until he had gone some distance, then he turned tail and walked abjectly homeward.

One morning a week or two later, I heard the challenging voices of a cat-fight, and hurrying to a window saw the encounter. It was teeth and claws now between my cat and the golden aggressor. The cats had chosen a flat open space sparsely grassed and in full view of the window. When I first caught sight of them they were in the centre of the arena walking slowly round each other, jaws rigid and tails lashing—black panther, golden leopard! Suddenly with one accord they wheeled about and went to opposite corners of the grass-space. Shouting a war-cry, each one leaped forward. Midway they clashed like two knights in a tourney. Each was seeking a throat grip on the other. With the force of the impact both cats came to the ground and holding fast with their teeth brought their strong and terrible hind claws into action. The golden cat had the advantage here: his legs were longer and he had all his claws. Fardoraca, an old and experienced fighter, knew this and quickly disengaged himself. Again the cats circled each other, again they sought opposite ends of the arena—again they clashed! And so the fight went on. The yellow cat was larger and heavier, Fardoraca swifter and more high-spirited. He secured a grip, brought the yellow cat and himself to the ground, disengaged himself, challenged, and repeated the tactics. The fight was not equal between these two: the odds were against Fardoraca, and I thought of interfering, but the yellow cat seemed to be slacking a little and I decided to wait. Every now and then the cats walked round each other in the centre of the arena. They did not strike with tooth or claw—they growled and stared fiercely as they circled—it was an effort on the part of each to intimidate the other. After one of these encounters the golden cat did not take his place at the end of the arena. He hesitated and stood midway.

Fardoraca promptly sat down with his back turned. He was offering the enemy an honorable retreat. The golden leopard took a few paces in the homeward direction, then he hesitated, stopped, turned back and approached Fardoraca, who sat resolutely with his back turned. The golden cat, prodding himself to an act of valour, came close to Fardoraca and gave a defiant howl. Fardoraca sprang to his feet and the fight began all over again.

By this time I knew that my cat would win, he had courage enough to fight to the death: the other cat, heavier, younger, longer-legged, armed with all his claws and all his teeth, had not the will-power or the spirit of Fardoraca. Again and again they sought the throat grip, again and again they rolled on the ground and disengaged. At last the yellow cat had enough. He got slowly to his feet and did not seek his corner. Fardoraca sat down with his back turned to the enemy. He never looked around, he did not move an eyelash. The golden cat retreated a few paces, turned towards Fardoraca, faltered, and again retreated: very slowly and ceremoniously he moved away. Fardoraca maintained his magnanimous attitude, silent, unexultant, unthreatening.

When the golden one had gone I came out with praise and refreshment for Fardoraca, but he could not eat. He could not even maintain his victor attitude, he lay panting on the ground. All day he lay in the one spot too exhausted to move. Towards evening he recovered, and next day he took in a lot of new territory and sat sphinxlike on the edge of it. The golden one never dared thereafter to cross that territory.

Only one cat dared to cross that territory—the black cat that belonged to a neighbouring house. He came to beg for his breakfast. His owners were on a vacation and had asked me to feed their cat, leaving tins of salmon for that purpose. I explained matters to Fardoraca, and that champion actually resigned his position on my front porch and pretended not to hear the raucous demands of a person whom he must have regarded as a guttersnipe. He insisted however that

"Smuts" must not approach my house and begin meowing early in the morning. He must wait till ten o'clock, the time when I bestirred myself and got my own and Fardoraca's breakfast. At ten o'clock loud and unabated meows heralded the arrival of Smuts. I thought that worthy should eat breakfast in his own house, so at ten o'clock I opened a can of salmon and set out for my neighbour's house, followed by the two cats, Smuts hungry at my heels, Fardoraca, who had not yet had breakfast, following after Smuts as an honour-guard to me.

After two or three days of this, Smuts began to fancy himself a hero: so he shouldered up to Fardoraca and spat at him. Fardoraca took no notice. Next morning, as we walked in procession, the same thing occurred. I took notice. I caught the ill-mannered Smuts, held him close to Fardoraca, and said: "Box his ears!" but Fardoraca declined. Next morning, when Smuts halted the procession with a growl and a snarl, I boxed his ears myself. I boxed his ears with double vigour on the morning following. Fardoraca seemed to be concerned about the matter—grieved if anything! Next morning he refused to be rear-guard. The procession started without him—without him every day after that! He would not humiliate the guttersnipe.

I said at the beginning, "This chapter is about a very noble cat."

THE DUNES

How SHALL I describe the Dunes and the great sea-beach at Oceano? I have seen so many sunsets, vermilion, rose, or flame-magenta, turn those multitudinous drift-piles to purple valleys and moon-white eminences; to gray-green trackless expanses and velvet-black crevasses! My memory vivifies picture after picture so varied that no one picture suffices.

I think of the Dunes at my first coming when a silver mist concealed the sea and the outlying mountains, and I could only be aware of a nebulous immensity. The sand at my feet was golden-yellow, the wind had toothed it in patterns and ridges, there was neither beginning nor end to it. With a whimsical suddenness the mist lifted: long green waves foamed on the sea-edge. The golden Dune-peaks retreating in battalions gave out a light as though the sun, still sky-obscured, were burrowing underground as Kepera, the Sun of Egypt, burrowed from West to East to emerge triumphant at the dawn-hour. In that memory of the Dunes no living thing takes part: sky and sea and sand, wind-toothed or foam-washed, renew themselves in a mutation unassailably changeless.

I remember another morning with mist drifting here and there: the auto in which I sat, the only car on all those flat sands that reach southward for ten miles. The car slid along the very edge of the waves: little pattering sea-birds rose in flocks as it advanced and sped away to alight again on the foam-edge, but the large gulls, moved by some whim of chance or destiny, chose to follow the car, circling it in a cloud, coming so close to the wind-shield that at times I feared for their safety: all through that journeying on the wet sands they circled the car, abandoning it only at the timbered slip which lifts to the highway—a day it was of light that played with shadow, foam-patterned, cleft with bird-wings, whitened with wave-crests hurrying to lose themselves in the shallows: life and movement everywhere, rhythmic and tireless.

I remember the Dunes—all sun-slant, sea-going pelicans, and perturbed sea-swallows and sand-pipers—on a day when the folk of the Halcyon Temple gave a picnic. John and Agnes Varian took me in their car to the beach. Gavin Arthur was there and Ellen Janson, the poet, with her husband, Maurice Browne, and their small boy-child, Praxy. They had a car, and soon we all piled into it, and raced southward to where Point Sal showed purple-blue against a sparkling sea and a sun-filled sky. Ellen and Maurice told us (Gavin and myself) of hermits who lived in that sky-devastated wilderness. Lived year in and year out, for they had found hidden oases where willow trees grew and water could be had for the digging. Every hermit had an oasis all to himself. It was his territory. He needed to be about two miles away from his nearest neighbour. His little tent or cavelike shack must be securely hidden: it must not affront any eye, even his own. He must feel that he discovered it, stumbled upon it by accident so to speak, when he returned from a foray, seaward with net and clamfork, or landward to a lettuce field or carrot pleasaunce. The hermits, nurtured by Providence, could meditate on eternity, write verses, or in beneficent mood ray out blessings to the Universe. There was Hugo Seelig, the poet, who knew at what hour the evening primrose opened and in what place one might surprise the first blue gillia; there was George Blaise who went about long-haired and bearded, clad in sun-tan and a loin-cloth, George the Evangelist who had attained health and salvation in the Dunes and longed to spread the gospel of it to others: meat-eaters, dwellers in cities, their hide-shod feet ignorant of sand and sea-wave; there was Arthur the Navigator who had wonderful tales of the sea and could carve dragons in a stone, and construct galleons full-rigged with the aid of cord, some oil-soaked paper, and a piece of driftwood. "Some day," said Gavin, "we must go in search of them!" That day we were content to race along the sands and talk of them.

One last memory of the Dunes is of swirling water when the car raced against the incoming tide: the sea a sullen silver, the wet sands platinum colour, the sky, dove-gray, smouldering slowly to pale rose.

As I write, other colours, other memories flash upon me clamouring for recognition, changing and mingling with
236

each other as the wave-crest slips to the hollow. Perhaps this unstable medley is the truest memory one can have of a wilderness of waters wind-patterned, and patterning a wilderness of wind-strewn sand.

BLUE AND GOLD

PERHAPS IF I HAD a sense of direction this night-trip would not seem so strange and magical. Gavin Arthur is plunging through the dusk at random in his auto in an attempt to find the house of Maurice Browne and Ellen Janson. We started in the late afternoon encouraged by directions from all and sundry. We entangled ourselves in fields of blue lupine, dug ourselves out of sand-slides, and came suddenly upon the house of Hugo Seelig, an oasis in a sea of lupines—Hugo's town house when he absents himself from the Dunes. Hugo stood with bare feet deep in blossoms and issued fresh directions as to the whereabouts of the Janson house. As we were about to renew the pilgrimage, he said, "But first you must see a beautiful flower that I have." He led us among the lupines to where one solitary golden-splendid flower took the light. "I sowed many seeds," said Hugo, "but only this one broke ground: It is called the Blazing Star."

Night overtook us before we found the Janson house. The red lights of it suddenly flashed between tall eucalyptus trees: so black those trees are—lifting pointed heads among the stars! The two poets, Maurice Browne and Ellen Janson, sat in a room that was papered in gold and had one Japanese Dragon on the central wall. It was warm and exotic, this room, with the night sky so cold outside. Ellen recited poems, and Maurice read his play founded on the ballad *Annie of Lochroyan*. We talked for hours: as we came away a blue passion-flower drooped pale in the light from the open door.

237

Gavin touched it and said: "Today I have seen the Flower of the Sun and the Flower of the Moon—it is good omen, for I hope to make my home in Halcyon."

When Gavin speaks of Halcyon he thinks of the Oceano beach, that ten-mile stretch of water-purified sand with the sea brightening one edge, and a wilderness of drift-hills forming a barrier on the other. Between the hills there are reedy lakes and willow-grown oases: districts where hermits can live with two or three miles of elbow-room. South, North, and East are barren ranges of mountains. The sunlight races along the flat sands finding wet hollows to fill with gold, and little foam-pools that glint with silver: the wind races there making patterns that are like wave-patterns; birds and even insects leave their footprints.

Gavin has been camping in one oasis, sleeping under the stars, gathering driftwood for a fire—clam-hunting, forcing the wilderness to sustain him. He plans to live after this fashion for a while, and write a book.

LIFE ON THE DUNES

GAVIN ARTHUR AND Carl Beckstead are living in an oasis on the Dunes. They have not even a tent. They have a well, and something to set on a fire—something to boil water in or cook a fish if they catch one. They journey to my Halcyon cottage at times and tell me of their adventures. It makes me wish to be a hermit. As the next best thing I've come out to spend some hours on the Dunes. We sit on the sun-baked sand: Gavin, Carl, Hugo, and John Doggett. I am looking at cloud patterns, but the others are talking of Plato, of cosmic cycles, and recurrent periods of civilization, talking of Atlantis and the lost continent of Mu. We do not succeed in solving even one cosmic problem, and presently Hugo and

238

John go their ways each to his own territory. Carl stretches himself on the sand, and Gavin proposes that he and I set forth on a visitation to George the Evangelist and Arthur the Navigator.

First to George who is sitting cross-legged like a Hindu pundit. George, however, does not believe in Hindu religions. He is the one Christian in a scatterment of neo-pagans, and feels that he must expound to them his own particular gospel of salvation, at times opportune, or inopportune.

Today George is in a mood of elation as he sits cross-legged in front of his cabin. His little cabin is swept and garnished. It is always swept and garnished, the broom in the place where it ought to be, pots and pans scoured. He even has a cellar to keep his parched corn and home-made wine. His elation today is that of a saint who has snatched a brand from the burning. He has rescued Arthur the Navigator from Hugo Seelig and set his feet on the path of righteousness. "I told him," said George, "that he must build a house for himself. He must come away from Hugo's territory. He must leave the past behind him and begin a-fresh."

He had begun a-fresh in a little clearing in George's territory. We went to see his house. Arthur, up to this, had lived in a tent. When we arrived he was sitting hunched in the shelter of the tent, his manuscript book on his knee, a pen in his hand. He was making pen-and-ink drawings for the book. His shock of tow-coloured hair fell about his eyes. It had not been cut for some time. This was a sign of grace. According to the Gospel of George, hair is beneficent. It has an occult significance: Arthur is growing a scanty beard. He rose to do the honours of the house.

The house, about the size of a large dog-kennel, stands on four stout legs. It is a frame-work of wood thatched on the top and sides with stiff reed-grass. It was George who discovered and recommended the reed-grass. Arthur had cut it, carried it in bundles and fastened it securely to the frame-work. A short ladder leads to the door of the house. It has no windows and is only large enough for Arthur to crawl into and stretch himself full length. His meagre bed fills the whole of it. A narrow shelf runs round the walls within hand-reach. Arthur keeps his galleons, his little boats made of walnut-shell, his cordage, his oil paper, and his paints on this shelf. He carves everything with a jackknife. At times, when he finds a piece of driftwood that appeals to him, he will carve an Oriental face: the face of a Siamese dancer, or of a Chinese courtesan. He imparts a smoothness to these faces with infinite patience. Discerning people take possession of them. People who are less discerning try to order replicas. Arthur can do nothing on order. He just has to have the wood in his hand and an idea in his head. He never knows just what the idea is till the thing in his hand takes shape. I came away with some wonderful galleons shaped of walnut-shell, and a promise that when a bigger galleon appeared I would get a chance to secure it.

George hurries us back to his cabin. He is all on fire to show us a chart he has made to illustrate his discourses on food and the right way of living. A truly lavish expanse of paper, that chart, a thing calculated to hit and enthrall the eye a-far off! It is dominated by a fearful and terrible cow which George, borrowing Arthur's paint box, has painted in lively colours. Below it one reads:

"BEWARE! Milk is poison. Butter should not be eaten by the righteous; nor should cheese."

George is in a mood to amplify the gospel. Meat is no food for humanity: it entails the slaughter of cattle; but a cabbage has a life of its own, so has a carrot, the leafy and exuberant innocence of spinach is entitled to protection. Only what a tree or a plant discards of its own free-will can be used by those who would walk in the way of the just. A tree drops its ripe fruits; an ear of corn scatters its seeds; nuts burst their shells. Plainly a beneficent Providence provided these for Adam in Paradise and expected Adam's descendants to sustain themselves thereon.

240

We take farewell of George and cast a backward glance at him as he sits in the orthodox attitude with sunlight on and about him, a bronzed and bearded Master of Wisdom. How soon would Arthur weary of his new Guru? Hugo, a poet himself, lent always a kindly ear to the unbelievable tales of shipwrecks, palisaded cities, Tibetan Adepts, monsters of the deep, starvation rafts, and other episodes with which Arthur embroidered his conversation in moments when he relapsed from silence and a strict avoidance of spirituous liquors—would George, seeker and expounder of Truth, be as tolerant?

We think that George will lose his chela, but he can afford to. He has many disciples, folk who pilgrimage from cities, eager to make short trial of a new way of life. George allows his disciples grain of any kind. It must be cooked whole, and cooked on water. He allows them little cakes, unleavened cakes baked with flour ground in a handmill by George or by the disciples. Fruit he allows, dried or fresh; also nuts. For drink, water: for the hours of the day, meditation and work.

George is at once the exemplar and accomplishment of this regime. A drunkard and wastrel when first the word of the Lord overtook him—a sick man, marked for death—he is now young and strong and joyous. He can run on the sand-dunes like a deer. He can snatch up a log of driftwood that a younger man would not lift single-handed—snatch it up and run with it on his shoulder. As he works in his house or on his territory his voice can be heard in song.

In twos and threes folk come to follow his way of salvation. He makes them sleep under the stars and go about in loincloths. They stay until this way of life fills them with energy enough to revolt and depart in search of other foodstuffs.

LOTUS-BY-THE-SEA

*A*FTER ALL THOSE YEARS IT IS A STRANGE
thing to meet Kenneth Morris again and find him, as if no
years at all had passed, still the Palmerin, the eager young-
hearted poet-knight that he was long ago, when life for
most of us held the lure of Helen, and fire had not blackened
the ramparts of Troy.

Kenneth came with others from the Theosophical Headquarters at Point Loma to hear me lecture at La Jolla, but,
with the shyness that he used to have, he did not wait to
speak to me after the lecture. It was Carrie Coates, the irre-
pressible Carrie, the early friend of Æ, who rushed up to say
that Kenneth had stolen away, and would I not come to
Point Loma where they all lived and worked and meditated:
would I not come especially because Kenneth wanted so
much to see me?

The stronghold of Madame Tingley at Point Loma is
well guarded. Colonel Hinkle, his poet-wife, Marion Ethel
Hamilton, and myself had orders for admission. These were
scrutinized by wardens responsible for the approaches, and
scrutinized again when the tall iron entrance-gates had
closed behind us. I enjoyed those gates, and the guards in
uniform. I like cloistered places and my mind held a memory
of Irish pleasaunces shut in by ten-foot walls of hewn stone:
but the colonel, perhaps because the guards were not in military uniform, was impatient of the routine. Finally we were
ushered along a broad entrance avenue sentineled by date-
palms and flanked by blossoming trees. At the head of the

242

avenue, Carrie, with Bob Coates, her husband, and one or two others stood ready to extend a welcome by permission of Madame Tingley. They were laden with white flowers and green branches—all for us!

Kenneth wished to receive me in his own cottage, with the rose-garden about it that his hands had planted. In the room where his books displayed themselves so multitudinously, we talked of many things—and through the open door we saw the roses, multitudinously red and white. From the doorway the land sloped away to a grove of eucalyptus trees, beyond them was the sea, and over them brooded a sky pale and dream-stricken with heat. "It will hold a star, and show itself all violet-dusk at evening," said Kenneth.

When I had to go, Kenneth gave me a copy of his book: *The Fates of the Princes of Dyfed.* It has his version of one of the most splendid of the Welch hero-tales, and is, to my delight, a bulky volume. On the way home the sky was violet-dusk indeed, and the mountains were (to use an epithet of Kenneth's) "grape-dark" against the waning light.

That talk with Kenneth brought sharply to my wind the young green of beech-woods in Springtime, brought song of blackbird and thrush. Kenneth must be thinking of them too, for in a letter he asks: "What bird is it that sings Gaelic, as the blackbird sings Welch?"

In a little sheaf of illuminated poems which he has sent me, there are many where skylark, thrush, and ousel disport themselves; several in honour of Wales; and a number of translations from the Chinese: for Kenneth, among other accomplishments, is a skilled Chinese scholar. Indeed he has almost a Chinese way of proffering the beautiful handprinted pages, so richly coloured: "I take the liberty of sending you a few pages out of an old notebook, that a sick man once spent hours trying to illuminate; his efforts will make you wish to burn the pages as soon as possible; but please, if you are in the mood, read the translations first!"

The translations are a joy indeed, but I love best of all in the book, Kenneth's own poem:

243

Between the Hills of Quietude—
Gray, sun-kissed hills—and seas a-gleam
Iris and mysotis hued,
Griefless, the dead folk dream.

The meditative waves uprise,
O'ercurve, and fall away in foam:
These are the Priests that sacrifice
Where our dead have their home.

With genuflexions toward the shore,
In the wild Latin of the seas
They anthem forth forevermore
Their sonorous liturgies.

O'er the pearl-gray, slow-glittering deep
I saw five pelicans go by
Low-winging,—noiseless as deep sleep
Knowing the dead so nigh.

PENDRAGON

KENNETH HAS SENT me so many Chinese poems that I begin to think the garden about my cottage has lotus-ponds, and lute-players, and, perhaps, tree-peonies!

But Kenneth is not concerned with Chinese poems today. He is filled with indignation because he has received an advance proof of his folk-tale, *Shon ap Shencyn*, which I persuaded him to allow the use of in a series of stories for children. The proof was accompanied by a copy of the illustration in colour for the story. It depicted what the artist

244

thought a Welch peasant with a turn for song-making, and an ear for faery music, must look like. Kenneth had imaged a different figure. He sends me the illustration in a fine fury:

"For the love of Saint Michael and all Archangels—look what we have here!

Will you please summon up strength by meditation and look at this picture they propose to damn 'Shon ap Shencyn' with—

Oh goodness! Great Angus Oge!
Glory be to God!"

There is, however, news of a more heartening kind to be had. Miss Gunterman is considering *The Book of the Three Dragons,* Kenneth's version of one of the greatest of the Welch sagas. Miss Gunterman has a high opinion of the manuscript, and will take it if Messrs. Longmans, Green and Co. can see their way to publication. If they accept the book they will bring it out most worthily, with fine printing and Kenneth's choice of an artist.

I have by me a portion of the saga, and cannot resist putting down here, in mingled delight and despair, the description of Caer Harlech:

"They came to the gates of the caer, and there was neither porter nor dog to withstand or to welcome them. They went forward by court and corridor, voiceless places full of silence and sunlight. On the walls were pictured hangings: the mighty of old, scarlet-raimented, moving in the green-wood, moving by the shores of the sea. Proud faces, white as ivory, wary-eyed, looked out: as if, at a sudden spell a moment since, the power of motion had gone from them. Hall and court and corridor, all was mute as a song just ended; all empty, as if the singers had but now gone down to the sea."

The Queen of Sheba was not more humbled before Solomon!

245

YANG KUEI-FEI

KENNETH SENDS ME a play, one of several that he has written in verse. The central figure is Yang Kuei-fei, beautiful and death-fated; Yang Kuei-fei for whose sake fire took hold on the Imperial palaces, and the Emperor, Ming Huan, endured the hardship of desert places—Ming Huan who had lived so long with flowers and poets and beautiful women! Yang Kuei-fei endured the hardship of death—she had drawn it down on herself! Perhaps she chose it so, dying young she keeps about her the enchantment of her beauty—strange as Deirdre of the Sorrows, more ill-starred than Helen whose loveliness candelled Troy.

Kenneth has stressed the tragedy in his verse but I like best to remember Yang Kuei-fei in the peony garden on a day of those days when the world was under her feet. On that day the Emperor, Ming Huan, strolled in the garden of his palace. With him strolled some of his most favoured courtiers, gay as butterflies in their broidered coats. The garden had peonies everywhere: great tree-peonies firmly rooted in the earth, peonies nurtured in fantastic jars, peonies housed in marble and jade. Ming Huan had decided that year to take the tribute of the provinces in peonies. He was pleased with his choice. He said to his courtiers:

"This is the most beautiful garden in the world. Let Yang Kuei-fei be conducted hither, that the peonies may gladden the eyes of the loveliest lady under the sun." When she came, the Emperor said: "The garden lacks yet one thing—the greatest poet, and a worthy poem! Where is Li Po?"

Search was made in the palace and its precincts—without avail! There was a whispering among the courtiers, and one suggested that the wine-shops in the town might have news of him. Messengers hied to the wine-shops, snatched Li Po from a drunken reverie, doused him hurriedly to a semblance of sobriety, huddled him into court garments and presented him to the Emperor and the Lady Yang Kuei-fei. The most lovely lady in the world smiled on the greatest poet, but the Emperor said with a touch of indignation:

"Did I not give you in this palace-garden a house worthy of you? How is it that you frequent instead the taverns where beggars and horse-thieves guzzle in company?"

Li Po spread his hands in a deprecating gesture: He was not without gratitude. The Emperor's gift was as gold of the sun, but something had tarnished the gold. A certain court official, Kao Lishih, chief eunuch, to be exact, had turned a haughty face in the direction of Li Po; he had spoken with contumely; his shadow was sinister on the flower-framed walls and on the door-threshold.

"Enough!" cried Ming Huan. "You will make a poem in honour of the peonies; in honour of Yang Kuei-fei; and of this one moment. Yang Kuei-fei who can put music to words so fitly, will sing it—Kao Lishih will stand, as a slave might stand, and hold the ink as you write!"

Li Po made the poem; to the music of a jade flute, Yang Kuei-fei sang it; the peonies opened their tasseled hearts languorously, the goldfish swam under the porcelain bridges that were lazuli and emerald—no one dreamed that Ming Huan would be driven from the lordship of China; that Yang Kuei-fei would hear the soldiery clamour for her death; that Li Po would find peace at last under moonlit waters; that in distant barbaric lands an alien people and an alien culture would catch a shadowed splendour from the peony garden: be aware of a faint far-off fragrance.

The verse that Li Po made that day in the peony garden has come down to us: so has a poem made about Yang Kuei-fei by Po Chü-i, a later poet. In *The Everlasting Wrong* Po Chü-i tells us how Ming Huan, mourning for the woman he had been forced to abandon to the executioners, blind to the loss of his kingdom, sought among priests and sages and such persons as were skilled in magical arts for sight of Yang Kuei-fei, and at last by virtue of an invocation saw her —glittering for a moment—in a spiral of incense smoke: and thereafter was reconciled to what might chance—since he had learned, that in a country where death is not, she waited for him.

Kenneth knows these poems well, but has not worked on them as yet. I find however in the multicoloured booklet:

MING HUAN PASSES

Like meteors streaming through huge night
The golden cohorts hurry by;
Their broad halberds frosty white
Gleam in the awed moon's solemn light,
Their dim pennons fly
Like blown clouds moon-glazed at the rim.

And keen and throbbing up to a sky
Keen and throbbing, star by star,
The impatient silver war-fifes cry
Their mincing-dancing march—and die . .
And the noise dies a-far,
And Night sinks back to her broodings dim.

Did not Ming Huan, himself a poet and philosopher, have this word:

"When the string is pulled the marionette is alive—till the end of the play——

"Even such a puppet is man, till the dream-play ends— the play that we call life."

JADE SCEPTRE

KENNETH ON THE SUBJECT of cats endears himself by a phrase: "I love all—or most—cats for the sake of one, now with God."

But we are not on the subject of cats for the nonce.

Chinese poetry engages our attention. My comparatively ignorant admiration of Chinese poetry is being remodelled and at times minutely instructed. I ventured in a letter the opinion that since the rhythm and cadence of one language cannot be successfully imitated in another, the safest thing, perhaps, is a quite unadorned literal translation. Kenneth made haste to correct this misconception:

"Free verse! I hate it royally—Chinese verse is far more intricate even than any of our Celtic forms. Where in English verse we depend on the rhyme, which has to correspond in sound to one other syllable, in Chinese every syllable in the poem has to correspond in sound to some other: making a ripple of chiming music it's impossible to get an idea of from western poetry; but our Celtic alliterative forms perhaps come nearest. They can't be written, as you know, in English; at least I know the Welch ones can't, and judge the Irish by analogy. But the old French forms, with their chimes of ever-recurring rhyme and phrase, can; and they give some suggestion of the Chinese intricate music; that's why I have used them so often; and made forms of my own that follow their idea, such as:

There where the brook comes down in a white cascade
From the gloom of the pines to the green of the mountain
    glade,
Suddenly I was aware of the heart of Tao.
I was making a poem—simple thoughts enow—
And choosing the simplest words—and then, somehow,
There where the brook comes down in a white cascade,
At the sound of a lute blown down through the pine-tree
    shade
The spirit within me thrilled and stirred and swayed,
And suddenly I was aware of the heart of Tao.
First there was one came bent, with the sweat on his brow,
Bearing a load 'twixt low-hung bough and bough
There where the brook comes down in a white cascade;

249

And then, that one, unseen, in the wood who played;
And then—this one who heard, in the woodland strayed
Was suddenly wholly aware of the heart of Tao . . .

But suppose I had only striven and searched and prayed,
And not gone forth where my fancy led me—how
Should I so have suddenly come on the heart of Tao
There where the brook comes down in a white cascade?

The sound effect got by those chiming repetitions comes nearest to giving the music of the Chinese that I can think of; so you see how free verse must always fail to give any true representation of the true effect of a Chinese poem? Beyond the enjoyment of the picture, and the thought, there is always in them also, furthermore and in addition, an enjoyment akin to that we get from a ballade, a rondel, roundel, rondeau, villanelle or virrelai; a satisfaction in the sweet amazing *cleverness* of it all: something unlike any effect possible in free verse, even when it is the free verse of the one Master of it, Walt Whitman."

I am setting down here a poem or two—recensions, Kenneth would call them. He says: "The business of making these is difficult sometimes and interesting always. Chinese poems mean as much as you can see in them. There is no definite end to the meaning." And again he cautions: "There is a thing to remember about the Chinese script and its difference from alphabet-writing such as ours; and that is that it is magical. You read an English poem, and say, Yes, I have the meaning. Not so with a Chinese. You look at the glyphs, and grow interested. Your face lights up suddenly, and you say, Good Lord, does he say that? Startled you watch; and the images of beauty, humour, strangeness and delight come stealing out of the characters, and amaze you. No two translators seem to get a poem to mean the same thing. And I am content to make it mean whatever pictures I see come glimmering out of the characters; secure that if the result is beauty, and poetry, the poet meant it too."

WANG WEI BIDS FAREWELL TO HIS RELATIVE WANG SUN
WHO IS GOING INTO HIDING AMONG THE MOUNTAINS

Swing the gate to! The flames and glory wane
Where the red sun's gone down beyond the pass.
These brown hills will be rich again with grass
When green spring comes and birds sing through the rain;
But you must go. The times are bitter-souled,
And peace hides in the wilds. Swing the gate to!

And I, that watch you ride off down the lane,
Note how the mountains loom, vast, dark and cold
Where chill gray clouds and twilight hide the blue;
And know the sun will rise again, gold, gold;
And know the vale will glow green, green;—but you?
When shall I hear the voice I loved of old?
Wang Sun will come again—or never again?

HSÜ HUN, ON AN EARLY MORNING IN AUTUMN, THINKS IN
EXILE OF HIS NATIVE MOUNTAINS

Somewhere lute-music ceases: the last bars
Die through night's end; and somewhere the east grows gray;
And far up by the waning Milky Way
South-going wild geese brush against the stars;
And half-way skyward the dark tree-tops sway
To a slow somnambulent wind that rising, sighs
And whispers through the wu-tung leaves, and dies;
And in a long while dewdrops turn gray jade;
And in a long, long while the last stars fade
And the clouds slowly whiten—How the skies
Would flame with dawn, and day grow golden bright,
Were this a land I yet should see—gone blind—
And these dark trees those mountains crowned with light
Where no leaf falls this Autumn, day or night,
But my heart swells like waves 'neath a great wind!

251

THE DESERTED CITY OF STONE
BY LIU YÜ-HSI

Forever the unchanging hills look down
And see no motion, year by year
In this Stone Ghost that once was a town
And day and night the sea draws near
And fumbles at the gates; and then
Listening awhile—and naught to hear—
And muttering, stealthily ebbs again.
And birds drift by, crying in their flight;
But never are heard voices of men.
And the slow moon steals night by night
Up o'er Huai Stream, and slowly o'er
The battlements, and sheds cold light
Along mute streets feet pass no more;
And slowly in her deep mood goes down
And the light goes from river and shore
And this Stone Ghost that once was a town.

And here is one by Li Po, the poet whom Kenneth loves in especial.

THE HILLS OF KINLING

Here's a song for Kinling, and three libations poured
For the six olden kingdoms that rose and fell therein:
The rites and pomps and pleasaunces—the sceptre and the
    sword—
The high thrones overthrown—the splendour and the sin!
A song, and three libations poured to the worlds gone down
'Neath the blue hills of Kinling, and the old, old town!

There the Lords of Tsin built their faery dreams in stone,
And their silks and jades and sapphires took the glory of the
    morn;
The ruins of their dreams are laid low and nettle-grown,
And their pride's with Kiang waters to the dim seas borne;

But the hues of silks and sapphires and their gleam still glow
On the blue hills of Kinling when the sun sinks low.

And ah, the gardens that the kings of Wu made of old,
Where the peonies hung bloom-globes opulent with dream,
And Autumn levied armies of chrysanthemums, all gold;
And Spring snowed its plum-blooms and sweetness on the
  stream!
Fallen is all their loveliness, as the plum-blooms fall;
But the blue hills of Kinling have dwindled not at all!

I have been trying to persuade Kenneth that his Chinese recensions and the poems he has written in his own person deserve to come out in book form, but he says he prefers to be discovered—if discovered at all—a hundred years or so after his death. Meanwhile I hope that the poems are not fluttering about on sheets of paper and losing themselves! Headquarters at Point Loma surely must have copies in a place of safety. They have not needed a hundred years to discover the poet in their midst.

MAESTRO

OUT UPON MOCKINGBIRDS! This garden with its ubiquitous shade-devouring sunshine is infested with them! They don't sing. They don't maintain a decent silence, or any sort of restful quietude. The young birds have left the nests, and the father bird, the great Maestro, the rival of the nightingale, has constituted himself Guardian-in-chief, Inquisitor, Warrior-without-let-up—and half a dozen other things. His hunting cry, *"Che" "Che" "Che,"* rings all day long; his savage swoops on stray dogs, unwary cats, and unarmed humans continue without intermission. It is going to be like this till the young birds are strong enough to fly South with their parents. Who would ever wish to have mockingbirds in a Halcyon garden?

To hear a mockingbird sing, one must go South in the days of his courtship. His song in the darkness before dawn is passionate and strange with a strangeness of palm trees and lemon orchards; shot through with the colour of roses; heavy with spices that no cloister of the nightingale is acquainted with.

I have heard mockingbirds in the South, and when these pestiferous gangsters go farther a-field I shall think kindly of mockingbirds. I shall remember that an English enthusiast once sent nightingales to a spot in America judged likely to make them forget their homeland. They were kept in cages till their custodian could be sure of the forgetting. He judged that song would be a token of forgetfulness and reconciliation. At last the nightingales sang. The mockingbirds of the locality took up good listening-posts and repeated the song. A cablegram summoned the English enthusiast: *"Come quickly to hear the nightingales."*

He came quickly. The nightingales had fallen dumb, and did not again break silence, but the mockingbirds, faultlessly efficient, rehearsed the song.

This outburst is written to an accompaniment of *"Che"* *"Che"* *"Che,"* and is provoked by Kenneth's enthusiasm about mockingbirds. They sing at Point Loma and come North to build nests. In Halcyon there is a little owl that cries in the night: a soft melancholy sound. I love to hear it. This owl, and the frogs, make the music of nighttime at Halcyon: but hark to Kenneth who has lain awake at Point Loma!

> *"When afar the forest 's stirred*
> *With new silence, and unheard*
> *Is that high Mage Mockingbird*
> *Whose glug-glug and treeo-tree*
> *Pricked groves, hillsides, moon and sea*

254

> *With sweet pain and mystery*
> *All night long; and beryl-dight*
> *And silvered Nuncios of the Light*
> *Camp along the coast of Night,*
> *And soon with linnets' glad to-do*
> *And quail's chuckling talk, and coo*
> *Of mourning-doves, morn's thridded through,*
> *Let naught rise in the heart to stay*
> *The Dawn there, or lure thought away*
> *From the Brotherhood of Day."*

I wish I could hear the birds that make music at the coming of the first light in Ireland, and again when dusk falls—such a violing and fluting of blackbird, thrush, and robin, mingled so often with the sound of moving water: water that sings to itself over stony reaches or among rushes and water-weeds—little streams that hear the soft-feathered owls calling softly to each other, that know to what meadow the skylark sinks when he has poured out those golden notes of his, prodigal-fashion, in the face of the ever-prodigal sun.

THE DESERT HAS JOSHUA TREES

WITH THE SUDDENNESS OF SPRING'S FIRST swallows, Ansel and Virginia Adams have arrived. There is a blueness of lupines in all the meadows, but their talk is of the desert and Joshua Trees. They are on their way to Taos and Santa Fe where Ansel is to make a series of photographs for a book that Mary Austin is bringing out. They are driving half across the continent in an open car. Mountain-peaks, desert-immensities—the Grand Canyon itself—lie as it were by the roadway. They urge me to be of their company. Lectures can be had in Santa Fe, in Albuquerque, in Taos, in a dozen places, mayhap. The mountains will have snow upon them, and the desert will have blossoms all cunningly set in colour harmonies. I decide to go with Ansel and Virginia.

Fardoraca is my chief concern. A friend who lives near, and has a sense of his merit, offers to feed him; receive him as honoured guest at hearth and home, and give him freedom to come and go as he pleases during all the hours of the day and night. He could visit my cottage and take note of the fact that no stranger occupied it—an omen of my return! He could—but I am sorry to leave him! Some good days have come to an end for both of us.

THE OPEN ROAD

It CERTAINLY IS a fine adventure, all in the Spring of the year! Sunshine and flowers in California: snow on the divide, miles of snow glittering blue-white; after that, forests of small trees, beautiful little trees growing each apart from its fellows. Miles of desert. Then New Mexico, a faery country all rose and violet, showing itself miraculous and sudden as a mirage. There is one snow-covered mountain, double-peaked like Shasta. Ansel Adams knows it—the Sacred Mountain of the Navajos.

Navajo Indians ride on horses: everyone in this country of rose and amethyst rides on a pinto, a buckskin, or a golden-brown horse. I mean to ride on buckskin, mule, burro, camel, or llama—even a unicorn if the country possesses one! This stone-pure mountain-guarded land is one after my own heart: it reminds me of the stony reaches of Western Ireland—of Connemara where the white horses of faeryland thrust untameable heads from wine-dark shadow-encompassed mountain tarns. I shall love this country. Ansel and Virginia tell me of Indian dances: of warriors, saints, and magicians; of songs the Indians sing, of the sound of a flute heard on lonely mountains, of voices that mock or invite, of bears that are not bears, and deer that elude the hunters. This is a country that possesses, like Ireland, the ancient magic. I shall stay in this country as long as it will let me stay.

TURQUOISE MOUNTAIN

I DID NOT KNOW its Indian name when I saw it first. I did not know that the Navajo Indians revered it as one of the four mountains that are the Pillars of Heaven—the Red, Black, White, and Turquoise Pillars of Heaven! But at first sight I knew that it was a Sacred Mountain. I saw it from the window of a railway carriage as the train from the East bucked and snorted on its way to California. Sunset was colouring the sky. The mountain stood in the pathway of the sun. It was joyous and beneficent. It reached out in a greeting that seemed almost a greeting to myself.

"What mountain is this?" I asked a neighbour.

"It is Mount Taylor," was the reply.

Mount Taylor—the name meant nothing to me! I watched the mountain as long as I had sight of it. The sun flushed it with purple and rose, with ruby and violet, and the sky hung over it in a mist of rose and azure long after the sun had gone.

It blossomed in my mind for months and years till one day against a sunset in a land of rose and amethyst I saw it, snow-crowned, far off as I motored with two friends to New Mexico.

"What name has yonder mountain?" I asked, "the mountain double-peaked like Shasta—like Everest, the Goddess-Mother of the World?"

"That is Turquoise Mountain, the Sacred Mountain of the Navajos."

Its Indian name is *Tsodsichl.*

HOUSE OF THE MULTICOLOURED COCKS

MABEL LUHAN'S HOUSE sprawls on a plateau: below it lies Taos with its two hotels and its tiny plaza, beyond it the desert stretches to the foot of the Rockies. An irrigation ditch, a New Mexican moat crossed by bridges and gang-planks, separates it from the slanting fields and the entrance-road.

Girdled by this swanless water-fastness, the house progresses leisurely and fantastically from patio to patio, from court-yard to courtyard, from the tower at the North end to the tower at the South. Inside it has earthen floors; adobe walls; and ceilings upheld by massive pine trunks stripped of their bark and latticed each to each by criss-cross pine branches, also stripped of bark and in some instances stained in rain-bow colours. The central court has many dovecotes. Pigeons: blue, gray, and silver make a whirr of wings and strut cooing on the cobble pavement where, all the Summer, hollyhocks, self-sown, thrust to the sunlight and make a gladness in the keen air. But the great and splendid Presence is Taos Moun-tain. One can see it as one walks from courtyard to court-yard. I greet it as I walk: morning; noon; and night.

Life is primitive here. We have oil lamps and candle-light. The telephone is safely hidden in the kitchen. How did I come to be here? I had no thought of it when my friends, Ansel and Virginia Adams, proposed that I motor with them from Halcyon to Santa Fe in New Mexico where they had the loan of Mary Austin's house. I lectured in Santa Fe. Mabel Luhan and her Indian husband, Tony, came to the lecture, and as a result I find myself Mabel's guest. She has a houseful of guests: Ansel and Virginia are here, so is Georgia O'Keefe, the noted artist, and Rebecca Strand who works so cleverly in pastel. John Marin, whose fame is noised about America and beyond it, is here too. He is the slave at present of the Sacred Mountain, Taos. Every day he sets forth with paper, paint, and pencils, vowing that this time he will escape, he will not be captured by Taos Mountain. He comes back and somewhat shame-facedly ex-hibits another study of Taos. "I just looked at it in passing," he declares, "and the Mountain held me!"

Mabel Luhan makes me think of Egypt—an archaic Egypt. Her face, with the dark hair cut straight on either side, might have been the face modeled in that statue of the Fourth Dynasty Princess who sits by her Egyptian husband in all the dignity that can be carved into wood. Tony, it is

259

true, does not resemble the Prince: but given an Egyptian head-dress he might pass for one of the aquiline-nosed Pharaohs. These two people can sit silent longer than anyone else that I know—it is, perhaps, an Egyptian and an Indian gift.

Across Mabel's alfalfa meadow one glimpses a ring of adobe houses, each with its patio and orchard, each one quite unlike its fellows, all of them joyous with window-paint and the coloured clay that Indians use instead of lime-wash. These are Mabel's guest-houses: designed by her, and enriched with the old Mexican furniture, the carved wood, and the santos that she loves to collect. They have many books, for Mabel's library overflows constantly and from time to time she ousts a cart-load of detective stories and best sellers—a gift to the Taos Reading Room! More serious-minded volumes display themselves permanently on shelf after shelf, in bookcase after bookcase, worthily hostelled in "Los Gallos, the House of the Cocks."

People come and go in this house: writers from New York, passing through to the West; Indian chiefs, stately and taciturn; householders from Taos and Santa Fe. Spud Johnson, poet and critic, comes here on evenings from his own quaint cottage where so many pottery horses remind one that he edits the magazine, *Laughing Horse*. The Honourable Dorothy Brett "breezes" in (to use her own expression). That word exactly describes her entry. She makes a commotion in a room. She arrives like a mountain-nurtured wind and swirls joyously into the conversation, turning and changing the drift of the talk. It is a pungent wind, too, for she has inherited the wit of her witty father, Viscount Esher. Her voice is English, but she has the long pale face, the fair hair, and the sparse tall figure of a Scotswoman: she is, indeed, of Scottish and French descent, and proud of it. The first time that I laid eyes on her, she was wearing a black velvet jacket and the nearest approach to a Scotch kilt that she could assume: Scotch wool it was, woven in Scotland, in a tartan that she has an ancestral right to wear. As a general

ELLA YOUNG ON JOCKO

rule, however, she appears in baggy crimson trousers tucked into riding-boots, a cambric shirt, and a waistcoat made of calfskin, with the hairy side out. She sends to Brittany for the trousers, the kind that Breton sailors wear. They are dyed a very special crimson—perhaps with native dyes.

Her advent that first evening marked a cessation of hostilities, or at least a truce. Every now and then Mabel issues an ultimatum: Brett must not set foot again in the house of many courtyards! Brett makes a reply suitable to the occasion and stays away. In a little while, however, Mabel says: "Taos grows dull—after all there is only one Brett!" and Brett says: "That house with a thousand books, and people from everywhere, is not a house to cold-shoulder." She condescends to return, and is welcomed as if nothing untoward had ever happened.

Some time in the morning a cock crows; loud enough almost to waken the cocks that range themselves in a long line on the roof-edge of Mabel's house: cocks that are yellow, and green, and scarlet, and rose-violet. Pottery cocks from China. Indian servants are a-stir at dawn, and go about soft-footed, but Mabel's guests, for the most part, lie a-bed in the mornings. They see each other at lunch time.

On days when Mabel does not sit up in bed, propped with pillows, and spend the sun-climbing hours in writing chapters of her memoirs, she sallies from the house to ride on the nearby desert. She has a snow-white horse and keeps him at a sharp trot all the time, while two fawn-coloured Great Danes do their best, by example and loud-mouthed remonstrance, to urge the pace to a gallop. Tony rides a black stallion. When I go with them, Mabel lends me a milk-white and chestnut pinto with sapphire-blue eyes. He is quite charming, and very rascally. We like each other.

Dorothy Brett, at times, rides down from Lobo Mountain. She has invited me to stay with her on the ranch, high up there, that belongs to Frieda and D. H. Lawrence. She is taking care of it for them. She lives there, day in and day out, content with her books, her canvases, and the horses, until

261

snow drives her to an apartment in Taos. Living with clouds, tall pines, and hawks, for company, she paints her pictures of Indians; mountains; and horses.

I am eager to acquaint myself further with Indians, Mountains, and Horses.

BROTHERS OF THE SUN

THE TAOS INDIANS today have ceremonial races to hearten and strengthen the sun. Old men, young men, even small boys, take part in the race. I can see the racers standing about. They have beautiful feathered head-dresses and their bodies are painted in rainbow colours. Wound about their waists they have lengths of silk. Bright pure colours. The old women are sitting in seats of honour, the young girls are standing in groups. They are slender and shy as fawns. Their skirts are of bright-coloured cotton, apple-green, rose-magenta, blue, purple, orange—every colour. On their feet are doeskin boots that come up almost to the knee, white doeskin pleated over at the top. They are wearing black silk Spanish shawls embroidered in black. They will cry little cries of encouragement when the racers pass them. Very old men are standing in groups all along the race-course. They have green boughs in their hands and they will strike lightly at the racers as they pass, calling out "Oom-pah, oom-pah."

Now the race is about to begin. The Pueblo of the North is racing against the Pueblo of the South. At each end of the race-course the racers are grouped. They start. One racer from the North Pueblo darts forward. At the same moment a racer from the South Pueblo darts forward. They will pass each other almost midway. The racer who first reaches the goal at either end has won a victory for his side. Racer after

262

racer, sometimes tall young men, sometimes small boys, jewelled in feather and paint like hummingbirds. Excitement grows. The Pueblo of the North is winning! It has not won in the races for several years. The racers from the North run with redoubled vigour. Their comrades shout to them. The old men fan them with leaves.

Yes, the Pueblo of the North is winning. The last racers have reached the goal. Shouts now for the Pueblo of the North.

The winners form into a procession. Behind them the Pueblo of the South forms into a procession. The victorious racers are silent at the head of the procession, which will march round the Pueblo of the North and the Pueblo of the South, going first round the Pueblo of the South. The defeated racers of the Pueblo of the South are singing and laughing and shouting congratulations to the victors. As the procession passes among the houses, women shower fruit and flowers and sweet-meats. The young men catch them as they pass.

Now they are going around the Pueblo of the North with shouts of acclamation. Everybody is delighted. And gayest of all seem to be the losers.

These races hearten the sun. Every Taos Indian knows that. Did it not happen a year ago that the sun was gloomy and hid his face day after day? Hard gray skies, no sun, no warmth. Something must be done. Something unusual must be done, for no usual ceremonies in the usual heartening of the sun had been omitted. The priests and wise magicians of the tribe were consulted. They remembered a ceremony that their ancestors practiced, fanning the sun-fire.

One of my friends saw the dance. She told me that a great fire was kindled in the centre plaza. Round it the young maidens circled holding their shawls as if to shelter the flame. In an opposite direction, young men started dancing and making gestures to hearten the sun.

Next day the sun came out.

263

THE BUFFALO DANCE

MABEL, TONY AND I have been invited by the Governor of San Ildefonso Pueblo to see the Buffalo Dance. It doesn't seem a very promising day. The wind is already twirling eddies of dust here and there in the desert. The wind is a potency in these parts. It can lift columns of sand and gravel almost sky-high. I begin to wonder what the Plaza at San Ildefonso will be like. Every Indian plaza has a plentiness of sand and grass and dust.

It becomes evident as we drive toward the Plaza that the wind is strengthening. With a freakiness that seems malicious, it dashes handfuls of gravel and dust against the auto's windows. We have to keep them shut. When we reach San Ildefonso we find that the wind has preceded us. It is in the Plaza. It seems now to be indignant as well as malicious. Possibly it has taken note of the number of autos drawn up in a circle and full of "Whites" who have come to look at the dance. They are shining like black beetles, those autos. The wind spirals over and about them and slaps every "White" who ventures to put a head out of window with a handful of gravel in the face. We run for the shelter of the Governor's house, the wind slapping dust and gravel even through thick veils.

It is very quiet in the Governor's house. The Governor is there and some other Indian dignitaries. We sit down solemnly. The dance is supposed to begin at ten o'clock. It is past ten now. No dance could begin with a wind like that. Such a demon of a wind! The Governor and the dignitaries are unperturbed. An hour passes. The wind is still potent and vicious. Presently the Governor sends a messenger to the kiva where the Indians are in full regalia for the dance. In a little while an Indian from the kiva enters. He is wearing jewels, paint and ceremonial dress. The Governor says to him in English, in deference to his guests, "When is the dance going to begin?" The Indian replies, "We are waiting

264

for the wind to stop." "That is good," says the Governor. The Indian saluted and departed. We sat again in silence for about an hour. I thought I knew what the Indians were doing in the kiva—the ceremonial Indians—they were waiting for the wind to stop. That meant a promise from the wind. They had been asking the wind to stop, and the wind had promised to stop.

But the wind was dancing a war-dance of its own in the Plaza and in the desert. In the midst of this turmoil the warrior entered again. Saluting the Governor, he said, "The dance will begin." We made a hurried dash for our auto, but the wind was still in the Plaza and it slapped us each separately in the face with unabated virulence. How could the dance possibly begin? Every "White" sat in his auto with closed windows, but the Governor took his place in the Plaza. The Indian women and girls in gala costume were sitting on roofs and balconies. The children came out. They had every colour of brightness in their garments. In fact, the Plaza flowered with colour. The chants began. The young men were coming from the kiva. They lined up in the centre of the Plaza for the dance. And at that moment the wind took itself out of the Plaza. It didn't go very far. It played about in the desert, energetic and freakish. It stayed in the desert till the intermission of the dance when the young men retired to the kiva. Then it returned to the Plaza, slapped every "White" in the face until they sought refuge in their autos with closed windows. When the dancers lined up again in the Plaza, buffalos and warriors, the wind leaped over the low wall and played about in the desert. It returned to slap every "White" in the face when the dance was ended. The "Whites" were greatly impressed. I heard them muttering things about nature-magic and strange coincidence.

I went home thinking of a tale I had heard about this same Pueblo from a woman who was a trusted friend of the Indians. After the great ceremonial dance for rain had ended —The May Dance—she chanced upon this Pueblo and found the young men and maidens still dancing. She said to an

Indian who stood near her: "Why is the dance continued?" "We are dancing for a rain," he replied. "But the rain-dance is over. It ended yesterday." "Not for us," said the old chief. "We must dance till we get the ceremonial rain." "I thought you always got it at the end of the fourth day." "We always do," said the Indian. "But this time the young men of Taos are dancing against us. They'll keep back the rain." "What then will you do?" said my friend. "We must dance till we get it," said the Indian. "Or maybe the Governor will send for the young men of Taos and settle the complaint they have against us." They got the rain. But whether it was extra dancing, or a peace treaty with the Taos dancers, is a thing that I don't know.

The Taos Indians are wise in magic arts. They are powerful and fortunate. They have now three real live buffalos, well-known rain-mascots. One of the National Parks had too many buffalos. It wanted kind homes for them and offered three to the Taos Indians. They received them with heartfelt gratitude. Now they would be doubly sure of rain. And if by chance a buffalo died, the head priest would have a ceremonial buffalo robe. Certainly they had rain, a double amount: all that the Rain-Mother, the Sacred Lake, the Mother of Waters had promised them. And an extra lot on account of the buffalos.

I wanted to see those buffalos, but when I went there, so lavish had been the rain, and so thick was the mud and deep, that my horse could not plow through it. From a distance only could I salute the Rain-Makers.

TOWER BEYOND TRAGEDY

I AM STAYING with Brett in the house that she has built for herself and named The Tower Beyond Tragedy.
266

Lawrence is dead, but Frieda is coming back to the Ranch where Brett so long kept vigil. Tall pines grow on Frieda's ranch, but Brett's house has little piñon trees and trees of incense cedar. They grow, each one apart, patterned on the austerity of the desert. They have but one fault, these trees —so heaven-aspiring are they that at high noon they cast no shadow. It is always a problem what to do at high noon. The only shade is to be found in the house, and the house insists on being hot. Brett doesn't mind the heat. She paints industriously, or works on the book she is writing about Lawrence. I bathe in the little stream that runs and leaps by the house, and wonder why God invented ants. They are everywhere—big black ants, far too friendly. They never bite, but they run all over one. Fortunately they are not early risers else I could not lie in my sleeping bag as I do by the little stream. Night after night I hear the little stream and the stir of birds and animals. One night a flock of wild turkeys slipped through the shadows close to me: on another the horses from Hawke Ranch thundered up the hillside, whinnying and trumpeting to each other. Azul, the big white leader, showed spectral against the blackness of tree-shafts.

Coyotes signal to each other with cries in the night: and yet there is a magnificent stillness. Rain-storms that purge the heat of daytime avoid the night: at times frost chills it. Always the stars burn undiminished as they move slowly over the sky-space, marking unhurried hours on the clock of the universe.

Brett gets up before sunrise and stands with bare feet on the scantily-herbaged earth outside her door. She stands so to greet the sun. I like the idea of someone going out barefoot to hearten the sun—I do it in imagination at times myself, but have never in reality been able to persuade my feet to the task. I wait till the earth is warmed up a little— not too warm! One must ride in the early morning if at all. Brett and I snatch a breakfast and catch the horses. Sometimes Deirdre Golden, who is practising to be a dancer, is with us: a tall fair girl, young and enthusiastic. When she is

267

here we capture the horses in record time. Brett says that Deirdre has genius and will make a name for herself in the world.

Deirdre sleeps in The Tower Beyond Tragedy. I have a little house higher up the hill—Brett's guest-house. Already my friends have put nice things in it: gay rugs; pottery; and even forks and spoons. Miriam Hapgood has given me a special house-treasure: amber-coloured glass from Mexico, very lovely!

On Sundays auto-cars toil up the mountain-road. People from everywhere coming to see Brett, and Brett's pictures. I like the way that Brett paints Indians and horses. She has imagination and a splendid sense of colour and motion. On week-days no auto climbs the road, but yesterday one descended—a battered-looking large car! My horse, Prince, who has a sense of humour, pretended that it was a dragon and pranced off the highway. As he did so, someone with a wealth of golden blonde hair leaned out of the window and called to Brett. When Prince sidled back, the auto was gone. "Who is the woman with that beautiful voice?" I asked of Brett. "Why, don't you know? That is Frieda."

So that was Frieda Lawrence.

THE RATTLESNAKE

DEIRDRE AND I are riding through the woods on Lobo Mountain. The trees in this part are fairly tall, and the trail is fairly easy. We are riding carelessly when suddenly my eye is caught by a very beautiful pine tree, tall, red-stemmed and straight. It stands a little apart from its fellows. Something at the root of it moves, a gorgeous something, green and gold, freaked and freckled with patterns.

"A gorgeous snake. What luck," I cry to Deirdre, who is

riding several paces behind me. Next moment I take note of the flat triangular head, and shout to Deirdre, "Go back, it's a rattlesnake!"

We wheel our horses about and are riding slowly away, when suddenly a thought occurs to me. That rattlesnake, so big, so splendid? Ever since I came to America I had longed to see a rattlesnake coiled and hissing. I had asked the Nature Powers to let me see one. I had explained to them that I wanted to see the rattlesnake when no person would kill it: I wanted to see it with someone who thought snakes were strange splendid things. I had waited for years for this gift from the Nature Gods. Here it was now, and I was riding away from it! I pulled up my horse at once.

"Deirdre," I said, "we are fools to leave that rattlesnake."

"But the horses won't go back," said Deirdre, "they won't stand. Your horse, Prince, will go wild when he sees it's a rattlesnake."

"No, he won't!" said I. "Prince is my good friend. I'm going to explain it all to him and ask him to go back."

A split second explained it to Prince—that is the good of being pals with a horse! He promised to go back and stand. When we went back, the rattlesnake was coiled and hissing. He had taken two twists and the rest of his body stood up. His head was bent forward and swayed from side to side. His tongue flickered, and his rattle, which had eight or nine rings, vibrated sharply. The sun struck the red bark of the tree and touched up the vibrant green and gold of the rattlesnake.

A snake, I had been told, can strike only his own length. I made a rough calculation of his length and halted Prince just outside of striking distance—Deirdre came to a stop on the mare, Bobchuile, much farther off. Prince stood without moving an eyelash.

The solitude of mountain-peak on mountain-peak was about us. The desert was stretched below, a multicoloured sea. The world held just ourselves, the horses, and the snake.

I think the snake knew that we were not deadly enemies.

He continued to sway, and he increased the vibration of his rattle, but he made no attempt to strike. He was marvelous to look at. When I had filled my eyes and my imagination with that sinuous splendour, I said to Prince:

"Turn quietly and go quietly away."

He went quietly away.

"Wasn't it splendid?" Deirdre and I chorused to each other.

"That green snake," said Deirdre, "is a very rare kind. If anyone knows that it is here they will come up and hunt it for its skin."

"We must swear an oath never to tell," said I.

"Good idea," said Deirdre.

We swore the oath.

THE LITTLE FOX

"Antonio has caught a little fox," said Deirdre. "I thought his traps always killed them," said I. "This one was caught by his foot and his foot is only bruised a little. Antonio wants to show it to you. It has beautiful fur." "He knows that I don't buy skins of trapped animals." "Yes, he knows, but he thinks you might buy it alive. He is just outside with it and wants to bring it in." "Tell him to bring it in."

Enter Antonio, a dark-eyed, lanky Mexican youth, with a box under his arm from which he skillfully extracted the little fox, the most beautiful little silver fox, with a sharp nose and frightened eyes. "I want to sell it with the life," said Antonio. "Antonio," said I, "if you can cure it so that it won't be lame, I will buy it." "I can cure it in a week!" said Antonio.

At the end of the week we consulted together as to what to do with the fox. We felt an unseen audience as we delib-

270

erated, for the neighbourhood had been discussing the subject of the fox. Why had I purchased it so easily from Antonio? I must know some place in Chicago or New York where people can get great prices for animals from zoos or circus-masters.

We decided, the Golden family and myself, that we would ride up one of the nearby mountains and give the little fox its freedom. It must know that mountain fairly well, and perhaps it would have sense enough to keep away from traps. Antonio brought the little animal in a box closed with chicken-wire. We could see it huddled in a corner with frightened eyes and bared teeth.

We had planned to ride on horseback, but at the slightest attempt to move the box the captive darted forward to snap, and drew back with a snarl. Quite certainly no horse would carry him. We took an auto and went as far as we could, then we carried the little creature in his box up the hill and took off the chicken-wire.

The little fox did not move; he did not understand that the sky, unbarred, was above him. I tilted the box gently and, so assisted, he rolled out, felt the earth under him, sat for a moment petrified with astonishment, and then began to run up the hillside. The hillside was of a rose colour, the little trees were blackish-green; they looked like spots on a leopard's hide; and from tree to tree the little fox ran. He was beautiful to look at, but he couldn't get over his astonishment—human beings who didn't hunt him, who merely stood and looked at him, wishing him well. Three times he stopped, turned, and solemnly regarded us.

When he disappeared in some of the scant underbrush, we turned about in search of our auto.

271

THE MEXICAN HORSE RACE

"Will you bet on the race?" Tony said to me.

"I never bet," I replied. "I'm too unlucky."

"This will be a good race," said Tony. "A black horse from Talpa and a white horse from Taos. This is the third time that they race. Once they raced in Taos—the first race—and the white horse won. Then they raced in Talpa and the black horse won. He belongs there. Now they race in Taos, and this race decides the winner."

Tony was going to see the race. The Taos Indians were riding down. The Mexicans would crowd the race-course, but the white residents of Taos showed a marvellous lack of enthusiasm. Brett announced that she was going, so I tumbled into her Ford and we started. When we got there, Brett explained that the way to really see the horse-race was to sit on the roof of the car. So we sat there, with our riding-boots swinging against the side (Brett's boots had a splendour of embroidery). We sat inglorious and not very comfortable.

Why hadn't we ridden down? We would have been objects of beauty in that assembly—at least the horses would! As it was, I wondered whether Mabel's guest—I was that—should not support the honour of the house and the supremacy of the white race more efficiently. But while I revolved this problem in my mind, a car swung within kenning distance. A woman sat in it, slim, elegant, faultlessly gowned, dowered with that poise and arrogance which have made the white race revered through the centuries—it was Georgia O'Keefe, and she, like myself, was Mabel's guest! The honour of the house was upheld, the situation saved! I returned, with a heart unburdened, to the sun-baked plain and the multi-coloured crowd.

What a crowd! Mexicans, men, women, and children. Taos Indians stately on horses, noise and laughter, movement everywhere—dust, hot sunshine, voices shouting.

The race was supposed to begin at two o'clock. The white

horse was led up and down the length of the course. So was the black horse. When Brett and I caught sight of the black horse, we changed our minds about betting. We thought we could pick a horse, and this was three-quarters thoroughbred. The white horse looked as if he might draw a cart or turn an adobe-wheel.

The Taos Indians were betting heavily on the white horse.

Local patriotism, I thought. Very commendable, but of course they will lose.

The Taos Mexicans were betting on the white horse. They too were patriotic. The Mexicans from the other town were heavily backing the black horse.

"What horse are you backing, Tony?" we asked, as he passed our grandstand.

"I back the white horse," said Tony.

"We will take you," said Brett and myself. We felt it was almost a shame, but then Tony prided himself on his knowledge of horses.

It was long past two o'clock.

"Why doesn't the race begin?" we asked Tony.

"More bets," said Tony. "They wait for that."

How bright the sunshine was, and what a gorgeously-appareled crowd! The excitement was growing. People shouted bets from every direction, shouted boasts about their horses.

Now the riders were taking them down the course, one at a time, at a showy canter. The rider of the black horse rode without a saddle; the rider of the white horse had an elaborate Western saddle. An hour went by. At intervals the horses cantered down the track. Brett and I got hot and tired. I began to understand why the white residents of Taos stayed away.

"Soon they will start the horses," said Tony.

It was about four o'clock. The umpire had arrived. He was a local dignitary.

The horses drew together. They started. They had barely gone a few yards when the umpire yelled, "False start!" They tried it again. "False start!" They argued about it in a knot. The white horse seemed half-asleep. He didn't care how much they argued, but the black horse reared and fretted on the rein. Again they started. This time, mid cheers, they got halfway down the course. "Hurrah!" chorused Brett and myself. The black horse was leading. He would win by lengths and lengths. "False start!" cried the umpire. The white horse went to sleep while they argued, but the black horse reared and fidgeted. His rider could hardly line him up for the next start. I began to understand why Tony was backing the white horse. Down they came again. "False start." Again, "False start." It was near six o'clock. Almost always the black horse stretched into the lead. "False start!" "False start!"

At last the black horse, fretted almost to madness, could not start at all. The even-tempered white horse got under way and went down the course entirely by himself at something a little more than an amble.

He had won the race.

There were angry cries from the backers of the black horse, scuffling, and a few free fights. Pistol-shots punctuated and enlivened the altercations. Brett and I headed homeward.

Next day we came upon the white horse taking his ease in a meadow.

"Good horse to win," said Tony.

"Horse!" I snorted. "He might as well be a cow!"

"I picked him to win," said Tony, "and he won!"

"Tony," said I solemnly, "the age of miracles is not yet past!"

PENITENTES
Holy Week

I AM SLEEPING in the Tower Room in Mabel's house. Or rather, I am not sleeping; I am listening to the noises of the night—distant coyote howls, noise of dogs, and the wind in a great cotton tree. I have heard them all several times over, for it is more than midnight. But what is that sound? That strange chanting, those deep voices, that shrillness as of flutes? I hurry to a window. There is nothing to see but the stark outline of the Rocky Mountains and the wide emptiness of the desert. But yes! there is the Morada, the Prayer-House of the Penitentes; it squats on the desert-edge darkly shapeless, and through chinks in its closely-shuttered windows light struggles. The chanting comes from the heart of the Morada. It has a rich, strange, inimical sound. It might be those sky-thrust peaks lamenting: it might be the Earth herself crying out.

Suddenly the doors are flung wide, and light from within flares on the darkness. An eruption of Penitentes streams forth with a sound of multitudinous chanting and the shrilling of flutes. It is a procession with lanthorns, and sacred images, and banners. In the lanthorn light the banners are blood-red. They are giant-tall. They sway and stumble from lanthorn to lanthorn beam, from light to darkness, like unearthly Beings half-confused by contact with humanity. The procession, a splendid snake, curves and slithers along the desert.

There is a tall wooden cross on the verge of the desert, a cross uplifted on a little mound. The procession is going there. At the foot of the cross it halts. I can just see the cross, immobile, and the mass of the pilgrims crowding ever more closely about it. For a long while the Penitentes stay there. I wonder how they can endure the cold. I am sheltered in a house that is heated, I am warmly wrapped, yet I can't stand the cold. I can't wait to see that procession with its lanthorns

275

and its boys' voices and men's voices and its sacred images coming back to the Morada.

I establish myself warm in bed, and fall to thinking. I have seen Indian dances here in New Mexico where an old Pagan religion still reaches out to a joyous comradeship with Nature. Once the whole peoples of Europe reached out that way, and then came the swing-back of the pendulum. Instead of reaching out, man reached inward. He was concerned, not with The Thousand and One Gods, but with his own soul. In the great swing-back of the pendulum, nations came to the doctrine of The One God.

"There is no God but Allah, and Mahomet is His Prophet."

That swing took man through martyrdoms to a heightening of self-consciousness, and to a certain amount of self-purification. He emptied his mind of demon-wars, angels, and gods, in order to elaborate the Calvinistic "Scheme of Salvation" and the doctrine of "The Elect." But he did not stop there. Having denied The Thousand and One Gods his enthusiasm prompted him finally to deny The One God, and then his own soul: the soul that he had been so concerned about.

Lushness of decay at the end of one pendulum-swing: skeptical aridity at the other!

The pendulum still swings; from aridity now to the joyous lover-union with Nature; back to The Thousand and One Gods! Perhaps because of that our sympathies go to the plumed and jewelled May-Dancers rather than to the sombre-hooded self-torturing Penitentes. Yet these complement each other!

Winter and Springtime—the Entombment, and the Resurrection.

PASSION-PLAY

IT IS GOOD FRIDAY: every Penitente Chapel, or Morada as it is called, will have a Passion-play today in the Chapel yard. I mount my big black horse, Tom, and set out for the nearest Morada. The road winds by rutty lanes past Mexican villages tawny and vacant-eyed in the sunlight, past Mexican farmhouses crouching behind irregularly planted orchards well shut in by adobe walls, shut in by hedges, or better still, by hedges on top of adobe walls. The desert stretches to the horizon on one side, on the other, the rampart of the Rocky Mountains shuts out the sky.

The Morada sits on the edge of the desert: a small unpretentious adobe building with nothing but a graveyard to keep it company. The sun is hot, and sand and dust throw back the heat.

In the yard of the Morada, groups of children and women are moving idly about, but nothing seems to be happening. The Morada is evidently full: people are gathered at the door, and there is a sound of chanting from within. Tom objects to the chanting, but makes up his mind to endure it. He behaves with decorum till he spies a ghost or something fearsome in the churchyard. It is more than a horse can put up with! He whirls about and heads for home. I spend quite a while soothing him and talking sense before he abandons the idea of going home, and consents to stand quietly in a spot where I can see the Passion-play and he can't see the graveyard.

Nothing has changed at the Morada. It is almost as if time had missed a beat while Tom plunged, and backed, and sidled in an effort to express his apprehension and indignation. Little groups are talking in hushed voices. Young men are leaning on the fence of the Morada yard. Solemn-eyed Mexican children are staring at each other.

Suddenly there is a wavelike surge—a commotion everywhere—and the congregation breaks from the Morada, hurtling from candle-light and overcrowded air to sunshine and the pungent fragrance of desert sage. The men are wearing red handkerchiefs round their heads. They are carrying a life-sized image of Christ—a Christ in a long red woollen robe. After him comes a very small and dainty image of the Virgin. She has a robe of black silk. The bearers of the images and those who walk in the procession which forms behind them sing strange hymns with a wild beautiful music. To the sound of this singing, to the sound of marching feet, the Christ and the Madonna are engulfed in the crowd that follows them.

Wilder and stronger grows the music. The crowd is perambulating the yard. People kneel here and there. The children grow more solemn-eyed, but do not kneel.

Now from the Morada a huge cross is being shouldered and guided. The cross is set up in the Chapel yard, and from two posts on either side a white sheet is stretched. This completely shuts the cross from sight. The images are drawn in behind the sheet. The chanting continues.

There is a dull sound of hammering: the image of the Christ is being nailed to the cross.

Many of the Penitentes now form a procession. They are going to circle a cross in the desert two miles away. They will kneel there in the hot sunshine chanting prayers. I do not follow the procession: I have followed it on other days, for every day in Holy Week that cross has been circled. Numbers of the spectators follow it. With a sound of singing that grows fainter and fainter, the procession winds slowly across the desert.

There is a dead silence now in front of the sheeted cross. Some women are on their knees praying. The young men who have not followed the procession are still leaning on the fence. They are silent. The round-eyed Mexican children stare solemnly in front of them. They are silent.

It seems a long while that one waits in the silence, but at last, far off, the faint sound of old Spanish hymns comes across the desert. The Penitentes are returning. Their strong-

throated chanting swells and swells as they throng the
Chapel yard. They go behind the screened-off cross. The
white sheet is lowered and one can see that the Christ is
being taken from the cross. He is laid reverently in a coffin,
which is placed on a bier to be drawn in procession to a
cross that lies too far off for the eye to discern it. The bier
will be set down at the foot of that distant cross, and Penitentes will stand in a group about it praying and singing
far into the night. All this night of Good Friday Penitentes
will be going in procession bearing a dead Christ to inaccessible crosses with only the desert and the mountains and
God to listen to the rhythmic chanting and the passionate
prayers.

There will be midnight Mass at the orthodox Catholic
Chapel of Ranchos de Taos tonight—a Mass especially for
Penitentes. The orthodox Church does not recognize the Moradas which are the Penitente Churches, but tonight the
dead Christ, mourned in both churches, brings a truce if not
a reconciliation.

In spite of the cold I am going to the Chapel at Ranchos
de Taos tonight. Penitentes will come there from the mountains and from the desert—long lines of Penitentes. The
Church door will be guarded, but if one stands in shadow
one may see the Penitentes.

There will be moonlight too tonight—and the dark chill
peace that the moon gives.

PENITENTES

Midnight Mass

A COUNTRY ALL black and white; whiteness of snow on the
mountains, black shadows. Cold whiteness of the moon.

Streaks of light from the windows of Ranchos Church, and the open door. Penitentes are guarding the door. We obliterate ourselves in the shadow of the wall. Spectators are not supposed to be here, but if we wait very quietly, we may see the Penitentes coming down from the mountain.

Yes, the Penitentes are coming. They are not chanting now, but in long lines from the mountains and the desert they are coming. Hooded figures, black in the black shadows, the flagellantes who have prayed and scourged themselves night after night of Holy Week. On other nights they go into the Moradas, but this night they will be in Ranchos Church. In Ranchos Church there is a great image of the Christ, robed in red, an image that has perambulated the mountain-paths for all the nights of the week. And there is the little Virgin too, who has accompanied her Son. Every procession of Penitentes has a Christ.

"It is strange," says Lucia, my Spanish friend, "it is strange about the cloaks in the Morada."

"What is strange about the cloaks?"

"The cloaks that are not counted out," said Lucia. "When the men gather in the Morada (the real flagellantes, the men going out into the desert) they are each given a cloak and hood from the store in the Morada. They go into the night and return, but they have more comrades on their return. These do not hand their cloaks to the man in charge, they speak to no one—they are gone! but not through the door. In the morning there are cloaks lying in a heap on the Morada floor—the cloaks of those unknown comrades."

"What do the Penitentes think about it?" I asked.

"They think," said Lucia, "that some souls have died with a vow unaccomplished, and they come to keep their vow."

Penitentes are slipping silently into the church. There are many wax candles there. The church is solid against the sky. It fills one's mind when one looks at it. But turn from it a moment, and it is lost in the vastness of the desert and the bulk of the mountains.

They say that the sun dances on Easter morning. On that

morning the sun will have two sets of worshippers, Pagan and Christian, for the Indians always hearten the sun at its rising, and the Easter sun rises and dances especially for Penitentes.

BLUE LAKE

(Taos)

WE ARE ON a pilgrimage to Blue Lake: Merriam Golden, Mariana Howes and myself. Quite a procession we are as our horses climb the trail among the mountains. Burros, laden with provisions and equipment, climb with us. (Never have burros: pack horses are better! But our Indian guides insisted on burros because they will keep the trail without being led.) Two Indian guides lead the procession. They sing as they ride, and the leader has a twist of green vines around his head. He is chanting a song in honour of the lake. The lake is very high up, 11,000 feet. Even then it lies in a hollow among hill-ridges. In the shelter beside it, some tall trees have found sanctuary, but the hill-ridges are treeless. They have thrust themselves beyond the timber line.

We are camping near Blue Lake. We sit talking with the Indians. We begin to talk of battles long ago. I tell them that I came from a country where almost every bit of ground has a story, stories of battles and victories.

"Our tribe fought a battle," said the chief Indian, "at a place a distance from here, and our people were defeated. It was a great loss to us because the man who had the most powerful songs was killed. No one else knew the songs. But our tribe needed the songs. We had to get them." ·

"How did you get them?" I asked.

"It was the old men who got them. They fasted and called

281

on the spirit of the dead man. He came to them. He said: *'In that spot where I died, I will sing for you the songs. But you must come; you must make a ring of power. You must give me power to sing.'*

"The old men went when they had fasted and prepared themselves: and on the spot where he had died in the battle he came to them; he sang the songs. Our tribe has still the songs."

I said, "In Ireland there was a great song once that was lost, and the poets fasted; they came to the place where the singer of that song died, and for three days and nights they fasted and prayed to him to come. He came to them. He recited the great song from beginning to end, and in our old books we have still that song."

"Song is a great thing," said the Indian. "It is very powerful."

Our Indians had brought rifles. They had forgotten about fishing tackle, however. Of course you could not fish in the sacred lake, but there were many other lakes, some near at hand. But how to get fishing tackle. Why, the gods had provided it. A party of "Whites," all young men, had crashed in from the other side. They had no right to be there. Pilgrims should employ Indians and set out from the Pueblo. These folk had come from the opposite direction. They were in search of sport and had been fishing in the sacred lake for about three days without success. They were well-equipped with fishing tackle. Our Indians promptly borrowed it, went fishing—not in the sacred lake—presented the first fish they caught to the earth, and caught a basketful thereafter. That night we had a great bonfire and the Indians sang songs. With their consent, we invited the inmates of the "White" camp, who had never heard Indian songs, but captivated by Indian prowess in fishing were ready and eager to listen. The Indians sang far into the night, and the flame leaped and blazed beside Blue Lake.

Blue Lake has heard many songs and glittered in the light of many fires. Ceremonies are held in its honour every year—

282

a month of ceremonies. No "White" has ever witnessed them. Indians, posted on all the trails, turn back intruders. The lake, the Mother of Waters, is powerful as the sun or the soil itself, a food-giver, a heartener of life.

If one listened as we sat there one could hear it moving softly, murmuring to itself as it had moved and murmured for centuries—with folk to listen, or without them! The giant trees lifted themselves into the darkness unperturbed by our presence. We made, with our fire, our songs, our little crowd of people, a small impact on the wide solitude of sky and mountain-peak—a little flicker against the magnificence of the stars.

CHRISTMAS EVE AT THE PUEBLO

IT IS CHRISTMAS EVE at the Pueblo. The little church has a big Christmas tree on either side of the door. Everywhere you see great bundles of firewood stacked for a bonfire. If you were to follow the trail of them, you would go right round the Pueblo, starting from the enclosure of the church and ending there.

The church is lighted and the door is open: a priest is saying Mass inside. Children and women are going in. The men are leaning on the low wall of the enclosure. They seem to feel that that is just as good as going in. There is a hush and expectancy. Presently the women and children begin to come out. They are carrying what might be dolls, but what are in reality santos (saints), dressed in lace and silk and muslins, some of them with bunches of flowers pinned on their dresses.

A procession is forming led by the women carrying santos. Soon the Virgin herself will come out. This night, of the nights, she has to be carried round the Pueblo. Now she is

283

coming, on a litter under a canopy. Musicians are playing on violins. They are not Indians, they are Mexicans, and the air they play has come from old Spain.

Sound of singing and the Mexican violins. They are crossing the enclosure, the walled enclosure, in front of the church.

But what is that sound outside the enclosure? That barbaric chanting? Masked figures are dancing grotesquely just outside the enclosure in the path of the procession. They are the Matazuma dancers. They wear masks of black cloth, and they have come to meet and greet the Virgin.

As soon as she passes the gap of the enclosure, little boys set fire to the wood piled on either side, and as the procession advances fire leaps from pile to pile. The Matazuma dancers dance in front of the Virgin's procession. There is a king there among them, and a little girl who is the bride of the king: there are knights and warriors and a strange beast to be slain. In and out among the leaping fires goes the procession, with Mexicans playing on violins, the Virgin stately on her palanquin, the sound of a Christian hymn, and the Dance of the Matazuma Dancers.

The sky above is velvet-black with many stars, the little river of the Pueblo makes a song to itself. Out of the silence of Blue Lake, high in the Sacred Mountain, the river came: out of what eyrie in the human mind came the Virgin, the Slain Beast, and the Matazuma Dancers?

K'YAKIME, HOME OF THE EAGLES

IT IS A DAY in December. Tony is urging his auto along the road from Albuquerque to Zuñi at seventy miles an hour—his usual pace. In the car there is just Tony and myself. We had started from Taos four strong: Mabel, Tony, Muriel

284

Draper and I. Mabel had organized the expedition, declaring that the Winter ceremonies of the Zuñi Indians are especially beautiful and worth seeing. We all four expected to see the House-Blessing Ceremony, but when we reached the nearest railway station we discovered that Muriel Draper's ticket was about to expire and she must return to New York at once. It was a disappointment to all of us.

After a night in Albuquerque, Mabel announced that she was going to remain in the hotel. Tony and I could hurry to the ceremony and hurry back to join her and return to her house in Taos where I was guest, as Muriel Draper had been.

We are whirling through a country of gentle slopes wooded with small trees. The road is a white ribbon empty save for Tony's Cadillac. There is no sign as yet of the Zuñi Pueblo, the city of K'yákime, the Home of the Eagles, the last stronghold of what was once a great Indian civilization.

Once the Zuñis had seven cities in the Valley of Shíwina— The Seven Cities of Cíbola! These were, all seven, rich and great but the years have wasted and betrayed them. Good fortune remained with one city alone. The City of K'yákime still takes the sunlight, still holds its place by the Sacred Mountain not yet deserted by eagles, To'yállanne the splendid Mesa of rose-red stone, To'yállanne the dwelling-place of the Two Brothers, Áhaiyúta and Mátsailéma, the War Gods, the rain and thunder makers of Zuñi.

There is a tale that Spaniards came once to K'yákime— after long wanderings. They had with them a giant Negro who bellowed forth words of power demanding the surrender of the city. He had the black skin and the rolling eyes of a Demon. Other cities had opened their gates, but the Zuñi warriors barred the approach, and their priests shot the Demon with arrows.

The Zuñi Indians are rich, their houses are spacious and high-raftered. They have treasures of fawn skin, woollen garments of bright colours, and strings of turquoise and shell beads. Their children are strong. Their flocks and herds in-

285

crease. Their fields are heavy at harvest time. The sound of hammering is heard on new timbers throughout the year. Eight houses waited for blessing at K'yákime.

THE ZUÑI HOUSE-BLESSING CEREMONY

No ONE KNEW when the Sun-God would enter K'yákime. There seemed to be an idea, however, that he would get there about four o'clock in the afternoon. Keeping this in our minds, Tony and I arrived about half-past three, but the Sun-God was swifter-footed. From the mountains he crossed the plain, he crossed the wattled bridge in front of the rose-coloured Mesa. A slender lad, naked save for eagle-down and paint, he carried a bow and arrows in his hand. Eight houses expected his blessing. They were decorated, and shallow trenches had been dug in front of each one. Swiftly and silently to each house came the Sun-God. He paused in front of each and shot an arrow toward the house. Then he disappeared. The Gods of the Mountain, later, would come with great ceremony, and the elders and notabilities of the village would go out to meet them. For four days and nights the priests in whom the Gods of the Mountain were to incarnate had been fasting and praying on the Mountain. We would see them coming from the Mountain. They would be seen a-far off.

All at once, the Young Gods were in the Pueblo. A burst of singing made known their advent. Marching in rank with a glad crowd before and behind them, they approached the first house. The crowd fell away so that a clear space remained. The Gods wore bird-masks and were gorgeous in paint and jewels. They held in their hands short staves or rods of power made of wood shaped to a curve and ornamented with eagle-down. In front of the house the Young

286

Gods separated into two companies, standing in ranks four a-breast. Each company had a herald—bird-masked too and carrying a long lance, the green upright stem of some desert plant with a sharp growth-point at the top. The heralds advanced, passed each other, paced the extent of the dancing-floor, and returned to their companies. Then the dance began. The Gods sang as they danced, moving toward each other, mingling and retreating. Their bright-hued garments, their gaudily-painted masks made a constantly changing pattern, beautiful and strange and joyous as the shadow-dance of leaves in sunlight.

At the time appointed, each God approached the house-trench, and threw into it some eagle-down stripped from the curved insignium he carried. After that, they fell into rank and passed on to the next house.

As they went, at every street corner, at every convenient standing place, they met gatherings of the townsfolk, who were waiting for them. In one place there would be young boys; at another place young girls, bright as flowers in a flower garden. At another turning, old men, and again at another place the aged women. While the Gods passed these companies of the townsfolk, pollen was thrown on them by each group. It seemed to me that pollen, which is an emblem of fertility and vigour, was thrown upon the Gods partly as a thank-offering for what they had given to the house. It was as if the people were saying, "You have blessed us with a blessing from the God-World. We in turn bless you with a blessing from our hearts and from our fields. Be strong and prosper. Pass on, pass on. Live forever!"

I don't know where the Young Gods went after they had blessed each house. It was growing dusk. People waited for the Elder Gods. After a while, word went round that they were coming. Yes, they certainly were coming. One could see them moving from the mountains across the plain. They were immensely tall. They had bird-masks. They appeared bulky; they advanced stiffly with a grotesque swaying motion. A deputation of the townsfolk went out to meet them. No one else was allowed to go beyond the village, where everyone stood filling their eyes with the sight of them. The Gods and the city notabilities halted in front of each other. There was much ceremonial greeting and ceremony. The Gods at times made themselves very small. They did this by getting off their stilts. Each God had a great mask and sort of wicker cage, inside of which was a priest who represented the God. To increase his height, he was mounted on stilts. When he discarded these and the edge of the wicker cage touched the ground, he looked small. When walking with the stilts, each God looked like a great, unwieldy bird-man. The ceremonies were long-drawn-out. Indians have an infinite patience. To an onlooker like myself, the ceremonies seemed to repeat themselves. The Gods made themselves small and anon took on their full height; the Elders of the city orated, and it went on endlessly. It was growing very cold. The Sun, in setting, struck the Sacred Mesa, turning it rose-red, and painting the river with gold. I wanted to see the Gods crossing the wattled bridge in front of that Mesa. They would cross it, all in good time.

The light faded to violet, darker, and darker. Still the Elders of the city orated, still the Gods moved and changed shapes. Still Zuñi waited. It was too cold to sit down anywhere; one had to walk.

I must have walked miles, always backwards and forwards, in a place where I commanded a view of the wattled bridge. Friends who had come to see these ceremonies went off in search of food and warmth. English-speaking onlookers who were not acquaintances of mine, but who also wished to see the bridge crossing, gave up one by one. There was only one man and myself left. We exchanged views. Those Indians might stay out there until midnight, and ceremonies went on until daybreak. We were wretchedly cold, and not having the patience of Indians, we decided to make for the hotel—a barnlike structure in the hands of some Germans. Tony had gone there long ago. I ordered something to eat, but had scarcely taken two mouthfuls and was but half-thawed, when Tony arrived.

"The Gods have crossed," he said. "They have not landed yet. There is a Ceremony of Greeting before they land. Come and see it."

I bundled myself into his car and we drove down to where the wattled bridge touched the land of the village. It was more than dusk now. One could dimly see the Gods. They were standing on the landing place of the bridge, and the notabilities of the town were standing opposite. It seemed to be a repetition of the ceremonial greeting on the plain outside of the city. The Gods made themselves larger and smaller, there were fine-sounding words and long silences. It was still freezing cold.

Close to Tony's auto another car drew up. Doctor Light from Ranchos de Taos was in it with some friends. She leaned from the window and said to me:

"The Myth of Creation is being chanted in the most important of the houses. We are going there. If you don't come and get a seat, you won't get in later. The house will be crammed with Navajos."

In the old days, the Navajos used to raid the Zuñi villages, but now they content themselves with coming in force every time there is a fiesta. At a fiesta an Indian community has to offer hospitality to every comer—warmth of fire, food and drink, and the greetings due to a guest. Navajos adore fiestas. In expectation of that advent, the Zuñis had slaughtered about two hundred sheep, and heaped up corn and flattened cakes. Of course the Navajos, when they give a fiesta, have to slaughter sheep and extend hospitality to all and sundry. But then, the Navajo fiesta is held among inaccessible mountain places, and Zuñis do not take the trouble to go to Navajo fiestas. Navajos think nothing of miles on horseback. They had come to this fiesta with their wives and children, and even their small babies. I was glad the Navajos had come. They are the handsomest Indians that I have ever

289

seen—tall, dark, stately, mysterious-looking, tricked out with silver and turquoise. The Navajos are great silversmiths, and know where to find turquoise. The women have a dress that they copied from Spanish ladies—long full skirts, black silk shawls. Their hair is elaborately braided, and they have many silver ornaments in their hair. They make a multitudinous splendour when they crowd a house.

What was I to do? The Gods stood there, mysterious in the dusk. The river lapped quietly. The notabilities spoke in low, sonorous, guttural voices. The night was very cold. I decided to go in search of the Myth of Creation.

The largest house was decorated and filled with light. We entered the main room directly, a long, broad, high room with a raftered ceiling. At one end there was a platform reaching nearly across the room. On this were three altars with bird-symbols painted on them. In the middle of the room, or not quite in the middle, for it was nearer the altar, was a shrine, so high that one would need a ladder to reach it. At the foot of this shrine a square cavity had been dug in the earthen floor. I could hear the singers chanting the Myth of Creation. They sat at the far end of the room, the end where the altars were. They were sitting on benches arranged in a half-circle. Each one was gorgeously apparelled and masked with a bird-mask. They were chanting the story of the beginning of all things. Rich, deep and splendid that music was. They would go on chanting it while these ceremonies lasted, and they would usually last about a week. The hall was empty save for those singers and a few "Whites" who thoughtfully secured seats for themselves. The master of the house, however, was there, robed as every Zuñi was, from the smallest child to the oldest inhabitant, in festal robes. The Navajos had not arrived. Afterwards, I learned the reason. They were in the feast-hall where ceremonies connected with blessings of food and welcoming of guests were going forward. This chanting of the Myth of Creation was like the sound the sea makes. It was like the wind in trees. It reminded me of Gregorian chanting, of the old traditional

290

music in Ireland, of something out of another world. Suddenly, there was a knocking at the door and a sound of running footsteps—footsteps of a multitude! The door was locked and barred. The master of the house advanced to it. As he did so, there was a burst of singing. The same high, sweet, musical singing that the Young Gods had made. The knocking was repeated, and the singing burst out more triumphantly. The Gods from the Mountain, the Elder Gods, had come.

Never for a moment did the singers who were chanting the Myth of Creation cease. Their voices made a sonorous undertone to the high, sweet singing outside.

The master of the house flung open the door. Two marshals, armed each with a long desert-grown lance, entered. They resembled those who had marked the ground for the Young Gods. Now they came into the room, holding their lances. One advanced toward the altar. The other went in the opposite direction. They were taking possession of the house for the Gods. When they had measured it, treading in opposite directions, they came to attention on either side of the open door where the master of the house still stood, and across the threshold of which the Gods waited, accompanied by a great crowd.

The master of the house drew backward, inviting the Gods. Their heralds stood on either side of the door. The Gods passed between them and entered the room. There were two of the tall Bird-Gods or Shalakos, a great company of the Young Gods, and a strange crowd with misshapen masks—human-shaped masks—and bodies daubed with reddish-brown ochre. These were the singers, and represented the mud-born humans to whom the God-Ray had not been given. Unmoved, at the other end of the room, the singers chanted the Myth of Creation, but the high, beautiful voices were silent. The lance-bearing heralds advanced to the shrine in the centre of the room. One of the Elder Gods mounted some steps and laid on the shrine some eagle-down. Then he placed in the cavity in the earth some more eagle-

291

down, and the cavity was filled in. The earth outside had been blessed by the Young Gods; now one of the Elder Gods blessed the earth within the walls.

After that began a ceremonial dance. The two great Bird-Gods danced stiffly toward each other from opposite ends of the room. They met, they retreated, they passed each other, and still the singers chanted the Myth of Creation. The Young Gods stood by the house-wall, for one side of the room was left free for the dancing. The Young Gods were silent, but the mud-heads, with ungainly gestures, were capering and singing.

I don't know what this dance meant to the Indians. To me it seemed that the giant bird-headed Shalakos were treading a measure from god-land, austere and strange and potent. The house would be blessed and changed by the rhythm of it. The mud-heads would also be blessed and changed. Dancing with clownish and uncouth gestures, capering excitedly, singing with those high sweet voices, the mud-heads represented a humanity excited and even distressed by the god-rhythm but eager to know more of it.

The Young Gods stood idly by, beautiful to look at, unhampered by impatience, uneager, eternally confident.

Unweariedly the Shalakos repeated their slow, austere, compelling rhythms, but ever the mud-heads capered more wildly and sang more distractedly. They were as yet clay-men. The divine soul-giving fire had not touched them. The Gods had brought that fire. I would witness the ensoulment.

Suddenly, the Young Gods stepped into the dance. They were singing, and the rhythm began to change. Slowly the divine influence was changing the earth-born, the mud-born, the clay-men. They caught touches of that higher melody. Now and then they could dance a phrase like the Gods. The great Gods, unmoved, threaded their first austere steps, but the Young Gods, partly touched by the frenzy of the mud-born, danced now a phrase of theirs and now a phrase of their own, and the steps were more intricate and the music more lovely till one could scarce endure the loveliness.

292

In the midst of it the Young Gods burst out of the room, singing, and the mud-heads, mingling with and following them, left only the Shalakos, and the masked singers who still chanted the Myth of Creation. Outside, one heard running footsteps and high sweet singing. The Young Gods and the earth-born were seeking another house. Throughout the night they would go from house to house of the eight houses, singing as they went, Gods and men together, accompanied by joyous runners holding lanterns.

"We should go out too," said Doctor Light. "There are so many other houses to visit and so many things to see."

We left the large house where the two Elder Gods solemnly advanced toward each other from either end of the room, retreated; advanced again, passed each other, advanced, retreated, passed, solemnly, slowly, purposefully, in accordance with some ancient ritual.

"Let us go to the house where the food is being blessed."

We went to it. Like all the other houses, it was brilliantly lit and decorated inside with green boughs and coloured streamers. At one end there was an altar. In front of it stood the master of the house, and in long lines the Zuñi women, carrying baskets of edibles on their heads, entered the house. They were clad in their brightest and gayest garments. When they came in they removed the baskets from their heads and set them on the floor in front of them. They gathered until the room was full. Then the master of the house turned to the altar and stood there reverently and silently. Soon the women would lift the baskets to their heads and file past the altar to receive the blessing which the house master was empowered by the Gods to grant. I wanted to see all of this, but my friends knew of so many other things that presently we found ourselves in the night again.

"Let's look in where the Navajos are feasting," said my friend.

We stood outside a wide, uncurtained window and saw within a large brilliantly-lighted hall. It had boughs of green and frescoes of fawn skin. The fawn skins had been carefully cured to preserve their shape and were arranged on the walls so that they seemed to be running and leaping. The Navajos were seated on the floor, stately, dark-visaged, gorgeously bedecked with silver and turquoise. Among them moved the Zuñi women, bright as tulips in a garden. Solemnly and daintily they offered meats and drink. Everywhere the windows were lighted, everywhere there was a sound of singing, a sound of running feet. In each of seven houses one of the Elder Gods danced. He would dance there till dawn. And the owner of the house, for sake of this, had to covenant to serve the God-Priest for the whole of the coming year. He must plant his corn, he must reap his crops, he must do whatever the priest commanded him. In the eighth house, two of the Elder Gods danced. One house always had to have two Gods. The owner of that house had to serve for a year two God-Priests, so the man who offered his house for the ministrations of two priests was looked upon with admiration and gratitude by the whole community. Every year in Zuñi this house-blessing was held because every house built during the year had to be blessed. It really did not become a part of Zuñi, it had no spiritual existence till the Gods received and recognized it.

Next day the nine Elder Gods would race to the wattled bridge, and whichever got there first would be a luck-bringer to the house and the man who had selected him. It was great bad luck if anyone fell; it meant a possible death during the year.

The eighth house was the last one that Doctor Light and I entered. Already the stars were paling for dawn. Three dancers only were in the room: the two Shalakos who advanced and retreated with rhythmic monotony, dancing slowly, and a young warrior who moved in the middle-distance between them. He was the only ceremonial dancer that I had seen without a mask. His face, however, was mask enough. He kept his eyes lowered and moved as if he were a bronze statue given the semblance of life, and upheld by a will not his own.

294

The cocks were shrilling for dawn as we left the house. Our feet made a sound on the frozen clay: redness had not come upon the Mesa. Doctor Light was telling me, as we walked, that day by day and year by year K'yákime's Priest of the Sun climbed the Mesa to stand there in the coldness of dawn and greet the Sun as he climbed the world-ridge. I was picturing that climb: from height to height, from rock to rose-red rock, colour-subdued as yet in a pallor that remembered the stars regretfully.

Like the flash of a sword, like the beat of falcon wings the sound of singing swirled and scintillated, lit and filled the air. Sunrise and that sound were intermingled!

"Is it a dawn-chorus from the Mesa?" I asked Doctor Light.

"No," she said, "it is the Young Gods. They are in the Plaza."

We hurried to the Plaza. On every roof against the dawn-sky stood Navajos, but the Zuñi folk were on the ground, holding themselves back so that the Gods would have room to dance in interweaving rhythms. I could not see the God-Dancers very well because of the crowd, but I had seen them before. They were young and slim and eager. They had bird-masks and those beautiful, unearthly voices. They made me think of Gods of Egypt with bird-heads; of strange genii from Babylon, eagle-featured. Truly because they did not appear to be human they were symbols of Gods. Greek Gods were merely beautiful men or women, with faces unlit by ecstasy, unmarred by sorrow. Martyrs or Hebrew prophets could be stranger and stronger, but even these were human, and the earth limitations crowded on them and held them down. The Bird-Gods who came so suddenly were kin to those Gaelic Bird-Gods, splendid-coloured, who flashed out of the Country of the Ever-Young. I had listened to tales of those Gods, I had dreamed of them—and now, suddenly, they were real! Here was a religion that all my life I had longed for—perfect, generous-handed, touching the fringes of the oldest myths, laying a finger on the great dreams of the visionaries, bringing the tang and savour of another world.

After all, I was glad that I left at dawn. I did not see the race of the Elder Gods. I took with me the memory of the dawn-dance.

BEADS ON A STRING

SUNSHINE AND KEEN AIR ON A CLIFF-EDGE, AND
two autos speeding southward. The leading one, piloted by
Molly O'Shea, has Robinson Jeffers and John O'Shea and
some well-filled wine hampers and luncheon baskets. Una
Jeffers is driving the second car, Tony Luhan's beloved
Cadillac. Tony, on the front seat, is hampering Una with
advice and sudden ejaculatory commands. On the back seat,
Mabel Luhan and I sit silent, occasionally wishing ourselves
somewhere else.

This is no road for an altercation between rival chauffeurs.
We are on the old coast road to the Big Sur, swinging in
detours by dizzy canyon chasms, disentangling ourselves
from the clutch of tree-roots, and feigning indifference to
the malignant glitter of a sea thousands of feet below us.
Tony distrusts the sea. That is why Una is driving the Cadillac. Tony has not had a lifetime to study the sea, but on a
short acquaintance he has found out a few things about it.
The sea has a grievance. No one has offered it pollen, or
made a song for it—worse even, garbage and poisonous
sewage have been thrust upon it. The sea is dangerous, and
would clasp a victim willingly.

Tony is aware too of another menace—Point Lobos, that
strange promontory, heavy with memories of heathen ceremonies and potent incantations! Lobos is a Dragon with
keen mouth unpropitiated. Lobos is to be approached with
caution. I agree with Tony. I have myself approached it with
caution, not to say reverence, and found it gracious. Once

297

on a time when I was there with Dane Rudhyar, composer and astrologer, and the artist, Mrs. Young-Hunter, she led us to a deep pool in the Lobos rocks that had flashed with the many-coloured splendour of a Nature Spirit. It was a large pool with one edge little raised above the sea-level. At the bottom of it the image of a great serpent lay coiled in stone. As I had more than once spoken of mountain-tarns in Ireland that shelter mythical serpents, known as Piasts, my companions said that I must greet the pool in Gaelic. I agreed to chant the most suitable words I could think of, provided that Rudhyar followed with a Hindu incantation. He did so, and while his voice rose in the chant, the sea, which had been drawing steadily nearer, sent a wave crashing over the rock-barrier, breaking the smoothness of the pool and giving to the coiled serpent illusory motion and life.

Not a car has met, or shouldered past us, on this cliff-road—a fortunate circumstance, for the road is narrow! We are on our way to a canyon owned by the O'Sheas and some friends of theirs who have clubbed together to keep it from being swallowed by real-estate dealers and cut into "home-sites." It is a narrow canyon with a stream threading between heavy-foliaged banks, but it climbs to hills that are bare of trees. When we reach it, I know what will happen—it has happened other times—Robinson Jeffers will hand up the weightiest hamper and then disappear in the tree fastness, like water slipping through sedge grass. Molly will take charge of everything. John O'Shea will busy himself with fire and a barbecue while the rest of us stand about, more or less useful or useless. Tony, with a woodsman's instinct, will recover Robinson Jeffers before we eat. Robinson will sit silent with the secret smile and shining eyes of one to whom the wild has extended more than the prodigal's welcome—though he came with the elder brother's righteousness! Later we will climb in a straggling procession to the hill top and Tony will cry out in his strong melodious voice an Indian greeting to mountains that crane, head over head, to look at the sea.

298

"You are driving too fast!" Tony says in a fretful voice.

Una slows down. She is not driving too fast. She knows every inch of this road, and is a marvellous driver: but she is also marvellously good-tempered.

"You should not interrupt your driver, Tony, you know that," says Mabel.

There is silence.

Snatching a glance at a ravine-depth, I surprise a group of redwoods, sturdy and unsubdued though somewhat mauled by wind and smarting from the bitterness of sea-spume. I am sure that John O'Shea, in passing, notes those trees: he has a passionate sympathy with the will of a tree to thrust skyward, the will of a cliff to endure. He has caught on his canvas the weight of a bough; the impatient frustrated surge of the sea; the very muscle and texture of rocks. John O'Shea comes from a part of Ireland that I know well. He has the pride of a man who can count his ancestors back for a thousand years: this proud untamed California enthrals him.

John and Molly rank among my earliest friends in America. I owe my first meeting with Una Jeffers to them. How well I remember it! Una with her beautiful long plaits of hair, and pale, distinguished face. In company with Molly and John I first had sight of the tower and the thick stone walls of the house that Robinson Jeffers built with his own hands: a stronghold where he might hope to live—comrade of hawks and mountains—enamoured of solitude and the sea.

Why have we, all of us, foregathered? Why did Mabel suddenly decide that she must see the West Coast, and begin with Carmel? We have slid together like beads on a string! Perhaps it is not wholly by chance. Perhaps there is a design somewhere, a pattern could we disentangle it! Who knows? We know, for the moment, that we are speeding south along the Big Sur road, sunshine is all about us, and Una Jeffers is driving Tony's Cadillac.

THE LUNCHEON

JOHN AND MOLLY O'SHEA are giving a luncheon. They are having it on the cliff-edge at the end of their peninsula in Carmel Highlands. Nature seems to have known in advance about John and Molly, royal dispensers of hospitality, known that one day they would own this peninsula reaching into the sea, since here at the end of it is a natural platform wide and guest-inviting, and a place a little higher up that just accommodates a wooden kitchen so that everything can be served hot in the face of the sea-breeze. On all sides the cliff rises, landscaped with little cypress trees that John has planted more daringly and more efficiently than they could plant themselves. On the platform there is a long table with benches on either side, and bright awnings over the benches. The people who sit today on those stone benches are well known. Mabel and Tony Luhan are there, with Dorothy Thompson, Robinson and Una Jeffers, Lincoln Steffens, and Ella Winter. There is a distinguished Austrian violinist. Everyone has to descend about a hundred steps cut in the rocks. Arrived, one might be on a desert island. No sound of a motor-horn, no glimpse of a roadway or of a house. A sound of the sea makes itself felt, the sea advancing in great waves and churning among the rocks. Far off, on Lobos magnificently thrust upon the horizon, there is the barking of sea lions.

Sinclair Lewis, a slender figure with contumacious red hair and an ironic smile, comes down those steps long after everyone else. He is in a holiday mood and catching sight of me declares that he is going to say a poem in my honour. He makes one on the spot, and follows it with another for good measure, proceeding thereafter to burlesque himself and mimic sundry Americans while his hosts urge him to be seated and fall to on viands, plentiful enough and rare enough to tempt a Roman epicure. "Not without 'Grace before Meat,' " says Sinclair Lewis, and assuming a new pose

300

and new facial expression he intones with a strong nasal accent what he warrants is "Grace" in the good old style.

It is a gay party, as gay as the sunshine, as gay as the coloured stripes on the awning, as light of heart as the circling sea-swallows. Sinclair Lewis is raying out the wittiest and most fantastic remarks. John O'Shea replies in kind. Lincoln Steffens is even more dazzling. So lightning-quick is thrust and riposte in this rapier play of wit that I find myself bewildered by it. Una Jeffers, at the other end of the table, is telling amusing anecdotes. Tony, tired of it all, is standing on a rock. He stands majestic in a scarlet serape. The sea curls in waves behind him, sapphire-blue except where churning foam transfigures it to chalcedony. Molly O'Shea, beautiful and gracious, is smiling and spreading that atmosphere of joyousness that makes her so renowned a hostess.

"What do you think of America?" asks Sinclair Lewis.

"America," I reply, "is a tawny lioness, beautiful, alert, and sinewy-muscled."

"And England?"

"England is a heavy-flanked bull: too long stall-fed."

"But Ireland," says Sinclair Lewis, with an air of believing it, "Ireland is a white unicorn!"

HOLLOW HILLS FARM

JOHN O'SHEA, MOLLY, his wife, and I are climbing the narrow road above the Carmel Valley that runs high up among the hills. We are climbing in an auto under Molly's efficient chauffeurship. Many autos have climbed this valley road since the day that Noël Sullivan roofed his house and fenced his twenty acres huddled in a hollow of the hills here. We are going to his house, and John is calling to mind Noël's long-eared Nubian goats. He thinks that he has been

301

remiss about sketching them. He has let opportunities go by, but today he feels that the time has come to do justice to those goats. In this idea he is heartened by Molly and by myself, chiefly, I think, because we admire John's work so much and are really curious to see what goats would look like on John's canvas. There is a black kid, we know, and one snow-white. There is a patriarchal Lord of the Herd, long-bearded and amber-eyed. John thinks much of him. He is prideful and arrogant, or would seem so if one had never encountered the lofty disdain of a camel. We urge John to sketch the whole herd, knowing well that in all likelihood he will not portray hoof, eyelid, or ear of any one of them.

As we approach Noël Sullivan's long low house with its balconies and patios, a riot of dogs erupts from every quarter: police dogs, bulldogs, dachshunds, all joyously barking and whirling in a dance of welcome. Noël himself, gracious and quiet-spoken, stands in the doorway. He wants us to meet his Irish gardener, a man much solaced by a word with Irish-born folks. John delights him by remembering places and names and news of the old country, and by showing a proper knowledge of the art of gardening.

Though Noël's house has welcomed so many guests it always has the air of receiving one for the first time with a shy invitation to enter. The house is like its master but it is difficult to say in what way it is like him, just as it is difficult to say what Noël himself is like. A sojourner in many cities, he has touched hands with many people, success-crowned or forlorn, yet he belongs to another era and other comrades. Sensitive to every phase of culture, to every colour of beauty, he cannot separate these in his consciousness from the grave-pall black, the underlying misery of life. He is concerned with agonies of the soul, as men were concerned in the days when they knew how to build cathedrals and palaces, and fenced themselves in cloisters from the fires of Hell and the more heart-piercing fires of Paradise. He might belong to the Italy of Saint Francis d'Assisi, or to the Florence of Pico

302

della Mirandola: indeed he well may die in a monk's habit as that young prince died.

Loitering in the afternoon sunshine among the flowers, we admire the fountain and its lilies. John speaks of goats, and we troop to the mountain-pasture where they have assembled themselves. There are goats a-plenty, and with them sheep enough to remind one of the scriptural parable. John moves affably among them, but disdains a sketch-book. He feels sure that he can envisage those countenances and those sleek bodies. He is learned in their ways, he is experienced in the moods and manners of goats. He can show them at will: grave or sprightly, friendly or cynical—long-eared, short-tailed, black, white, and yellow.

Noël Sullivan lifts a black kid in his arms, and carries it a little way. I shall remember him thus with Spring air about him, the greenness of grass, and the quiet amphitheatre of the hills.

There is a sound of bees in the valley as we descend. There is a fragrance of orchard trees and stream-delighting willows: a murmur and a fragrance more and more interfused with and overwhelmed by the sound and breath of the sea that glitters far out against the horizon.

THE ISLAND

I FIND MYSELF IN THE QUAINT OLD-WORLD town of Victoria on Vancouver Island. I have come here in order to re-enter America on quota status, and it seems that I may have to remain longer than I expected: the vice-consul having decided that I am not a suitable person to obtain a visa.

Though I am seeing the town of Victoria for the first time, I am not seeing the Island. Years ago I snatched from a lecture-tour some days to go Northward, and chanced upon a steamer that lay, for an hour or so, offshore at Victoria and permitted its passengers to scramble into the town and out again. I preferred to remain aboard and stare at the Island. It was green and silver. It had a withdrawn air as if it wished to avoid ships and the cargoes they brought, as if it wished to hide itself in a cloak of invisibility as faery islands do. The herbage of it was thin and fine with a thrust of stone through the grassland, even as Aran has, and quietude encompassed its slant meadows, such quietude as I had found in islands where the rim of the Atlantic touches Ireland; such quietude as islands have that lean from Scotland to the Western Sea. At sight of those islands once, hyacinth-blue on the blueness of sky and sea, joy gripped me so whole-heartedly that nothing else existed: it was as though I had thrown from me the weight of mortality and was free of the prison-house of Time and Space.

Since I am now inhabiter of the Island, and amply provided with leisure I can make discovery of its shy-blossoming

304

wild flowers. I can finger its mosses and lichens and mist-drenched rocks, and stand among its oak trees that gather in the hollow between two knolls—trees small of stature with delicately twisted branches—sheltered from the sight of too much sky or sun. Always I find myself believing that this Island is small, like Iona; that one could compass the length of it in a day's journey, as one might compass Inisbeg—or Eriskay. Perhaps it is because I know that this Island is really very large: possessed of unravished forest; lakes that have not been stared at by indifferent eyes; animals that have not lost a primeval confidence in the strength of tooth and claw and hidden lair; because, indeed, I would fain see all of this Island—and know that I shall not—for this reason, perhaps, I comfort myself with the pretence that it is small, and I have not missed a full sight of it.

The mosses and lichens are in bloom: one must kneel to see them. This is not Spring in California, a sudden greenness and a riot of blossom! Spring comes slowly, half-reluctant, here. The willows know about it first: their naked bodies flush to golden life, they show themselves bronze and amber before they don a cloak of silken-furred catkins, thick as snow upon them. Rushes stir uneasily in waters that are freeing themselves from the ice-lock, and into this austerity of stone and Winter-stripped branches the wild currant breaks with a joyance of rose and carmine: scarlet tassels are a-flaunt too on slender silvery trees that stand in wind-fenced places, dancers beribboned to timbrel-in the Spring.

Flowers that the Island has can thrive in rock-crannies; they thrust their heads scantly through the scant fine grass; they dispute a territory with moss and lichen. They have shaped themselves quaintly and delicately, not to dazzle with lavishness but rather to invite an intimate contemplation, so starry among the flowering mosses milky-white or azure: so intricate of curvature, so fringed of lip, in the miniature orchids amethyst-purple or paler chalcedony. Yet, at times, a flowering uncouth and almost inimical intrudes itself: the fleshy crudely-yellow calla lilies that flood the water-mead-

305

ows and marshy places are not sib to the willows or the dog-wood; the madrone trees that invade the devastated pine-areas, reproducing themselves avidly, their berries red as blood new-spilt, their branches heavy with voluptuous leaves —these, luxuriant and sinister, are not sib to the alders that pattern with stark branches the cold skies.

I am glad to be here in Wintertime: the colours are more lovely, and the beautiful lonely places have nothing to mar their solitude. I can abandon myself to the strange magic of the cloistered beaches that seem to have kept their still-ness and strangeness for centuries while forests of Douglas pine drew nearer and nearer the sea-marge; and sea-drowned trees and driftwood, dark with salt-rust or bleached to spec-tral whiteness, piled themselves beyond wave-reach. The sand of those beaches might be of powdered Labradorite stone, so clean and hard a silver it is! The bone-white trees, the skeleton branches, huddled at the tide-lip, might have come there when the sand came: ushered in by a turbulence that left a quietude of exhaustion no after storm may break. The sea creeps warily here—a sea of Labradorite silver when it is not Labradorite blue, the iridescent blue that stone has borrowed, once only, from the wing of a butterfly.

Dew drips from the trees, and the mosses are wet with it. The wind sends swirls of mist over the restless ever-moving waters of the inlets; over the dark still waters of meres and tarns—golden-dark waters like those of Ireland. The snow-mountains today loom ominously—white peaks against a darker snow-charged sky: their crevasses have violet shad-ows. Everywhere there moves a dark mysterious life.

Is there a potency in Northern lands to stir the blood of those who had birth there? Is it because this Island, at once like and unlike islands that had my heart's allegiance years ago, reminds me of my youth and the mist-swirl of impossi-ble dreams—is it for this, or for any poor reason at all, that the Island enchants me? I should have known it before the years overwhelmed me. Ah, if one only loved it enough, what master-tones of music; what jewelled and subtle manip-

306

ulation of words; what colours, burnt in enamel or spread upon canvas, could not this Island lavish on its idolaters?

SOUTHWARD HO

MY STAY IN Vancouver Island has overtaken the tardy flowering of the dogwood, has overtaken the tardier blossoming of the plum, but now I have leave to return to the United States. Washington, D. C., has issued an order that I am to be admitted, and the officials here have been at pains to speed the parting guest. This change of front is due to the untiring effort of my friends; to the wise campaign planned by Erskine Scott Wood, and abetted by Garret W. McEnerney; to the energy of newsmen who inquired at Presidential press-conferences: *"Now, concerning the Ella Young case?"*—and to the whole-hearted co-operation of librarians and friends everywhere. I am going back to the United States to become an American citizen, and perhaps to lecture in Berkeley at the University of California.

Safe on board the steamer I watch a sunset spilt upon the waters, and panoplied in gold upon the sky: fit arras for the serried snow-peaks! Music sounds as the boat draws away from the shore. I think of the kindly folk that I became acquainted with in Victoria: the collectors of Oriental china who allowed me to handle their rare and beautiful pieces; the Irish-born family of the Campbells from whom I had house-room; the Welch girl, Gwladys Richards, who took me so often to places in her auto; the librarian who permitted me to scan the pages of a treasured folio Shakespeare.

The steamer is churning southward; the light is changing from rose and amber to turquoise and emerald, darkening slowly as star by star comes out. Now, stark against the fading light, the mainland of America shows in a scimitar-curve, the edge set seaward. Seattle lies almost midward in the curve.

The sea is velvet-dark. The sky is galaxied with stars. The scimitar-curve is ebon-black: and mid-most of it the town of Seattle, lamped with ruby and sapphire, glitters like a faery stronghold, jewelling the night.

It was on an early mist-shrouded morning of Fall that I entered America, from the East. It is Springtime now as I enter at midnight, from the West.

Hail, America!

BERKELEY

BERKELEY IS A TOWN that one should see in the Springtime. Street after street has been planted with the Japanese plum tree, with the Japanese cherry, with almond trees and the japonica which is called fire-bush. Its hills are very green. Cloud shadows lie on the bay. And the town itself is full of young people: girls and boys with books under their arms hurrying to classes in the University. They are as gay as the Spring blossoms, those girls and boys: orange-coloured sweaters, rose-red skirts, shoes that tap sharply on the pavement. This part of Berkeley seems to have grown up around the University. It climbs the hill purposefully. It will go on climbing till there is no hill to climb.

I am lecturing at the University on Celtic Mythology and Gaelic Literature. It is a lectureship for a term of years, presented by Noël Sullivan in memory of his uncle, Senator Phelan. The students who come to my lectures are very enthusiastic. If they were not they would not come, for they get no credits for these lectures. They are purely joy-lectures: a joy to me to give, and a joy to the hearers. I make many friends among those enthusiastic students. Some friends also

308

amongst older people. Professor Lehmer and his wife come always to my lectures. Derrick Lehmer is a poet, a writer of plays, a composer of music, and a celebrated mathematician. Eunice Lehmer is a poet and lecturer. They are both interested in Indian folk-songs and Indian music. In my house at Berkeley we talk of these things, and at times Derrick Lehmer reads aloud from a play that he is working on. I have taken an old-fashioned house in Berkeley, one that was tattered and derelict. It had, however, quaint rooms and a garden with a pond, several trees, and a high fence that bestowed privacy.

When I decided to take it, and renovate it, my friend Zöe Fisk, and her daughter Sylvia, offered to help. They knew two very clever young students, Dick and Bob Peters, who could put on calcimine, match wallpaper, repair cement— could in fact do anything! We held consultations, mixed paints, and soon had a very colourful house. The hall was paneled halfway in dark wood; dingy torn paper bannered the rest of it! We took off the paper and put on a calcimine that had a warm glow as if the evening sun were touching it. The stairs we boldly painted in a colour that resembled a tangerine orange. It was a success in our own estimation. Zöe mixed for the upper rooms a beautiful turquoise-blue as paint for the woodwork. The floors were black. The walls against the turquoise-blue were pearl colour. I hung some of my treasured pictures on those walls.

But the great thing, after all, was the huge aquarium that Bob Peters made for me. I put it in my writing-room where I could watch the tropical fish. They soon became very tame. Two angel-fish would come to the front glass and do a dance when they saw me. It was a food-dance. They disdained anything but live food. They were so clever that I could beckon one at a time to take an ant-egg from a forceps. The chief person, however, was a Siamese fighting-fish, gorgeous in red fins. He was specially fed and would thrust himself high among the water-weeds and take tidbits from the forceps. Below him the wise angel-fish ranged themselves to be ready to pick up anything that he let fall. He never tried to retrieve anything; he just asked for another piece. I had silver danios who used to swim very fast and make a scintillating silver in the water. I had red tetras, too, but got rid of them because they bully the other fish.

The pond in my garden had goldfish, but alas, my neighbour had a handsome striped cat. Bozo found out about those fish and told all the other cats. A procession of cats came to try their luck: smoky Persians, silver chinchillas, alley cats. I think that Bozo was the only expert fisherman. Once I caught sight of him and went down to explain that he could not fish in my pond without a license. I thought that my advent and his own conscience would terrify him. But Bozo only raised his head, smiled affably, and came over to where I stood. He rubbed himself against my ankles with an air that said: "You could not possibly be angry with a cat like me." I had to fence and re-fence that pond! Finally some fish developed that Bozo could not catch. He got about twenty-five, however.

THE STRONGER ANGEL

This morning I awakened from a dream, all shaken with sobs, and while the dream is vivid with me I am writing it down. It is a gray, rainy morning. Outside there is a sound of hammering. This place is Berkeley, California, and workmen are putting up wooden platforms and enclosures in the Stadium near by for the Armistice Day celebrations tomorrow. The Stadium holds seventy thousand people. It is vacant now save for the workmen: vacant, gray, and rain-washed.

I do not know how my dream began. It was as if I had

been wandering in strange places for hours, and had suddenly taken note of where I found myself. I was going from room to room of a vast palace. I went without hurry or slowness, and there was no person in any room save myself, and this did not surprise me: it did not hasten or hinder me. Then, as I moved through a nobly-proportioned room, there leaned to me from the embrasure of a window a woman who had the charm of those frail and scentless blossoms that live a scant few hours in the length of a Summer's day: so, casually, she had leaned into my life years ago and leaned out again as those flowers lean the wind's way—but now it seemed as if no wind, of chance or destiny, stirred her, it seemed that she moved from an impulse within herself, so that now she came lightly and joyously toward me as one might come who had put away the languor and thralldom of life, and I was fain of her as one might be of some frail-petaled flower in the Elysian Fields.

Together we moved through wide and empty palace rooms till we reached one widest and loftiest. At the far end was a dais with heavy curtains drawn before it. The hall was vacant of people except for us two. I sat upon a low stool of ebony, and she on a silken pillow close by. Then began the music of a great and beautiful overture with a melody running through it like the wind's feet in the topmost boughs of a forest. It was Russian music. It was something concerned with what the curtains hid, something that shaped itself there mysteriously and splendidly to the pattern of the music—or did that hidden Splendour and Mystery shape the sound? Stronger, more complex grew the music moment by moment, and then all of a sudden I knew that the vast audience-room was full of people who thronged it invisible, for they were singing. They were singing words to the air that ran so lightly through the massed clangour of the instruments:

"When the little flowers break through the earth in Spring-time, my heart is broken by the thought of the Russian land.

311

A thought of the dead, the Russian dead, stirs and twists in my heart.

I remember the dead, I remember so many. My heart is twisted because of them. Blood is wrung from my heart.

So many that mounted the scaffold. They did not ask to be remembered. They asked that Russia might live."

"So many that mounted the scaffold"—yes! yes! in Ireland so many: so many that Ireland might live. And it had not sufficed—ah, God, it had not sufficed! Sobs choked me, and I was shamed that I should sob aloud while those others sang: yet intolerable grief shook me, and I sobbed on. Stress of sobbing woke me. I sat up in bed. Through my uncurtained window I looked across the narrow canyon to the curved hillside beyond, with its empty, sun-bleached golden spaces and its dark-foliaged flat-topped trees crouching in the shadow-creases. The morning was gray, heavy and sodden with rain. So glad of it the trees were, all the trees: the eucalyptus trees, the live-oaks, the bay trees, the heavy-needled pines, the little pine trees climbing the planted hillside.

Half a-drowse with all that rainy gladness, with the grayness of the morning, I fell to thinking of Ireland. I fell to thinking of Marguerite—so early dead! I saw again pale sunshine in a rain-washed sky. I felt the stir and traffic of a Dublin street.

Marguerite was with me. She had hurried down from a high-perched mountain cabin to find me in the research room of the Royal Irish Academy where I was working. Hurriedly she came through the door and beckoned to me.

"I have something to tell you—it is a message, I think. We can't talk here—come outside."

There is a grayness outside, but Marguerite is like a wind-blown flame; her eyes too bright—too bright the red spot on each cheek: too frail and slender her body.

"I have seen a thing that is terrible, but it is splendid also. I came to tell you."

312

"Before you begin to tell me, you must eat something: I know that you have come down without eating."

"Food chokes me. I want neither food nor drink. Let us go into the park, we can find a place without listeners."

"Close by is a little restaurant. It is empty at this hour. It will smell only of hot bread and tea and coffee. To please me you will sit there, you will try to drink some milk."

"Anything, anywhere, so that we can talk!"

We go through the green swing-door and choose a table in a corner. The room is empty. It has a warm stale stillness. There is a fly buzzing on the window-pane; and beyond the window-pane a dull sound of the street. Marguerite cannot swallow even a mouthful of milk. A tall glass stands before her with thick cream on the top of it, untasted. She is saying:

"Up there among the mountains and the pine trees, I know things. I can look at times into the other world. I have seen the Angel of our Country. I have seen the Great Sword of Light. My heart is broken!"

"Surely that Angel was good to see, and splendid?"

"So beautiful it is, our Angel! I cannot tell you how beautiful: but it needs help from us. It is not strong enough, all that we have thought of; all that we have worked for; all that we have prayed for, will go to another Angel—for there is another Angel, the strong Angel of a country not ours!"

"What country?"

"I have seen that Angel. It is beautiful, beautiful and terrible. We must lift up the hands of our Angel! We must get strength—how can we get strength? Tell me, how can we get strength?"

"We cannot get more strength than we have. We have done the utmost."

"Then it will go to the Strong Angel—to the Beautiful Strong Angel—but, oh, I wanted our Angel to have it!"

Yes, both of us wanted that! Do you want it still, Marguerite? Can that loss vex you, in Tir-nan-oge?

My thoughts go back to those voices singing:

313

"When the little flowers
Break through the earth in Springtime—
My heart is broken—"

Hail to the Stronger Angel!

"IN HIS WILL IS OUR PEACE"

IT IS THE Requiem Mass for Monsignor John Rogers, in his own church of Saint Patrick. I have come early but already the church is crowded. People are standing in the aisles and about the door. Pew after pew is somberly magnificent with dignitaries of the Church. Mingled with the incense is the perfume of many flowers. Sunlight strikes through the stained-glass windows and touches the rich sanctuary lamp designed and made by Mia Cranwill, the Irish artist who owed so much to Monsignor's recognition and patronage. On the altar are hand-wrought candlesticks also by Mia Cranwill. I am searching the pews for a sight of Albert Bender—surely he will be here—he valued Monsignor highly—but I do not see him.

The Mass goes on: how triumphant, how wonderful is the ritual of the Catholic Church. The grief of the people—for there is hardly one who sits dry-eyed—the rich music, the long tradition, the saints and martyrs of centuries, the angels and arch-angels, come together in a strange ecstatic moment that draws everyone into a magic one-ness. It is not death that is being condoned here. My thoughts go back to a ritual more ancient—the Egyptian one: *"I am the Resurrection and the Life, I Osiris, the ladder, and the god who climbs the ladder. I enter Amenti as one whose place has long been prepared for him—equal among equals, god among the gods."*

Outside, traffic is suspended. The people are standing in
314

a solid mass: so they used to stand with banners on Saint Patrick's Days when Monsignor conducted services. He would have a word in Gaelic for them. As I go out, I pause for a moment by the richly-coloured design for a processional cross drawn by Mia Cranwill. Beside it is a little notice, written by Monsignor, asking for contributions in old gold or silver or discarded jewelry. The cross will have no patron now, but at least the great monstrance has been completed. Monsignor had the pleasure of holding it in his hands.

So many people will be orphaned of Monsignor: the poor of San Francisco for whom he built shelters; the eager-faced Irish patriots who had help and counsel from him; the leaders whose decisions he more than once influenced. Slowly I pass the pillars of green and white marble—quarried in Ireland! I pass into the street. Albert Bender on the steps is looking back for the last time: why did we not see each other in the church?

Farewell, Monsignor: prince, and patriot—and saint!

WITHIN SOUND OF THE SEA

I AM DRIVING with Genevieve McEnerney over the great new bridge across the Bay. It is the last of many drives with her, for my lectureship at the University has come to an end and I have decided to leave Berkeley and find a cottage somewhere in the country. The water of the Bay is blue without a ripple today: it was green-gray and storm-tossed when I saw it first. Since then I have traversed it many times in ferry boats. In spite of its size it has always seemed to me more like a wide town-owned lake than a portion of the splendid-moving Pacific. Genevieve McEnerney gave me my first sight of the Pacific, ten years ago, in 1926. She had a Lincoln limousine, then as now, and a skillful and careful

315

chauffeur who threaded his way among old wharves and neglected streets until we came on a quaint old-world park, a quiet half-forgotten place that commanded a view of the ocean. There it was: luminous, wide-spread, sufficient unto itself—a dream in the mind of God! We shall see it again today from that same park. But Genevieve is saying: "I always find what excuse I can to drive over the bridge; it is strange-looking and has a beauty of its own." The huge pylons of it reach into the sky at this moment. They remind me of Egyptian pylons—but they, planted firmly on Egyptian soil, were earth-born—these pylons are fire-born and thrust themselves into the air as accredited citizens. We fall to talking of the æsthetic value of steel girders; of steel-clad monsterlike battleships, creatures that seem spawned of a whirlpool, not by any means descended from stately ships, four-masters curveting on the waves with their sails leaning away from the wind: though, perhaps, cousins of those many-oared Phœnician war-prows that quested the sea for spoils; or a-kin to the heavy-sided Roman galleys that rammed each other in the battle of Actium.

All this while, the car is edging along the route it has taken so often. We see again the wharves crowded with gaily-painted fishing-boats; the curve of the shore; and the seal-rocks. The park keeps its aloof sleep-tranced air, although, like one that stirs in his sleep, it senses uneasily the encroachment of the city. It has shrunken and withdrawn into itself. Walking there with Genevieve, I notice the touch of grime on its trees, but the stone mushrooms, the mannikins and bearded gnomes with which some fanciful-minded donor once enriched the place, are not affronted or time-frayed. The mushrooms keep their pincushion outline, the gnomes their optimistic smile.

The garden holds my attention on this last visit, as the sea held it on the first. "This enclosure," I mutter, "is an epitome of what we are doing with the Earth: slaughtering all the rare and noble animals, driving away the Nature Spirits, stocking it with cabbage-gardens and puny-minded orna-

316

ments of our own devising!" "Do not forget," admonishes Genevieve, "the sky-climbing cities; airplanes; cobwebbing power-lines; and the telescopes that stare a million light-years into space!" "Yes, but these things seem an incursion from another world. Are they indeed John the Baptists of a New Age, Evangelists of the Millennium?" "If we were not so wise," says Genevieve, "or so faint-hearted, we might risk a prophecy."

As we journey homeward the sea moves and glimmers iridescent against a sky of rose-pearl.

JOURNEY'S END

*A*FTER SEVEN YEARS I AM BACK IN HALCYON and within sight of the Dunes again. Technically I am a resident of Oceano, though Halcyon is closer to me. When my lectureship at Berkeley came to an end I cast about for a quiet place where I could write, and chanced upon this house that has one lofty large room and about an acre of sand-patch, fenced, however, and provided with a well. I am hastily planting young trees: pines, acacias, and eucalypti, and endeavouring to get the house (a wooden structure) into order. I have named my sand-patch Cluan-Ard (the Gaelic for high meadow). One climbs to it by a stony road: and the local wiseacres, who predict that one day a great wave will flood in from the sea and sweep the rickety hamlet of Oceano from its roots, say with confidence that the wave will not wash high enough to lap the hillside here.

I could walk through the eucalyptus wood and find my cottage at Halcyon again, but not the garden. The trees and flowers there are dead: and now, all on a May morning, comes the news that Kenneth Morris is dead in Wales—after seven years of crusading!

It is seven years since that letter of his, from Point Loma, trumpeted forth:

"The great thing has happened; and I am too excited to live.

I AM GOING BACK TO WALES! I'R HEN WLAD FY NHADAU!

318

Our new leader, Dr. G. de Purucker, is sending everybody he can possibly spare out into the world to work up the lodges of the society far and near and I am to sail via Panama in about three weeks, I should think. I am to work in Wales, Ireland, and England. I mention Wales first, because it is there I shall live. But I am instructed to be in Ireland some of the time . . .

Te Deum Laudamus! Hip, hip, hurramus!—as Cicero would say!

It is quite impossible for me to write a sensible letter under the pressure of this—or I should say the uplift, of this huge excitement. WALES. No; it is not possible for anyone but me to know what that little word means!

AND I AM GOING THERE!

After twenty-two years of absence."

After twenty-two years of dreaming about the Wales he had taken farewell of in a lover's sonnet:

"So, if I have no word but this farewell,
Deem not that while time is, my love may die,
(Wherein time is not, but eternity.)"

Kenneth could say: "It is a wonderful Wales I have come back to. It astounds me. The inhabitants of the Rhondda Valley are miners—and nearly all living on the dole. So you'd think the inner air would be heavy with depression: but instead, it's like breathing champagne to breathe it with the mind. In the Wales I knew years ago, the people were not intellectually awake. Their mentality was not flamingly and lambently active. It is now."

Later he could write—Kenneth who for years had been a semi-invalid at Point Loma—"Here am I, as strong at any rate as some horses, taking walks up and over the mountains, and working a good deal."

Wales had given her lover a great gift when she restored him strength to be among mountains: *The mountains are*

319

after all our Elder Brothers, and for aught we can tell, their Souls may be in some mystical co-relation with ours—Mountains proclaiming the Everlasting, with no sound." So wrote Kenneth of alien mountains. He made a special song for the mountain that looks on Rhondda Valley where he was forced to admit squalor, chaos, and misery existed beyond belief.

> *When I came down from the Mountain*
> *The wintry sun shone cold,*
> *And the windows in Blaenclydach*
> *Glowed to him rosy gold:*
> *And the hillside o'er Tre-alaw*
> *And the slopes of bare Pen Rhys*
> *Shone dimly up to the dim sky*
> *In a mauve rose-golden peace.*
>
> *And a pulse beat through the solitude*
> *Of winds and nibbling sheep*
> *As if somewhere a God were sleeping.*
> *(He will not always sleep.)*
>
> *When I came down from the Mountain*
> *Dusk brooded in the sky*
> *And the hideous vale beneath me bloomed*
> *In smoky lazuli:*
> *Blue as a periwinkle,*
> *O'er-starred with flames of gold*
> *'Twixt the darkening mountain outlines*
> *In the twilight mystery-souled.*
>
> *And a sound came up from the Rhondda,*
> *A throbbing low and deep,*
> *As if somewhere a God were weeping.*
> *(He will not always weep.)*

In seven years Kenneth founded seven lodges, lectured in remote places and in crowded towns, organized campaigns, and visited at intervals London and Dublin. I wonder if he found time to visit Amman Valley where his forbears lived and his own early childhood was spent.

Writing of his grandfather, Kenneth said once: "Morris is one of the commonest of Welch names; but a letter addressed to William Morris, Wales, would always get to him. They gave him the name: Tangnefeddwr y Dyffryn, the Peacemaker of the Valley; from the fact that during his 'reign' the English law was never appealed to in the Amman Valley; he stamped it out, among a very quarrelsome litigious people, and arbitrated on every quarrel that arose: and they say that his decisions were always accepted. He had Pontamman, a house in very large grounds; and his youngest son, my father, had Wernoleu, with grounds I fancy larger. Pontamman was down in the valley, Wernoleu was on the hill above it; perhaps three-quarters of a mile away: the road ran between the two estates.

My father died in 1884, and either then or in 1885, my grandfather died. From very rich, we became rather poor, and had to go off and live in a small way in London.

Of the three houses we had down there, only Brynhyfryd, smaller, but in a very delightful wild garden, was left. A cousin, Ivor Morris, but a few years younger than my father, remained at Brynhyfryd.

In 1886, I, being not quite seven years old, was taken down there to spend May and June or something like that, by an aunt. When this aunt took me through the village the old women all came out in the road. I was the youngest son of my grandfather's youngest son: but I was for some reason the one they adored. 'When are you coming back to us, Master Kenny bach?' was the question they all asked me. I made answer: 'When I am grown up I'm going to buy back Wernoleu and come back to you!'

A day or two after, I was called to the kitchen at Brynhyfryd, my cousin Ivor's housekeeper coming in and saying someone wanted to see Master Kenny there. It was an old woman; who went on her knees and cried over me a bit; she had tramped in from somewhere, because the news had gone

321

abroad that six-year-old I was going to buy back Wernoleu. These people keep a stocking hung up somewhere, and collect in it for their funerals; they never have any money to speak of. She had brought in her three-pence: 'To buy back Wernoleu with, my boy bach!'——

After a while Ivor noticed that I was always being called out to the kitchen by peasant men and women, and inquired into the matter. By that time I had collected more than a sovereign: in pence, halfpennies, three-pennies, perhaps even sixpences; all from people who had come to subscribe for the buying back of Wernoleu. Well; Ivor, as the last of the Morusiaid Pontamman, expected his orders to be obeyed in the Amman Valley; and he sent out the word that it was to stop.

Well, he had an adorable garden. A mountain brook flowed through it—all down the orchard and kitchen-garden, and then by a tunnel under the drive; a lovely tunnel for a small boy to adventure through! Also the pines grew thick beyond the brook; and it was the finest place in the wide world and Wales to play hide-and-seek in.

A few days after the order had gone out I was playing there as usual when a whisper came from behind some near shrub: 'Master Kenny bach!' Another old woman; she had come in from the other end of the valley; she had been in hiding there since early morning, waiting to catch me, and give her few pence. 'To buy back Wernoleu, cariad bach!' (little sweetheart). Then more and more came; and hid there. It wasn't to be known that they had disobeyed a Morris of Pontamman; but they were going to make sure that Wernoleu should be bought back!"

An old-world garden, and small silver coins pressed into the hand of a child! With those three-penny bits, and sixpences, and copper coins the old folk bought the soul of Cenyd Morus. He could not forget Wales, or the people of Wales. He had to return to them, bringing whatever of fortitude or wisdom he had gathered in a lifetime; return to

322

hearten and to love them before he flamed across the bridge
to Ceugant.

"*There never was a better bargain driven.*"

WAVE-PATTERNS

THE WAVE-RHYTHM ON the long beach here by the Dunes
has changed. I remember it as I first saw it: long, slow,
undulating foam that soberly claimed territory and receded
from it soberly; gray-green water; platinum-silver sand.
Last Winter the little stream that trickles over the sand in
times of drought, and swirls to the sea in days of plenty—
this stream, dignified amongst us for lack of a better, with the
title of river, took heart and leaving its bed scooped a great
amphitheatre of sand for itself. The sea also took heart, it
advanced in unwonted battalions and stormed the sea-wall.
Doubtless it scooped in the depths new channels for itself—
now it advances in curves and cross-waves with intricate
rhythms and gestures of invitation and denial. Sea-swallows;
long-legged sand-pipers; birds that have silver underwings,
and flutter and wheel like butterflies; birds that never
haunted the beach hitherto, have arrived. The giant sand-
dunes that used to flame at dawn and sunset are pale: they
have an unearthly whiteness as of saints renouncing the
world.

It is plain that a new demi-god, an archangel perhaps
from Bali, has taken command in the inner sphere: an angel
that might gaze with interest on the sculptures an Ankor,
and say to himself:

"*I make my sculptures move, my dancers are not foot-
tied.*"

323

SHADOW OF NIGHT

WHEN I WAS YOUNG and vigorous I had no thought of writing memoirs. I had planned to write a book on Celtic mythology: I had indeed spent about twenty-five years in preparation for it. I got no chance to write the book, and now if I got a chance I could not do it. In the limping end of life one can but shoulder a light-weight burden.

Few poets have written memoirs. They have something better to do! Perhaps if I were a really good poet I would not waste time on memoirs—for what, after all, can one put into memoirs? They must always have the most important things left out. The great things of my life were inner happenings: surges and fountains that renewed or inundated mind and soul. Of such events one does not write.

I have tried in this book to say what the Irish Rising meant to me; yet I have perforce given only the shell, being compelled to withhold the kernel.

I could of course fill the book with opinions—my opinions! But what use in that? Opinions, my own and other people's, bore me! There remains then to set down a few memories that are vivid, before the years press on my eyelids too heavily—yet I know that no one else will see the colours that dazzled me.

Here at Cluan-Ard, the name I have given the sand-patch that surrounds my cottage, I write when I can—half-heartedly, for I am not sure that the writing is good: or even worthwhile. It is past sunset hour and there is no flame in the sky.

324

CLUAN ARD

(High Meadow)

I BEGIN TO THINK that these memoirs are too staccato in style. They go from episode to episode like those books written chapter by chapter for some magazine: *"To be continued in our next."* I think a pleasant book should meander along like a happy river that flows without interruption between green banks, or swirls and pauses by a little inlet to permit a willow bush or a wild iris to mirror itself for a moment.

I am sitting in my garden at Cluan Ard. It really is not a garden, it is a sand-patch that I am striving to irradiate with trees: partly because trees were my earliest friends, partly because I want to shut out everything but the sky. Beyond the young pines that I am fostering are some sturdy well-branched wrinkle-trunk pines that someone, deserving of thanks from every passer-by, planted years ago. I pretend to myself that they are not single pines, or groups of pines— they are a forest of pines! I pretend to myself, as I sit with my back propped against a tree of my own planting, that I am walking in that forest of pines: and it has no limit but the sky-curve.

It changes as I walk there, this forest of my imagining. At times it is like forests that I have known in Ireland where the pines have red trunks, and the pine-needles lie underfoot with a tinge of redness in their bronze. At times it is like a wood that I used to frequent on a Californian cliffside, a wood well-remembered: the dusk of it, the sound of the sea in its pine boughs. At times this phantom forest blossoms into a wood that once I walked through as one trespassing on a wood of Faerie. Battalions that wood had, and squadrons, and phalanxes of rhododendron: all flowered in rose and pearl. The narrow pointed leaves made a burnished greenness, a joyance among pine trees blown to extravagant

325

shapes by the wind: sad-coloured trees, twisted and dwarfed. There was nothing but desolate country beyond that wood, and far-off the sea glittered.

There is desolate land here also, beyond my sand-patch: and far-off the sea glitters.

From where I sit I can see the glint of water in two ponds. They have blue water-lilies and the pearl-coloured Royal Shiroman lotus of Japan. These ponds were a birthday and Christmas gift from Gavin Arthur whose towered house is round a bend of the roadway. The ponds have strange-shaped and huge-finned goldfish, silver-scaled ones, and five jet-black fish that are not like fish at all. They have eyes that bulk from their heads, and such a plethora of tails and fins that they swirl in the water like ebon dragons. Claire Franklin arrived one morning, dragged a covered receptacle from her auto, and displayed the dragons, who were heartened and accompanied by several gorgeously-coloured fantails. Eve Riehle gave me the silver-scaled ones. Close beside me crouches Akbar, my huge cat and the mascot of the book. He has the flat ears and the large cheek-pouches of a lynx, and promises to have the ear-tufts also. Akbar is what might be described as "the reward of merit." At Cluan Ard I had decided not to have a cat, partly because I had so many things to attend to, partly, and chiefly, because the sand-patch by my house was full of burrs and stickers: and all the cats of the neighbourhood collected, from somewhere or other, stick-fleas in their ears. It did not seem an inheritance worth offering to a cat. At times a huge gaunt sable-coloured cat crossed my sand-patch talking to himself. He was plainly starving, yet he had a haughty and aloof air. Time after time I came out with food but he hurried away, expecting only to have a stone flung at him. One day, too tired and too starved to run, he sat down and I got his attention for a moment. I hazarded a name and ejaculated in my best voice "Tony!" He looked fixedly at me, then he solemnly walked down to where I stood, put his head on my palm, and as he lifted it gave my hand a small friendly bite. Thereafter he

326

THE MASCOT

was my cat! But where does the "reward of merit" come in? It comes because I worked so hard to get that cat into condition, not thinking that he would ever be anything but a quaint-looking somewhat battered yellow cat. His fur, owing to prolonged starvation, had fallen out in patches; his body had several poverty-sores, and of course his ears were full of stick-fleas. Unexpectedly he turned out to be a very strange-looking and very handsome cat, and a devoted companion. When I dictate chapters of the book (this accounts for the staccato style) Akbar insists on lending the lustre of his presence to the occasion. If I am at a loss for a word I contemplate him as he lies on a hassock, his body, uniformly the colour of Russian sable at its lightest, marked by darkest sable in what is neither stripes nor spots—an intricate pattern like that on a snake's back.

Friends to whom I have read portions of this book say that they like the staccato style. I am glad they do because I don't love it very much myself. They say too that I have not put enough of my own thoughts and feelings into the book. I had hoped that I was sparing my readers something by that abstinence: but sitting here with sunlight glinting among the ruby-hearted lilies and the white, with sunlight filtering through the boughs above me, I wonder what I could have written that I have not written. Only some things can be captured in a net of words: and captured, some things are like tropical fish that, lifted from the water, lose their radiance.

What wish do I keep now after seventy years of struggle, success, and failure? I think that I keep my first conscious wish: to see beauty always with keener perception and subtler understanding. I have wished to serve beauty as writer, gardener and citizen—though I have fallen far short of the wish.

Beauty is like flame—it lives by escaping: but where it touches one, like flame it leaves a mark. Burnt into my mind is the image of the first rose that as a child I really saw. At that moment, that epoch of consciousness, rose bush, garden

327

—the whole cosmos—disappeared: only the rose remained effulgent and heart-filling—only the rose remains in my memory. More lightning-fierce, more disturbing, was beauty when I first encountered it in human form. I was running along with my head down (for in those days when I wanted to go anywhere I always ran, with little skips and leaps let in between), running with my eyes on the ground, a thin long-legged child half-blinded by a tangled mass of bronze-gold hair, when suddenly on that little-frequented road I became aware of the beauty of a woman coming toward me. So strongly, so strangely did the sight of her impinge upon me that I stopped dead in my tracks like one who has received a strong-handed buffet and stands bewildered and half-stunned, unable to go forward or turn back. Through the length of a lifetime I have been astonished and delighted only by a few—a very few—beautiful men and women. This first comer triumphed for all of them.

Every lover of beauty becomes oversoon aware of that tragic shadow, the destruction of beauty: the destruction of joy which is in itself a kind of beauty—the fallen tree, the fire-scarred mountainside, the disease-eaten body. Since I saw many beautiful things destroyed, and sympathized keenly, for a time at least, with human misery, this shadow spread and blackened about me till it became a torture. At the blackest moment suddenly I understood that Beauty is outside of and independent of all form. It is imperishable. Here we see only the poor image of Beauty as one might see the sun reflected in a mud-puddle. A passing urchin stirs the water and the image is broken—but the sun remains! Reaching out toward this Beauty—conceived at once as formless and having every form, understanding it to be approached as much through sorrow as through joy one apprehends the fringe of it as an ecstasy, lifting mind, body and soul beyond the trammeled existence we mistakenly call life.

WHITE ASH

RAIN IS FALLING outside: it has a kindly sound. I hope
that it will keep on falling for days. The whole countryside
needs it. The eucalyptus trees have withstood the drought
most valiantly, but secretly they thirsted and now they are
drinking with feverish tongues. In Ireland I used to hate rain
—the sound of it, the wetness of it, the steadiness with which
it could obscure the sky—I welcome rain with outstretched
hands in California! I have put a massive log on my fire:
the flame makes a hissing song as it flickers and leaps. It is
a night on which I would not choose to be elsewhere, or
occupied more efficiently: it is enough to sit idle and let
thought inhabit bygone nights.

A night in that house by the sea that John O'Shea's pictures
and Molly's rose-damasks and blue enamels made so colourful.
Firelight glinting on copper bowls and hammered silver, a
wind in the twisted cypress trees, a wave-murmur from the
cliff-foot. The sound of a strange instrument on which a
young composer is playing, fingering the strings of it lov-
ingly: the long-necked rich-voiced instrument that his hands
had made. He is singing, or rather chanting, as he plays. He
is singing for Molly. She is like a lady in some far-off time.
Firelight makes the only colour in her face. Her long straight
gown is rose-red.

A Saint Patrick's night in San Francisco: Albert Bender is
holding open house, and one can see masked and fantasti-
cally-disguised figures threading the narrow courtway and
climbing the stairs. Albert stands in the doorway, a heavy
robe of crimson silk gathered about him, his black opal ring
on his finger. Behind him move masked bandits, spangled
Pierrots, Chinese ladies, Spanish hidalgos, Irish colleens,
damsels with guitars, comic-opera Irishmen—a changing
colourful medley. Almost everyone is somebody: painters,
singers, musicians, actors, writers, business-magnates unite

329

to honour Albert on what he whimsically styles his birthday. They recite verses specially made for him; they stage short plays; they sing his favourite songs.

Albert seems to be everywhere, dispensing hospitality, parrying witty thrust with one more witty, adding zest to song and laughter. His guests stroll from room to room: from the library, lined with rare volumes hand-bound in vellum and morocco, across the reception-hall with its pictures and bronzes, across the dining-room, drawing-room, and study, with their Chinese porcelains and ivories, across to the exquisite balcony-garden that Albert made for his cousin, the artist, Anne Bremer. A silvery fountain falls and flickers there, dancing as it used to dance when she watched it: the flowers that were her favourites are renewed from day to day as though she could walk among them still. The miniature lawn is clipped and tended: how strangely green it is in the artificial light!

From within comes a loud and strange burst of music. Someone has brought the Irish pipes.

One of Noël Sullivan's exotic feasts. This one is for Roland Hayes. The long narrow table has flat bronze bowls filled with blue lotus: one bowl after another for the length of the table. Those Nile lilies have a sweet foreign-seeming perfume. It might be a feast in Egypt. More than a dozen bronze-faced soft-moving servitors pour wine, and change the gold-patterned dishes. There is a murmur of voices and laughter. I am sitting beside Roland Hayes. We are talking of Africa. When he knew that he would be a singer, he went to Africa because he wished to touch the ancestral root there; to hear songs that had changed little since the jungle or the desert first hearkened to them. We talk of African magic, and I say to him: "Do you know, a strange thing happened in the concert hall when you began to sing: *Were you there when they crucified my Lord?* I saw you change, as you sang, to a tall thin old man with a scant gray beard." He became excited at once: "Why, that was the man who made the song! I knew him: he is dead." But champagne is being poured in Venetian glasses. They are going to toast Roland Hayes.

Again it is Saint Patrick's night in San Francisco. Archbishop Hanna has honoured me with an invitation to dinner at the palace. It is a small party: Mrs. Bassett, sister of the Archbishop; his secretary; and Monsignor John Rogers. The flowers are green carnations; the wine is poured in emerald glasses; the table-linen has green broideries.

His Grace the Archbishop, handsome and rapier-witted, is recalling days when he was not so high a dignitary: "Once when lecturing to a body of divinity students, I noticed that more than half of them were comfortably asleep. I stopped and said: 'Gentlemen, you bring to mind a Scotch compliment. A congregation during the absence of its pastor had a young substitute. On his return the pastor tried to gather what the congregation thought. They mostly preferred the young man, but one parishioner said stoutly: *"The young man did well enough! But for obscurating the subject and bewildering the intellect there is no one like yourself, sir!"* Gentlemen, the class is dismissed.' "

With a crash my log falls to ashes. Why does white ash make me think of early morning? Not tomorrow, for I hope it will be wet! I think of a morning at "The Cats," and breakfast out of doors there: breakfast in the patio with grapevines twining in the lattice-work, and a cherry-tree spiring into the blueness. Sara Bard Field and Erskine Scott Wood at home on their vineyard-crowned hillside. The talk is of poetry: and two police dogs, one black, one golden, stand by to listen.

The talk was of poetry too at a luncheon given by Senator Phelan at Villa Montalvo—the table set among lawns and porticos, all on a Summer's day: the grass shorn to a velvet smoothness; two macaws—gorgeously appareled in scarlet, jade, and lapis lazuli—clambering from column to column; a white peacock moving in the distance.

Do places, I wonder, keep memories, white and chill like fallen ash?

331

THE SERPENT BITES ITS TAIL

THE GREAT WHITE LOTUS, the Royal Shiroman Lotus of Japan, is a-flower this August morning in my pond. It is a long-dreamed-of blossoming: one faultless head towering above an opulence of leaves that glint and change as though damascened with emerald and malachite. The heart of the lotus is jewelled in topaz and emerald, and set round with multitudinous stamens that look like pearls and glimmer pearl-like, shedding a dull radiance: burdened with so much riches, overpowered with curved and perfumed petals, the languorous exotic blossom leans sideways. It has a strange troubling beauty. I ask myself to what can I compare it—and suddenly I know! It is like the smile of the Saint John—demon, angel, saint—that Leonardo painted with his last strength, to betray for ever, and for ever keep inviolate, the secret of his own enigmatic heart.

I should have had for this long-nurtured blossoming in my pond the hieratic red lotus, the red upward-growing sharp-petaled lotus, if only for sake of my worship of things Egyptian—perhaps a petal even, for my love of Chinese art. This lotus was, I thought, hieratical also—only white! Would I have chosen it, knowing what it is—en-spelled by an alien loveliness?

The Rose had my earliest homage, as a child in my mother's garden, but the Lotus, procrastinating its advent, held me by a stronger and more ancient lure. Now, weighed upon by the years, in a country far from my birth-land, I have a lotus in my garden! It is full cycle round. The Serpent bites its tail. But it seems that I have exchanged Monsignor the Archangel Michael, for a Lord, who goes under a courtesy title, incognito.

332

HALLOWE'EN

(Samhain Eve)

A KNOCK AT MY DOOR and a murmur of voices. It is Peter
Thorp in a paper mask; a hollowed pumpkin in his hands,
grotesque and shining with its lighted candle-heart; a
childish song in his mouth—for this is Hallowe'en. In the
country places of Ireland tonight companies will be going
from house to house. Companies wearing masks and straw
disguises; song in their mouths, old folk-songs: or verses of
their own making, set to any tune that fits them. Light will
be in every farmhouse that is not owned by a curmudgeon or
an enemy of old customs. A fire will be burning on the
hearth, the pewter and the kitchen table newly scrubbed will
smile at each other. On the table in the place of honour there
will be a shallow bowl heaped with apples; beside it another
amply plenished with nuts; and in front of both an eye-
delighting dish filled with small silver coins. I spent Hallowe'en once in such a farmhouse set high among the
Wicklow hills.

When a sound of feet and a sound of voices drew near the
house the farmer himself threw open the door. A company of
stalwart farm-lads entered. They had sacks drawn over head
and shoulders, sacks with eye-slits cut in them, and the chief
man had a mantle of straw. They greeted the house with
verses they had made in its honour, and then the chief mum-
mer danced with the farmer's daughter. Everyone danced;
more verses were recited; and as they took leave the farmer's
wife gave to each one an apple and a handful of nuts, and
the farmer gave to each one a piece of silver. We could hear
them singing as they stumbled along the rutty hillside lanes.
How many centuries had blustered or slipped away, fortunate or ill-omened, since the nobles of Ireland, masked and
wearing gorgeous ceremonial robes, danced in the light of
the Samhain fires the god-dance that insured good fortune to

333

man and beast, while the stars watched them, as they had watched the mastodons stamping—as they watched the farm-lads this night in their homespun disguises tramping the roads.

Fifteen years ago I leaned from a window in Yreka town the better to see the lanthorns in the street below and the masked children all so joyously and unknowingly commemorating in America a Gaelic festival. I had come to Yreka to meet Ann Hadden that we might together visit Shasta which we revered as a Sacred Mountain. While Ann leaned with me to listen to the song and laughter of the children, we knew that we would drive southward on the morrow, November Day, the great day of the ancient Festival, and we would see Shasta—shaped like a Pyramid, crowned mayhap with clouds, or with a gesture of sovereign courtesy bare of them—see Shasta at almost every turn and winding of the road. It was on November the second, 1926, that we lit a small ceremonial fire in honour of Shasta and brought away some twigs of incense cedar that the Mountain had blessed.

I did not think then that fifteen years would slip away before I could sit in the shadow of Shasta again, but it was not until this year that I could again visit Shasta in such a fashion. I went with Marion Peters during the May Festival when the water-meadows were pranked with iris, amethyst and purple, and little starry flowers showed themselves by the roadways. The Samhain Festival among the Pagan Celts was held in honour of Mannanaun, and whosoever ate of the meat and drank of the ale of Mannanaun attained to immortality. The May Festival was in honour of the Gods who came to renew the earth—the festival of youth, of adventure, of hero-deeds. I thought of this as I sat in the shadow of Shasta.

Peter is singing as he goes along the stony lane. He has an apple and a piece of silver, but alas! no nuts.

LUGHNASSA, 1942

WAR RAGES—the war presaged by the Golden Storm;
envisioned by Margaret O'Grady in Achill; and foretold,
years and years ago, by that night-wandering Gaelic patriot
who talked with an Angel on the roadside.

Why have I written nothing about the war? It is because
I have nothing to add to what I wrote in an article, published
in *Welfare* December 6, 1919.

"Nation after Nation is girding itself for achievement, and
filling its imagination with new splendours. Every thought,
every act of ours, must help or hinder the Nation to whom
we belong. If we but knew, the Grail is unveiled already; the
riders have gone forth upon white horses; the Abyss trem-
bles; the lowliest blade of grass, the poorest soul, today companions itself with angels and archangels in preparation for
a storm such as the Tree of Life has never before encountered
—makes ready for a blossoming such as the world has never
known."

Remembering Margaret O'Grady's words: "*A resistless
Force is descending. I cannot name it, this Great One! I
cannot bear it—this Light that consumes! Nothing can stand
against it,*" I ask myself was it such a Great One that the seer
of the Apocalypse looked upon:

*"And I saw heaven opened, and behold a white horse; and
he that sat upon him was called Faithful and True, and in
righteousness he doth judge and make war.*

*His eyes were as a flame of fire, and on his head were
many crowns; and he had a name written, that no man knew,
but he himself.*

*And he was clothed in a vesture dipped in blood: and his
name is called the Word of God.*

*And the armies which were in heaven followed him upon
white horses."*

335

ALL ON A MAY MORNING

TODAY IS SICK with heat. No place indoors is endurable: no place in the garden even, save the ridge of the swing-seat which catches whatever wind there is to catch from the sea. It is mid-May. Trees in Ireland are in leaf-bud. Wild hyacinths and primroses star the young grass. Marsh-marigolds burgeon by the water-ways. Here the lupines have gone. Roses hang heavy in every garden. The air is spiced with desert-sage, myrtle, and eucalyptus. In my ponds wine-red lilies and ruby-hearted ones have opened to the sun. I would go to look at them if the day were not so heat-burdened. Instead, ensconced in the swing-seat, I shall scribble pencil portraits of my garden. I feel that mention should be made of Africanus. Everyone leans over the palisade to stare at Africanus, and ask what his name is.

Africanus is a tree. His name is Erythrina Africanus, and just now he is flaunting on leafless branches the most incredible scarlet blossoms. Some day he will reach skyward mightily, but Africanus is tardy in the up-reach. He understands that nearby pine saplings shelter him, and he has no wish to out-top them. Alert and wary, he twists and turns, looking at his world from every angle and fencing himself with knobbly boughs that are as solid-seeming and as grotesquely beautiful as though carved from semi-precious stones, agate and chalcedony. The contrast between these boughs, which scorn to sway in the wind, and the piled-up splendour of the blossoms is what compels folk to pause and contemplate Africanus. No one, seeing those velvet blossoms, would imagine that Africanus has thorns curved like the scimiter claws of a panther: weapons unexpected, and disposed in hidden places. They are useful: Africanus had rested one bough upon the grass. An ignorant and presumptuous dog rolled there once on a time. He bemoaned himself and crept humbly away. Africanus wore a virtuous and self-congratulatory expression.

My garden has Brazilian fuchsias; and Japanese iris, spearing to purple; it has even a tree-peony, and the rare Chinese iris, fimbriata: but the savage beauty of Africanus puts them out of countenance. These notes must end with him, as they began.

A KING ABDICATES

PERHAPS MY BOOK concerns itself overmuch with cats! Anyone who thinks so may skip this chapter: it is about my yellow cat. Akbar is dead. Perhaps this is an evil omen for the book. Akbar was its mascot. Akbar, who disdained to come into the house and did not think the garden was jungle enough for a habitation, insisted on being present when Helen Becksted came to type for me, and I dictated chapters. He sat on a tall hassock, and never yawned through the knottiest altercation as to spelling, punctuation, and a thousand other trifles that trouble authors who, like myself, can't spell and have iron-bound notions about punctuation. Since he was the mascot of the book, I have persuaded my publisher to put in a portrait of a cat: a portrait that some folk have accepted as one of Akbar. It is not a portrait of Akbar. It is the portrait of a lynx, but Akbar was more like a lynx than this lynx is.

When Akbar walked abroad, every dog, every cat relinquished the pathway to him. Akbar accepted this as a right, but he was a gracious monarch and there was peace in his demesne until this last year when an immense platinum-gray cat came from nobody knows where! He was young and very strong and had a new technique in fighting: he bit the front legs of his opponents. This method enabled him to blitzkrieg every champion in the countryside, and cat owners talked wrathfully of poison and shot-guns. Akbar was re-

337

covering from a shoulder-wound when the cat showed a face in his territory. He had no chance from the first, and could scarcely stand on his feet when I found him. I kept him indoors until he insisted on limping from the house. Truly it was a high-hearted mascot, one that showed more courage than I ever did in my literary enterprises.

I hoped that someone had settled accounts with the gray tiger, but, alas, he was still a-foot and I was soon to know it!

Idly from a window I regarded the platform at the back of my house. Akbar sat there. His front paws were tucked under his breast, and he wore an air of almost exaggerated nonchalance. His eyes occupied themselves, uneagerly, with the distance. Behind him the garage door gaped open; in front of him my sand-patch, with its dear-won trees, stretched acre-wide to the palisade: beyond lay a territory where Akbar had fought off two cats at once, and reaching away from that battle-ground sand-lupine and scrub-brush huddled to the horizon where the sand dunes slip to the sea. Following Akbar's gaze, I caught sight of a gray beast parading across the far-away end of my sand-patch. I judged it, by size and colour, to be the blitz-krieging tiger-cat. But as Akbar never moved I thought myself mistaken. In a few minutes the beast again paraded—much nearer this time! Then I understood: it was the conqueror's challenge to Akbar. My yellow cat, though maimed in both front legs and terribly mauled, had evidently not made submission according to the proper ceremonial in the cat-world: this parade was to give him a chance of renewing the fight if he wished to. Akbar did not move. The blitz-krieger stood, as if taken a-back, for a moment, then he slowly approached the platform. Aware of that approach in every nerve and fibre, Akbar maintained his air of nonchalance. His steady eyes took in the territory that he had ruled so long: not a hair bristled.

The gray beast, walking warily, came close to Akbar and stood well within striking distance. He did not invite combat by so much as a glance, he kept his head averted and looked into the emptiness that filled the garage. He stood thus, with a semblance of gentleness, for a few seconds: then, without turning his head, he uttered one of his best war-howls. Akbar sat without the quiver of an eyelash. The gray cat gave a second war challenge, and a third, with head averted but standing well within reach of any buffet Akbar might bestow on him. Akbar sat motionless. The gray cat, still without looking at Akbar, walked slowly away. I had seen a king relinquish his territory to an adversary who was not ignorant of high ceremonial usage, however unchivalrous and unorthodox his fighting methods might be.

In remaining weeks Akbar did not regain strength. Feeling death upon him he stalked into the wilderness, holding himself erect, and going proudly as he was wont to go. He never came back.

"DREAM OF TENTED FIELDS NO MORE"

THE AIR HAS a tang of frost, a sense of Autumn: elsewhere there would be falling leaves, but Californian trees cling sturdily to their raiment. I am glad that such is their custom, for the trees that I have planted shut in my garden now. It is a cloistered place where I can lie on the warm earth and idly regard the sun-warmed sky. It has few cloud processions, this California sky, but birds interrupt the sapphire calm of it now and then: vultures ominously circling and poising themselves on nothingness; little birds that rise up suddenly into the air and fly confusedly, many of them together, like dead leaves whirled in a sudden tempest of wind. They are not always in this part of the country, those little birds: they are gathering now for a journey—I know not whither!

At times a hawk fans the air, its body under the curved wings, silver, or cinnabar golden. But for long intervals the

339

sky is empty of aught save blueness, a deep violet blueness without beginning or end: blueness that saturates mind and body with a honeyed lassitude, a Nirvanan contentment.

Once I surprised a lovely flight of birds in wedge formation, forging steadily ahead and making a sound as they flew. They were dazzling white of body and breast, but the wings had a bold pattern in black feathers. Knowledgeable people maintained that they were wild swans, but they bore no likeness to wild swans as I had seen them rise in Ireland from river inlets and reedy meadows: a crowded whiteness, winging heavily to the next alighting-place. These aëronauts had no thought of a speedy alighting. I am content to remember them without a name, beautiful in wedge formation, winging with such surety of purpose to a place far off. I too shall soon be setting forth to a place far off: a joyous and winged adventure, be it through sunshine or through storm.

EVALUATION

THE DAYS AND YEARS of my life, fair-faced or evil-countenanced the good gifts, the bitter honey, the mandragore, the forgotten and unforgotten, what do they mean?

Black teeth on white, and a child to wonder at them!

At end of all, what does one have when one is old? Some wisdom—perhaps; many memories, certainly; and if one is lucky, a feather shaken from the Phœnix-Bird.

PORTRAIT OF ELLA YOUNG
BY OSCAR MAURER

I walked in the Land of the Ever-Living with my Ladye. We walked in a wood. It was a wood that had the naked loveliness of Springtime, and yet the boughs were glad with blossoms. A wind moved with us, and where it touched the delicate grass under foot slender-stemmed hyacinths sprang up. There was music everywhere and changing colour and motion. The trees changed shape and stood a-tiptoe for very lightness of heart.

I have said that we walked in the wood: equally the wood walked in us. It moved with us, the trees blossomed in us. The music, the wind, the flowers in the grass patterned our mood; and we patterned the trees: growing tall with their tallness, reaching out joyously with their branches. The music that surged and sounded everywhere was like the heart-beat of our blood.

It would seem as I tell this, that I was thinking more of the wood than of my Ladye, but I was thinking more of my Ladye: for walking beside her again I was whole. I had no wish unfulfilled.

INDEX

343

347

348

351

352

356